THE CHANGING MIDDLE EASTERN CITY

CROOM HELM SERIES ON THE ARAB WORLD

Edited by
P.J. VATIKIOTIS
School of Oriental and African Studies, University of London

THE INTEGRATION OF MODERN IRAQ
Edited by Abbas Kelidar

PALESTINE IN THE ARAB DILEMMA
Walid W. Kazziha

The Changing Middle Eastern City

Edited by
G. H. Blake and R. I. Lawless

CROOM HELM LONDON

BARNES & NOBLE BOOKS · NEW YORK
(a division of Harper & Row Publishers, Inc.)

© 1980 G.H. Blake and R.I. Lawless
Croom Helm Ltd, 2-10 St John's Road, London SW11

British Library Cataloguing in Publication Data

The changing Middle Eastern city —
    (Croom Helm series on the Arab world).
    1. Cities and towns — Near East
    I. Blake, Gerald Henry
    II. Lawless, Richard Ivor
    915.6'0973'2   GF670

    ISBN 0-85664-576-1

Published in the USA 1980 by
Harper & Row Publishers, Inc.
Barnes & Noble Import Division

ISBN 0-06-490451-2
LC Card number: 79-56647

Typeset by Leaper & Gard Ltd, Bristol
Printed and bound in Great Britain

CONTENTS

FIGURES

Figures

Photographs appear between pp. 114 and 115

TABLES

Tables

PREFACE

It is pleasant to be able to acknowledge the assistance of numerous colleagues and organisations in the production of this volume. We are particularly grateful to the contributors for their co-operation, especially perhaps to those who met the original deadline for the receipt of manuscripts. The staff of the Drawing Office and the Photographic Unit of the Department of Geography at Durham University gave us a great deal of assistance, and Mrs Nancy Smart typed and corrected the manuscript with infinite care and patience. We are extremely grateful to them.

We also acknowledge with grateful thanks permission to reproduce illustrations. Karl Krämer Verlag, Stuttgart-Berne for Figure 8.3; John Wiley and Sons Ltd, for Figure 10.1; Werner Dubach, Architects for Figure 10.3; the University of Durham for Figure 10.4; Gazzard Chipchase Consultancy Services B.V. for Figure 10.5 and 10.6; and Blackwell Scientific Publications Limited for Table 11.5.

Gerald Blake and Dick Lawless
Durham, England

A NOTE ON NAMES, UNITS AND MEASURES

One of the problems encountered in studying the Middle East is the spelling of place names, particularly where languages are written in the unfamiliar Arabic script and different systems of transliteration have been employed. Most readers are likely to be confused unless some standardisation is achieved. As far as possible, therefore, place names have been spelt in the form used by *The Times Atlas of the World* since this is generally accessible. Where reference is made to places not marked on the maps of *The Times Atlas*, the versions employed in the English language literature have generally been accepted. To avoid the inconvenient term 'Persian/Arabian Gulf', 'the Gulf' has been adopted throughout. Where Arabic words have been used in the text, they have been transliterated, but for the non-specialist ordinary English plurals have been added. For example, *madrasas* (sing. *madrasa*) is preferred to *madāris*, and *sūqs* (sing. *sūq*) to *aswāq*. The metric system has been adopted for most quantities, in line with current British practice. For financial matters, however, a variety of currencies is used. Standardisation over a long period of time is almost impossible given inflation and fluctuations in exchange rates.

INTRODUCTION

The Middle East, defined here as extending from Morocco to Iran and Turkey to Sudan, lies at the crossroads of three continents − Africa, Asia and Europe. With the largest reserves of petroleum in the world it ranks as one of the most important world regions − an importance well beyond its physical size or scale of population. Whereas the urban experience is a relatively recent phenomenon in many regions of the world, cities and city life have been an element of Middle Eastern society for millennia. What Gordon Childe has called the 'urban revolution' began here in the fourth millennium BC, and cities then became characteristic of successive civilisations in the Middle East, each leaving its mark on urban structures. Today the Middle East is one of the most highly urbanised regions in the Third World, with some 44 per cent living in towns, and rapid urban growth and rapid rates of urbanisation are dominant elements in the complex process of modernisation and change affecting Middle Eastern society. Already there are at least a dozen Middle Eastern cities with over one million inhabitants, and Cairo, with a population of some nine millions, is now a major world metropolitan region. Present trends suggest that by the year 2000 at least half the region's population will live in towns and cities.

Yet paradoxically scholarly research in Middle East urban affairs has lagged behind both the growth of urban studies for other regions of the world and interest in other aspects of Middle East society. Thus Bonine, reviewing the current state of urban research in the Middle East in 1976, concluded that 'The traditional Middle Eastern city is still being explained in clichés and stereotypes . . . The modern city and processes of urbanisation have barely been touched upon.'[1] Nevertheless, although important gaps still exist in our understanding of the structure and function of the city in Middle Eastern society, substantial progress has been made in recent years, as evidenced by a growing number of individual case studies and monographs. However, studies which provide general statements on the major themes which characterise the region's specific urban phenomena and patterns are lacking. Within the last ten years although the papers resulting from three symposia on the city in the Middle East have been published,[2] remarkably there is only one study that examines Middle East urbanisation from a single viewpoint.[3]

The aim of this volume is therefore to review some of the major

1

issues of Middle East urbanisation in the light of contemporary evidence in order to provide a comprehensive and up-to-date statement about the current position of research into these topics, to indicate the work that has already been carried out, and to identify those areas that deserve more detailed attention in the future. Because of the growing volume of scholarly work on this subject and the increasingly specialised nature of research techniques, it was decided to invite a group of specialists in various fields of urban research to contribute a chapter, each drawing on their own particular expertise. As most of the contributors are geographers, attention focuses on the spatial dimension of a complex and multifaceted subject, though other dimensions, the historical, social and political, are by no means neglected. Consequently this perspective has influenced both the choice of the themes discussed in this volume and the way in which they are analysed. Even a cursory review of the literature reveals that in recent years geographers have been major contributors to analyses of the Middle Eastern city, particularly to processes of urban growth and to the physical and spatial structure of the contemporary city.

The opening chapter traces the evolution of the Middle Eastern city from its origin in the first half of the third millennium BC to the beginning of the twentieth century, and describes the emergence of new urban forms and the development of urban systems. As there are few studies of the continuities and similarities between the Muslim city and its antecedents, J.M. Wagstaff begins by discussing the emergence of the first towns, their basic structure, and the radical changes that occurred with the intrusion of Macedonian and then Roman power into the Middle East. The Arab expansion and conquests of the seventh and eighth centuries AD have been credited with significant increases in the degree of urbanisation in the Middle East and with the introduction of a new urban form, the Islamic city. Wagstaff, after reviewing recent research, concludes that neither claim can be fully sustained. The Arabs gave a certain impetus to Middle Eastern urbanisation without causing a general increase in the level of urban development, and without identifying the city with Islam. The Arabs did not introduce a model Islamic town and many of its typical features were either inherited from pre-existing towns or evolved gradually over time. After two centuries of considerable socio-economic strain and readjustment, expanded trade and contact with Europe in the nineteenth century led to a restructuring of urban hierarchies and the deliberate planning of new urban development.

In Chapter 2, by contrast, J.I. Clarke presents an arresting summary of the nature and scale of contemporary Middle Eastern urban growth. In previous centuries the urban life of the region may have been stimulated by substantial population levels. Today, it is one of the most urbanised regions of the Third World (possibly 44 per cent), and one of the most rapidly urbanising at about 5 per cent per annum. A significant feature is the concentration of population in cities with over 100,000 inhabitants, and even more notably in cities with over one million inhabitants, of which there are at least a dozen. These cities are growing exceedingly rapidly, with one or two main centres accommodating a growing share of total national populations, largely as a result of migration. J. I. Clarke concludes that the only real solution to metropolitan expansion must lie in more effective economic planning for each country as a whole.

In Chapter 3, A.M. Findlay looks in detail at migration from rural to urban areas and the increasing permanency of migrant residence in the city. He points out that throughout the Middle East the absolute number of migrants arriving in cities will certainly continue to grow even though the importance of migration as a component of growth is less predictable. He argues that the significance of rural-urban migration lies in the quality as well as the quantity of newcomers entering the city. His contribution demonstrates that the location of migrant activities and the behaviour of migrant populations are functions of the distinct and different demographic, educational and occupational characteristics of migrant communities. He concludes that although the debate over the optimum spatial distribution of population in cities of different sizes is important, the most serious problems facing urban and regional planners in the near future will arise from the widening gap between the high economic and social aspirations of migrants and the severely constrained occupational and societal roles open to them.

In Chapter 4, J.S. Birks and C.A. Sinclair draw attention to differences in urban employment structures in the Middle East, particularly between capital-rich states (exemplified by Kuwait, Bahrain, Qatar and the United Arab Emirates) and capital-poor states (exemplified by Egypt, Yemen AR and Sudan). The former are characterised by heavy concentration of employment in the tertiary sector, at levels normally associated with post-industrial development, and scarcely any informal sector employment. The creation of numerous public-sector posts for nationals commensurate with their traditional status in society is largely responsible. With government thus absorbing national labour on a large scale, the private sector has had to recruit immigrant labour. In capital-poor countries a large tertiary sector is again evident because of the growth in government employment, but also because of a rapidly expanding informal sector. It is argued that the process of labour migration from capital-poor to capital-rich countries is actually fostering a large informal sector in the former, while militating against its growth in the capital-rich countries.

D.W. Drakakis-Smith stresses how little we really understand about urban development processes in the Middle East (Chapter 5). There is very little information, and comparative studies within the region and with other parts of the Third World are rare. Interpretation of urban problems is too frequently Eurocentric, and inappropriate planning policies are adopted. This is particularly true of housing and unemployment among rural migrants. Conventional housing provision, both private and government-financed, is usually too expensive. Non-conventional housing in the form of overcrowded slum properties and illegal squatter settlements have received too little serious consideration. Housing the urban poor needs to be seen as an integral part of the development process in the Middle East, and not merely as a resource-absorbing activity.

Ethnic quarters have long been recognised as characteristic features of Middle Eastern cities. T.H. Greenshields in Chapter 6 investigates the processes involved in their formation and development. He focuses specifically on quarters as spatial, ethnic clusters rather than on quarters as social entities, and argues that explanation of cluster formation must lie in the relationship between population movements and the socio-economic environment in which they take place. His investigation highlights the diversity of processes involved in cluster formation and development, and the dynamism of ethnic clusters. Far from being static features, merely the physical expression of a social system, ethnic clusters can expand, contract and shift their location. He concludes that while there may be some local tendency to disintegration, ethnic clustering remains vital in a number of Middle Eastern cities today.

In Chapter 7, V.F. Costello examines the traditional pattern of retailing in the Middle Eastern city, and the transition which has taken place in that pattern to the present day. He concludes that most cities in the region possess a mixture of ancient, traditional elements and modern elements of a purely Western pattern, and notes that although Western acculturation is taking place in some respects, a 'reorientalising' process can be identified in others. If the bazaar or traditional trading centre has lost some of its importance, in most cases it still retains a large part of its retailing if not manufacturing functions. Physically, socially and functionally the traditional commercial district is no longer the centre of urban life. Modern commercial districts have developed in the newer suburbs of most towns, supplementing rather than competing with the bazaar and providing services for the more Westernised sectors of society. He predicts that in the future shopping for the wealthier, more mobile sections of the urban community will increasingly follow North American patterns of out-of-town shopping centres.

Urban planning policies and problems are discussed in Chapter 8. B.D. Clark reminds us that urban planning can refer to interventionist policies at a variety of scales including the relationship of urban land-use planning to regional and national planning strategies. In most Middle East countries, however, the concept of planning usually relates to physical land-use planning at the city scale. The city master plans which have resulted from this approach are in many cases design orientated and fail to take into account social and economic considerations, while lack of legislation and enforcement procedures remains a major weakness of planning. He argues that until a more integrated overall planning strategy can be implemented, a range of small-scale actions such as road-building, provision of low-cost housing, sewerage systems and piped water will continue to be the dominant theme of urban planning in the Middle East. There follows an evaluation of the processes which as a result of recent rapid urban growth are increasingly necessitating the introduction of a range of interventionist policies – policies which have had to be related to the scale and spatial form of growth in an attempt to try to solve what has been described as a malfunctioning of individual cities, or parts of towns and cities, and in some countries the whole of the urban system. An analysis of the development and nature of urban planning in three selected countries (Iran, Morocco and Kuwait) illustrates the form that planned intervention has taken. Finally, certain key planning themes are selected to evaluate the strengths and weaknesses of current planning policies and to suggest what form future strategies may take.

Chapter 9 highlights one of the most regrettable problems associated with rapid urban growth – the deterioration and destruction of the fabric of the historic *medina*. R.I. Lawless argues that conservationist policies, and schemes for the revitalisation and reconstruction of these historic cores, have so far been very disappointing. The experience of Tunis, Jerusalem and Eşfahān illustrate the difficulties. Too much has been done for tourists, too little for the lower income groups of the medinas, many of whom are migrants. Policies are needed to encourage revitalisation of social and economic life at the neighbourhood level as well as the conservation of historic buildings. Urban land reform, new forms of local participation in planning, curbs on speculation and other radical changes should accompany modernisation. The problem is that powerful interests are often benefiting from the destruction of historic urban centres, and the process continues.

G.H. Blake draws attention to the neglect of small towns in the study of Middle East urbanisation (Chapter 10), and the uncertainty that surrounds the causes of their population change and their functions within urban networks and hierarchies. He indicates that there has been a considerable increase in the number of settlements with 5,000 to 20,000 inhabitants, though these centres probably contain a slightly smaller share of total national populations than previously. He notes that the thousand or so small towns of the Middle East represent an immense variety of urban types, including modern foundations, traditional regional centres and urbanising rural centres, fulfilling a great range of functions. He concludes that small towns need to be more fully integrated into national urban planning, partly because the population of some is declining, but also because many of them still function as vigorous regional centres representing considerable potential for the implementation of the development policies of central governments. Planning should be devised to stimulate the social and economic life of small towns without striving to turn them into small cities.

Peter Beaumont examines a problem associated with urban growth which is often overlooked (Chapter 11). Scarcity of water in many parts of the Middle East could impose absolute limits upon urban growth unless new sources are discovered, more effluent recycled for irrigation, and new techniques evolved for more efficient use of fresh water. Per capita domestic water consumption has risen from 50 litres a day 50 years ago to 150 litres a day. With rising standards of living, and the installation of piped water to more households, this average is forecast to rise to over 250 litres a day. At the same time industrial demands are increasing. New sources of water are having to be found for several major cities. The costs of discovering, storing and distributing water to towns, together with the collection and treatment of waste are already enormous and will continue to grow.

In the concluding chapter (Chapter 12), the editors reflect on the urban future of the Middle East. While acknowledging that the rapid pace of changes makes forecasting difficult, they argue that one fact about the future urban scene which seems beyond dispute is that the level of urbanisation will continue to increase. The desirability of continued urban growth may be a matter of lively debate but the polarisation of urban and national populations in a few dominant metropolitan regions appears inevitable. The detrimental consequences, particularly for cities outside the oil-rich states, are already exemplified by the appalling problems of Cairo which could contain 20 million inhabitants by the end of the century. Increased numbers will aggravate already serious pressures on urban infrastructures and housing, and although little is yet known about the relationship between economic development and urbanisation, a significant part of the urban population has been excluded from the material benefits of economic growth. The social and economic inequalities and tensions within the Middle East city could, they believe, find political expression in the future. Though a major reappraisal of development goals could bring about unexpected changes in the pattern of urban growth, we foresee a continuing urban bias in Middle East development with the cities receiving priority in development strategies, thus tending to reinforce rural-urban disparities. The chances of a new urban revolution are remote, and they predict a continuation of contemporary trends to breaking point.

These contributions also help us to identify gaps in our knowledge and to define some of the major topics and issues which need to be investigated in the future. If the significance of urbanisation in the Middle East is to be properly assessed, a wider chronological perspective must be pursued. The city in the Middle Ages has received attention, but surprisingly we have less understanding of the pre-modern city. For example, there is no comprehensive treatment of the city in nineteenth-century Qajar Iran, and the Ottoman city is only now beginning to receive attention.[4] We need a more sophisticated and penetrating analysis of the city in the past, recognising the subtle differences and similarities of urban societies and morphologies in different regions and periods. Only when the principles which governed traditional urban spatial organisation are clearly understood can we determine whether they have any applicability for solution of present-day problems of urban planning.

Many of the cities of the Middle East have been experiencing rapid rates of growth in recent years and yet the diagnosis of growth has been relatively superficial and sometimes incorrect. Urban planners have ignored growth generated by natural increase, and birth-control programmes have been concentrated in rural areas. If birth-control programmes are to be effective in urban areas we need to know more about the diffusion of fertility decline. At the same time the effects of migration on the city and the city on migrants have only just begun to receive attention, and there is a dearth of research on the critical interaction between spatial and social mobility. One of the most neglected fields of urban research in the Middle East concerns the relationship between urban growth and economic development. We must examine more closely the workings of urban economies in the region, and the major features of urban economic organisation. Furthermore the urban economies of the Middle East need to be analysed in the context of the wider world economy. Studies are urgently needed on variations in employment structure of cities, occupational mobility and marginality, the scale and style of state intervention in urban economic development, and the effects of contemporary urban planning on city economies. For too long, discussion of these vital issues has by-passed the Middle East and has been concentrated in Latin America, Africa and Asia.

On the nature of social organisation in the city, there are still entire sections of the urban population about which little is known, and it is among the mass of the poor citizens, the overwhelming majority of the inhabitants of Middle Eastern towns, that least research has been done. The relationship between socio-economic status and ethnic clustering has also been neglected, and we are ignorant of the processes involved in spite of growing recognition of the indispensable role which such small subsystems can play in mediating between the individual and the large-scale society and perhaps averting those symptoms of social breakdown so often associated with urban life.

In the complex and constantly evolving urban planning process, there is considerable scope for further research. The functioning, or in some cases, the malfunctioning of the region's urban systems, the concentration of population, production and investment in a limited number of cities and the neglect of others, deserve more attention. Although squatter settlements and inner-city slums are becoming a focus for research, their relation to the entire city and urbanisation process must be examined, while the relationship between land ownership, land speculation and planning, and the role of *waqf* (*habous*) in urban land-use patterns have been virtually ignored. There have been few in-depth analyses of hinterlands of Middle Eastern cities, although the pioneering work of German geographers on rent capitalism provides a valuable theoretical framework for future research. The regional functions of towns and cities in the region are still incompletely understood, especially the role of town dwellers in agriculture, land ownership and in marketing. Work on the city in its regional context, on the economic, social and political inter-relationships between the city and its surrounding settlements, is only just beginning, and there have been few attempts to apply central place theory in the Middle East. The relevance and role of the periodic market has been similarly neglected, and many traditional markets are disappearing before being studied or properly understood.

An emerging field of research concerns the city as a major user of water. In a region characterised by water deficiency, severe competition exists between agricultural demands for water and the fast rising domestic and industrial needs of the major cities. The problems which some Middle Eastern cities are now facing in terms of water use are likely to become more widespread in the future and require urgent study.

Lastly, the idea and image of the city in the indigenous literature, and the ways in which contemporary urbanites perceive the urban environment have yet to be explored. But above all urban research in the Middle East must abandon its isolationism — an isolationism which many have sought to justify in terms of cultural specificity. Enormous advances have been made in urban research in other parts of the Third World resulting in new methodologies and exciting new theories which those working in the Middle East can no longer afford to ignore. New conceptual tools must be adopted if urban research in the Middle East is to progress from the stagnation of empiricism and acquire a more dynamic theoretical basis.

One fundamental problem, however, remains critical to the success of future urban research in the region — the constraints which result from data deficiencies. Government statistics on the city are generally inadequate, often inaccurate and in some cases non-existent. Greater interaction with practising planners and architects could open up some new sources of data previously restricted to these professions, but there is no doubt that in the future much vital data on the city must be collected in the field by the researcher. This demands both time and financial resources and is likely to remain a major obstacle to the progress of urban research for many years to come.

Finally, national institutions within the region must begin to play a much greater part in the formulation and execution of the urban research programmes. The continued participation of foreign researchers is important, but it must be in co-operation with Middle Eastern colleagues. Without underestimating the difficulties inherent in such an approach, it is nevertheless essential if research on the Middle East city is to yield significant developments in the future.

Today the Middle East stands at a new turning point in its history. The historic peace treaty in March 1979 between Egypt and Israel, and the seemingly impossible 1979 Iranian Revolution have thrown the region into turmoil. For many, the rise of Ayatollah Khomeini signifies the failure of the existing order in the Middle East and of those imported Western institutions and ideologies by which national elites hoped to bring about change and development according to their own prescription. The modern Middle Eastern city, for long promoted as the catalyst for change and progress, is now condemned by the new Islamic revolutionaries as a veritable cancer, alienated from its own environment, and the very embodiment of the region's moral decay. They have recoiled from recent social changes and in particular from modern city life with its gross emphasis on conspicuous consumption — calling for a return to the land. It remains to be seen whether the ideals of these Muslim fundamentalists succeed in engulfing most of the region as some observers predict. Whatever role the city is ultimately called upon to play, it will remain a fundamental element in Middle Eastern society. Circumstances may change the direction of urban research in the future but it could well become even more exciting than in the past.

References

1. M.E. Bonine, 'Urban studies in the Middle East', *Middle East Studies Association Bulletin*, vol. 10, no. 3 (1976) 19-20.

2. A.H. Hourani and S.M. Stern (eds.), *The Islamic City: A Colloquium* (Bruno Cassirer, Oxford, 1970); I.M. Lapidus, *Middle Eastern Cities: A Symposium on Ancient, Islamic and Contemporary Middle Eastern Urbanism* (University of California Press, Berkeley, 1969); L.C. Brown (ed.), *From Madina to Metropolis: Heritage and Change in the Near Eastern City* (The Darwin Press, Princeton, 1973).

3. V. Costello, *Urbanization in the Middle East* (Cambridge University Press, Cambridge, 1977).

4. M.E. Bonine, 'From Uruk to Casablanca: perspectives on the urban experience of the Middle East', *Journal of Urban History*, vol. 3, no. 2 (1977) 169.

1 THE ORIGIN AND EVOLUTION OF TOWNS: 4000 BC to AD 1900

J.M. Wagstaff

Origins and Early Development

Considerable difficulty attends any attempt to define *town* adequately in such a way as to be able to discuss morphological characteristics over a long time period and, arguably, for different cultures.[1] Rather than enter the debate, it is proposed to cut the Gordian knot tied by numerous scholars with a pragmatic definition. For purposes of this chapter a town is defined as

> 'a concentration of population larger than neighbouring agricultural settlements', in which there is a substantial non-agricultural population, which may be concerned with defence, administration, religion, commerce and/or industry, though not necessarily, of course, in that order.[2]

No longer can urbanism, the idea of living in such settlements, be conceived as a contagion spreading into neighbouring lands after incubation in southern Iraq around 4000 BC.[3] If the claims of Kenyon and Mellaart are justified, then towns existed around 7000 BC in the Jordan valley and in Anatolia[4] and if there, probably elsewhere as well. It is equally clear that no explanation for the rise of towns can be wholly adequate.[5] Certain prerequisites probably existed. Amongst these are the predisposition of men to settle, the emergence of a loose web of exchange, the development of settled agriculture in the Middle East circa 8000 BC, and the stabilising of farming villages in the period *c.* 7000 to 5000 BC. The production of food beyond the requirements of the cultivators themselves[6] may not have been so essential to the existence of the traders, craftsmen and others whose local concentration is part of our working definition of town, since complete specialisation may have emerged only slowly and the necessary support could have been extracted by force or through customary obligation. Finally, in southern Iraq, Iran and probably elsewhere the emergence of towns was accompanied by the desertion of other settlements in the immediate vicinity. This implies a gathering together of scattered communities, or *synoecism.*[7] The motive may have been religious,

11

political or economic, as current theories suggest, but the role of some 'leader' with possibly coercive power may have been important.

Whatever the explanations for the emergence of the first towns, by the first half of the third millennium BC, South-West Asia was dotted with towns and cities.[8] So, too, was the Nile Valley, despite the views of some Egyptologists.[9] The situation in the rest of North Africa is obscure, but the first towns may have been the Phoenician and Greek colonies established at points on the coast during the eighth and seventh centuries BC.[10]

The earliest towns, those of the third millennium BC, may best be described with the aid of a model derived from research on Mesopotamian towns (Table 1.1, Figure 1.1).[11] The core of the town was an area surrounded by massive, towered walls which were not only, or even primarily, for defence, but were meant to display the wealth or power of the urban community and its ruler, as well as to give a ritual definition to the community. The large and ornamental gateways were used as meeting places for the governing and judicial authorities; markets may have been located near them. The walled area contained temple and palace complexes. In Mesopotamian towns these were separate, but in northern Iraq and Syria they often formed a combined unit, the citadel nature of which was emphasised by location on some eminence and by its own walls. The dominant feature in many ordinary Egyptian towns may have been just a temple.

Around the dominant structures were the residences of various officials and the houses of the ordinary townsmen. Little is known of the layout of these residential areas, since excavation has tended to concentrate on the monumental structures. Elements of regularity have been detected in street systems,[12] but the dominant impression left by such areas as have been examined is of a cellular structure built up of units comprising small rectangular rooms and courtyards bounded by narrow lanes.[13] Outside the walls lay a suburban area combining clusters of houses, farms and cattle stalls surrounded by fields and gardens. In Mesopotamia the suburb contained a commercial area, literally a harbour settlement lying on an arm of the river or a navigable canal, where merchants had their factories; in Syria these appear to have been situated within the walled area. A secondary temple existed in the suburbs of some towns and was occasionally linked to the core area by an elaborate processional way. Although suburbs often remained unwalled, in several Egyptian towns they were subsequently included within an outer ring of defences.[14]

Most third millennium towns were small, perhaps covering four to

Table 1.1: Principal Characteristics of Successive Types of Town in the Middle East

Characteristics	Early	Hellenistic	Late Antique	Islamic
Walls	—	—	—	—
Street system	?	orthogonal	transition	irregular
Zonation		—	—	—
Public space				
Agoras		—	transition	
Religious buildings	temples	temples	churches synagogues	mosques medreses churches synagogues
Municipal offices		—	transition	
Gymnasia		—	transition	?
Baths		—	—	—
Theatres		—	transition	
Markets:				
open	—	—	—	—
covered	—	—	—	—
Caravanserais	?	?	kaisariyas	—
External authority				
Citadel	some	—	—	—
Palace	—	rare	transition	—
Public water supply		—	transition	?
Private space				
Residential quarters	?	—	—	—
Courtyard houses	—	—	—	—

Note:

— = presence of characteristic
? = evidence uncertain

10 ha, if information from the lower Diyala plains and Khuzistan can be generalised, but some covered as much as 20 ha.[15] A few were considerably larger. Ur, for example, covered 89 ha at its peak *c.* 2100 BC, whilst the famous walls of Uruk enclose 502 ha. The size and elaboration of their monumental buildings varied considerably, as did the richness and sophistication of other aspects of their material culture. Many of the artefacts discovered in them were of local origin, but others were clearly imported. Cuneiform tables of slightly later date than the third

Figure 1.1: Model of an Early Town

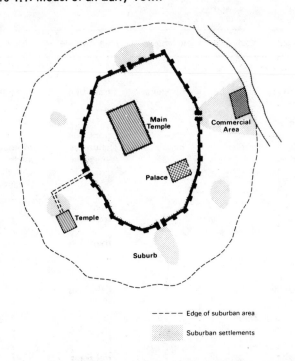

Main
Temple

Commercial
Area

Palace

Temple

Suburb

– – – – – Edge of suburban area

Suburban settlements

millennium point to the careful organisation of the trade.[16] Of course, even on a time scale calibrated in centuries rather than years, not all the known urban sites were occupied simultaneously, and towns seem to have risen to prominence and decayed to relative insignificance remarkably quickly, perhaps indicating the importance of royal courts to their flowering. None the less, the variations pointed out above are *prima facie* evidence for the existence at the subregional level of hierarchically organised and interconnected urban systems. Such systems have continued to exist in the Middle East, though their configurations fluctuated greatly over time (Figure 1.2).[17]

Urban form, in general, remained more or less as described for the third millennium until the third century BC. Various innovations, however, were introduced. One of these was increased formality.[18] Walled areas were made to approximate regular geometrical figures; citadels were carefully sited; and street systems were formally laid out, perhaps even a gridiron plan, as at Megiddo II following the Assyrian conquest.[19] Second millennium Holep Sesostris (Kahun) in

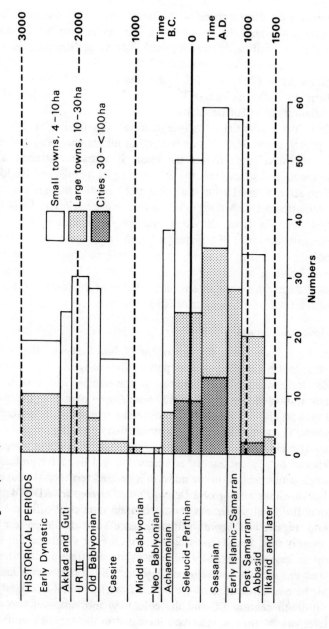

Figure 1.2: Fluctuations in Town Size and Number in the Diyala Plains (from data in R.M. Adams, *Land Behind Baghdad*, 1965)

Egypt even shows traces of deliberate social and economic zoning.[20] Although found in small towns, formal layouts were particularly associated with such large imperial capitals as Nimrud, laid out on a 360 ha site by Assurnipal (883-859 BC), Nineveh (729 ha) built by Sennacherib (704 to 561 BC) and Babylon, which was given its final form by Nebuchadnezzer II (604 to 561 BC).[21] The lack of overall planning at the Hittite capital, Hattusas (Boğazköy),[22] and its absence from the residential units of ephemeral Akhetaten (Tel el-Amarna) in Egypt[23] show that the rule was by no means universal. A second and related development was the clear, if sporadic, attempt at urban renewal, as distinct from the refurbishing of temples and the like. Both Sennacherib and Darius the Great (522 to 486 BC) are credited with such attempts.[24] A third development, more obvious in Syria/Palestine and Anatolia than elsewhere, was the emergence in the tenth and eleventh centuries of a system using the outermost line of houses as a defence. This is significant because its systematic use, as at Bethshemesh and Debir in southern Palestine,[25] implies at least an overall concept of the size, shape and internal articulation of the town — a rationalising of the traditional, irregular cell-like structure.

Hellenistic Towns[26]

Radical change came to parts of the Middle East with the intrusion of Macedonian and then Roman power. The change involved three related developments — first, an increase in the number of towns, second the elaboration of new urban forms stemming in part from the third development, the introduction of a different socio-political concept of the town. The Greco-Roman concept was that of a self-governing community (Greek *pólis*), bound together not just by religious obligations or kinship but by contractual relationships, and living for preference in a single settlement set in the midst of a defined territory.[27] Pausanias, the Lydian-Greek author of a *Description of Greece* (c. AD 174), thought that the focal settlement should contain municipal offices, a gymnasium, theatre and *'agorá* ('gathering place') and should possess a public water supply. Pounds has suggested that the list should be supplemented by an *'acrópolis* (literally 'high city' but in effect a citadel), walls, at least one temple, and religious objects.[28] Such settlements had existed in the coastal districts of the region from the initial Greek settlings of the tenth century BC and the colonising movement of two centuries later, whilst their number was increased in districts like south-western Asia Minor be creeping Hellenisation. A major increase in numbers came when the successors of Alexander the Great and after them the

Figure 1.3: Spread of *Pólis*-type Organisations in Palestine under Roman Rule (After M. Avi-Yonah, *The Holy Land*, Grand Rapids, Michigan, 1966, Figure 8)

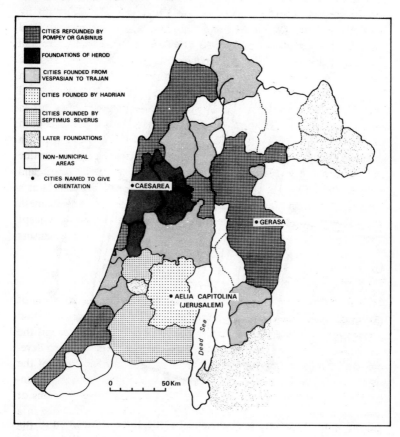

Roman emperors used the Greek type of town as a mechanism for controlling, administering and civilising the peoples of their various provinces (Figure 1.3). Greek forms of local elective government were extended to many native towns, some of which were rebuilt following destruction in war, and were endowed with suites of public buildings. *Pólis* communities which, like Smyrna, had decomposed into separate villages, were reunited. New towns were founded, but it is difficult to determine just how many because of the processes already mentioned, as well as the custom of renaming older foundations to honour current

Figure 1.4: Model of an Hellenistic Town

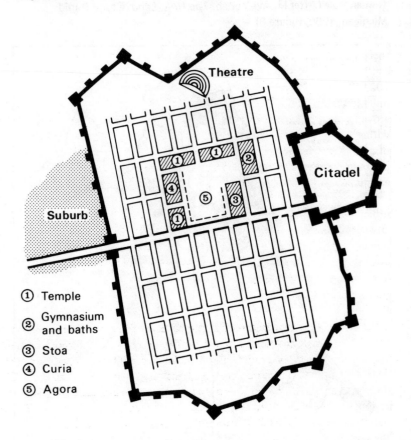

① Temple
② Gymnasium and baths
③ Stoa
④ Curia
⑤ Agora

rulers. Some, however, were created by the forced synoecism of pre-existing village or small town communities, as in the case of Halicarnasus (Bodrum) around the middle of the third century BC.[29] Others were founded by the settling of veteran troops; the Roman *coloniae* in Asia Minor, Syria and North Africa are particularly good examples.

Whatever their precise origins, the various urban settlements of the Greco-Roman Middle East assumed common morphological features (Table 1.1, Figure 1.4).[30] Under the Hellenistic monarchs the spatial positioning and grouping of public buildings was used to enhance the coherence of the urban layout, while under the Romans full play was given to the dramatic effects of massive buildings seen in architecturally contrived vistas. The Romans also added bath suites to the gymnasia and built aqueducts. Many of the public buildings, together with *stoás* (covered markets) and the forerunners of caravanserais, were located on or close to the *'agorá*, which was often made the focus of the town plan, as it was already of public life. Leading from it to gates on opposite sides of the town was a particularly wide street along which were shops and workshops. Herod the Great probably introduced the idea of providing it with colonnades, and from simple beginnings at Antioch in Syria before 4 BC, the concept reached great elaboration in Roman Gerasa, laid out in the third quarter of the first century AD, and in the last, third-century stage of Leptis Magna. This street served as the principal axis for laying out the rest of the town, where formal planning was introduced. In Greek towns rectangular blocks were normally used, but the Romans generally preferred squares. One of the great merits of such a standardised orthogonal framework was that it allowed piece-meal development of the town into a coherent whole over a number of centuries as local wealth or the ruler's beneficence allowed.[31] The example of Priene, laid out on a mountain side in western Asia Minor during the second half of the fourth century BC, shows that the rigid formality of the plan was capable of skilful adaptation to site. Enclosing many of the towns, and linking with the citadel, was a strong wall. Configuration and location were frequently unrelated to the ground plan of the town, but were determined by current military ideas and technology.[32] This characteristic makes particularly hazardous the use of the walled enclosures to determine population, as attempted by Russell.[33] None the less, metropolitan cities existed in the shape of Alexandria and Seleucia/Ctesiphon, joined later by Constantinople, New Rome. Important regional centres included a revived Carthage, Ephesus and Antioch-in-Syria.

Something of the expansion of the urban system in general can be learnt from the lower Diyala plains (Figure 1.2). All categories of town showed a considerable increase over the previous period and there was a corresponding elaboration of the urban hierarchy. Further development and some restructuring of the hierarchy took place during the succeeding Sassanian period (AD 225 to 637). The Sassanian kings were reputed to be great builders of towns, though some of these must have been reconstructions necessitated by wars with the Roman Empire. Round circuits, perhaps taken from Assyria via Parthia, seem to have been favoured, but the regularity of internal layouts may have been adopted from Hellenistic towns. However, all vestiges of elective government and corporate responsibility had probably long since vanished.

On the Roman side of the frontier, the socio-economic crisis of the third century AD, as well as reorganisations of imperial and local government, had a profound if creeping effect on towns. Local autonomy frequently broke down under the heavy responsibilities placed upon town councils by the imperial government at a time when inflation and periodic confiscations of civic land reduced their resources. By the time of Justinian I (AD 527 to 565), imperial governors had become responsible for running most of the towns. Some towns evidently became too small to be viable administrative centres and their populations were amalgamated with others so that, overall, the number of towns appears to have declined. Further losses in numbers resulted from reorganisations of the military districts in the east, the abandonment of sites as a result of man-induced ecological change (for example, Harran), the slow deterioration of harbours by silting (Ephesus) and the shift of trade routes (Palmyra).

Those towns which survived underwent considerable internal modification (Table 1.1). Public buildings fell into disuse as town councils ceased to meet, games and plays were abolished or discouraged, and paganism was disestablished. Most striking was the encroachment of commercial and domestic buildings onto public open space, as on the *'agorá* at Dura-Europos well before the town's destruction in AD 250,[34] and along the colonnaded axial streets of Damascus and Aleppo during the fourth century.[35] These are surely consequences of the weakening of town government, for we are told how a particularly efficient governor of Edessa (Urfa) in AD 496 to 497 'cleared the streets of filth and swept away the booths which had been built by the artisans in the porticos and streets'.[36] Where such vigorous action was not taken the result was the partial, or sometimes the virtually complete replacement of a rigorous gridiron street system by the tortuous, narrow alleys and culs-de-sac considered typical of the Islamic town.

Islamic Towns to c. AD 1500

The expansion of the Muslim Arabs during the seventh and eighth centuries has been credited with significantly increasing the degree of urbanisation in the Middle East and with the introduction of a new urban form, the Islamic town. Neither claim has been fully sustained by recent research.

Protagonists for increased urbanisation develop three arguments. The most fundamental is religious. Islam means submission to the will of God, and man's duty is best performed, it is claimed, in an urban environment. The Qur'ān contrasts the virtues of settled life with nomadism, whilst the Shari'ah maintains that the Friday midday prayer, the main integrative community ritual which all Muslims should attend, can be performed only in a permanently inhabited settlement with 40 legally responsible men present. Urban living is, thus, an ideal to which Muslims should strive.[37] A second argument stresses the military needs of the invading Arabs, and points to the establishment of military camps which gradually grew into towns – for example, Basra (founded AD 635), Kūfah (AD 639), Fusṭāt (AD 641 to 642) and Kairouan (AD 670) – and the case could be further supported by adding various fortress towns established later on the frontiers with Byzantium and the Khazars.[38] A third argument takes up the idea of the fourteenth-century historian, Ibn Khaldûn.[39] It is the observed tendency for Muslim rulers to establish new capitals for themselves. The pattern was perhaps best developed in North Africa after the break-up of the united Caliphate,[40] but it may be traced earlier in South-West Asia where Baghdād and Sāmarrā' were produced in this way.[41]

Each argument has been challenged, particularly by Lapidus.[42] Without citing comparative statistics, he contended that relatively few towns originated during the Muslim era. During the first century of Arab rule, for example, none was established in Syria or in Iran, apart from Fars, whilst the establishment of such undoubted new towns as Basra, Kūfah and later Baghdād simply involved a transference of population from pre-existing urban communities. Adams' work on the lower Diyala plains supports the argument (Figure 1.2). Many of the *villes de gouvernement* were either ephemeral creations or established as twins alongside already existing towns.[43] Neither added significantly to the degree of urbanisation in the region.

Lapidus has also shown that the conquering Arabs did not settle exclusively in new towns.[44] Some attached themselves to existing urban settlements as both settlers and garrisons, whilst others settled in villages, notably in Iran. Despite the disparagement of the Qur'ān,[45] though, many Arabs remained nomads and their intrusion into the agricultural districts of Syria was associated with a regression of settled living, as well as a retreat in cultivation. This diverse pattern of settling refutes an alleged Muslim Arab preference for urban living. Lapidus concludes: 'The Arabs gave a certain impetus to Middle Eastern urbanisation without causing a general increase in the level of . . . urban development and without identifying cities with Islam.'[46]

Except in the case of the new foundations, the Arabs did not introduce a model Islamic town. Its typical features are well known and can be summarised by Table 1.1 and Figure 1.5.[47] Many of these were

Figure 1.5: Model of an Islamic Town

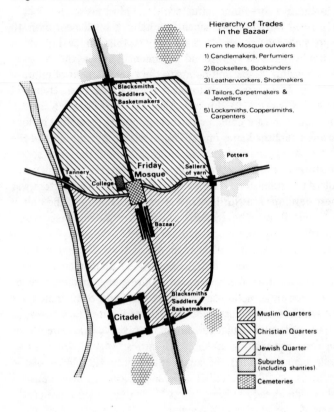

Hierarchy of Trades
in the Bazaar

From the Mosque outwards

1) Candlemakers, Perfumiers

2) Booksellers, Bookbinders

3) Leatherworkers, Shoemakers

4) Tailors, Carpetmakers & Jewellers

5) Locksmiths, Coppersmiths, Carpenters

Blacksmiths
Saddlers
Basketmakers

Potters

Tannery

College

Friday Mosque

Sellers of yarn

Bazaar

Blacksmiths
Saddlers
Basketmakers

Citadel

Muslim Quarters

Christian Quarters

Jewish Quarter

Suburbs (including shanties)

Cemeteries

either inherited from pre-existing towns or emerged gradually over time, through a process of convergence.[48] The most distinctive Islamic feature, the mosque, appeared in purely Muslim towns from the beginning and was added to existing towns at the moment of conquest, usually by confiscating the most prominent church or temple. Residential quarters existed in the early Arab foundations and were certainly extended by Muslim settlers in conquered towns. Lapidus has argued that convergence was strengthened by sharing the same socio-political developments in the later Middle Ages. Between the ninth and eleventh centuries most townsmen, who had previously resisted Islam, were converted and mosques began to proliferate.[49] Meanwhile, the pattern of small but distinct residential communities was consolidated in response to both a fissioning of the Muslim community itself and also

an alienation of the administration from the mass of the people resulting from a seizure of power by alien groups, often Turks but also
Mamluks in Egypt and Syria, and Mongols in eastern Anatolia and Iran.

Although the existence of residential quarters is as much perceptual
as anything else, they were given coherence by their recognition as
convenient fiscal units; generally they do not appear to have been given
physical definition by walls and gates until after AD 1500.[50] In the
larger cities of South-West Asia, where the mosaic of communities
became particularly detailed, the number of quarters could be large.
According to Ottoman tax lists of the early sixteenth century, Aleppo,
with a population estimated at about 67,000, contained 50 'quarters'.[51]
Apart from fiscal obligations, cohesion was given to the quarters by
definite social acts, whether participation in the frequent street fight-
ing[52] or, more constructively, in the maintenance of some facility for
community use.[53] In part, this explains the proliferation of the
mosques and other Muslim religious buildings so noticeable in the
mature Islamic town from the twelfth century onwards. Conspicuous
consumption on the part of the wealthy was another factor.[54] Some of
the quarters were clearly of higher social status than others and, in
general, rich and poor do not appear to have lived side by side.[55]

Such conglomerate urban communities did not exist in a vacuum.
Although cities such as Cairo and Aleppo were sustained by inter-
regional trade in AD 1500 and many towns developed manufacturing
specialities which entered regional trade, the basic support for the
tradesmen, artisans, labourers and servants who made up the bulk of
the urban population was more basic. In part, it consisted of providing
goods and services for the surrounding villages. But the main support
was the influx of wealth from the countryside in the form of the landlords' shares of the harvest and delivered in kind, technically either as
tax or as part of sharecropping agreements. This helps to explain the
importance of the court, or its equivalent, to the *villes de gouvernement*, and their speedy decay when the administrators, who were also
landlords, moved elsewhere.

Urban hierarchies are difficult to reconstruct for the period, but the
writings of Al-Muḳaddasī (c. AD 985 to 986) and other Arab geographers show that they were recognised,[56] whilst the lower Diyala plains
again provide a concrete example of spatial patterning.[57] In the tenth
century the whole of the Middle East was dominated by Baghdād, the
capital of the united Caliphate, with a population estimated at 200,000-
500,000.[58] This is considerably larger than both Constantinople at its
Byzantine peak (c. 150,000-200,000 in the eleventh century),[59] as well

as Seleucia/Ctesiphon (*c.* 38,000).[60] Cairo in the thirteenth century had a population of about 500,000.[61] Other cities were much smaller, indicating a primate rank-size structure at the subregional and regional level, even if all its levels cannot be specified from currently available data. More quantitative information is available after 1500.

Islamic Towns, c. AD 1500-1900

Largely on the basis of Ottoman statistical sources, Tekeil has argued for the existence in sixteenth-century Anatolia of a clearly defined urban hierarchy integrated by carefully organised trading and administrative structures.[62] The imperial capital, İstanbul, dominated the system — and the entire Middle East — with a population estimated at 400,000 in the period 1520 to 1535.[63] It remained dominant throughout the period under review, with its population estimated at about 700,000 in the middle of the seventeenth century and at over one million in 1900.[64] Below İstanbul in the sixteenth century came a number of regional centres with populations between 20,000 and 40,000. These were located at the intersections of major routes or at break-bulk points, and were frequently major manufacturing centres with famous specialities. Around these centres were arranged two sets of lower-order towns, settlements with populations of under 10,000 and those with under 5,000. The sultans took care to maintain the health of this urban system, even to the extent of drafting settlers to reconstitute town populations. The urban population grew during the sixteenth century in the western provinces of the Empire,[65] though in Syria and Egypt stagnation may have been characteristic in the lower levels of the hierarchy. Decline took place in such major regional centres as Cairo, Damascus and Aleppo, partly because of the draining attractions of İstanbul to elites following conquest from the Mamluks and partly because of the decisive shift in the lucrative spice trade following the Portuguese break into the Indian Ocean.[66]

According to Tekeil the integrated urban structure of sixteenth-century Anatolia disintegrated in the following two centuries,[67] a period of considerable socio-economic strain and readjustment for the whole Middle East, as well as of political decentralisation. Relatively closed subregional urban systems emerged, perhaps similar to those prevailing in Iran, where political centralisation was much less developed. None the less, towns appear to have increased in population and area throughout the Ottoman Empire, partly by the growth of what today would be called shanty-towns to house crowds of dispirited rural migrants. During the nineteenth century, expanding trade with Europe

Figure 1.6: Distribution of Towns of over 5,000 in Iran, *c.* 1900
(Note: International boundaries are those of the present day.
Data from J. Bharier, 'The growth of towns and villages in Iran,
1900-66', *Middle Eastern Studies*, vol. 8 (1972) 51-62)

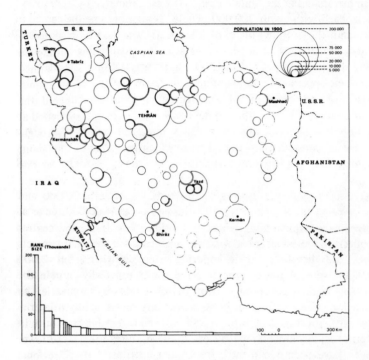

led to a restructuring of the urban hierarchies in the Middle East. Ports
such as Smyrna (İzmir), Beirūt and Alexandria began to emerge as
major cities, each with populations of over 200,000 by 1900.[68] The
spread of railways revitalised and reshaped urban systems in western
Asia Minor, whilst elsewhere in the Middle East new towns emerged,
either to meet the needs of increasingly efficient administrations or,
more organically, in response to expanding local economies.[69]

Population estimates for settlements with over 5,000 people assem-
bled for the territory of present-day Iran by Bharier[70] allow the reconstruction of at least the major elements of several subregional urban
systems before they were much affected by Westernisation. Around
1900, the urban population of Iran was about 2.08 million out of a

total estimated at 9.92 million (21 per cent). The urban system of the country was strongly primate (Figure 1.6), perhaps reflecting both the colonial nature of the country's economy at the time, as well as the importance of political and administrative control in shaping urban hierarchies in the Middle East.[71] It was dominated by Tehrān and Tabrīz, each with about 200,000 people. Tehrān became the capital in 1786 and the settling there of the court was largely responsible, through its demands for goods and services, for quadrupling the population in the next 114 years.[72] In 1900, Tabrīz was not only the residence of the heir apparent and a major administrative centre, but it was also the leading commercial city of Iran, benefiting from trade links through Turkish and Russian territory to the Black Sea.[73] The rest of the urban structure of Iran was composed of many small and middle-sized towns arranged in constellations around cities which performed higher order administrative and economic functions for their relatively isolated regions.

The socio-economic aspects of this type of spatial structure have been revealed for Kermān. By 1900, this city of some 60,000 souls had emerged as a major trading centre for south-eastern Iran. Not only did it collect the produce of a wide region including several lesser rank towns, and distribute goods imported from elsewhere, but it also handled large surpluses of manufactured goods, especially carpets, and high-value agricultural produce from its own rural hinterland.[74] This involved a close relationship between the city and a tightly organised system of socially and economically dependent villages.[75] Similar patterns of lower-order spatial organisation, integrating towns and villages, have been documented from other districts of Iran[76] and can be paralleled from elsewhere in the Middle East.[77]

Just as urban hierarchies were not stable during the period 1500 to 1900, so the extent and internal planning of towns fluctuated. Three major tendencies can be observed. First, the urban structure was dynamic: This can be illustrated on a large scale with reference to Cairo, but it may be paralleled in many smaller towns whose development has yet to be investigated. Whilst Cairo declined in population to reach about 250,000-260,000 at the end of the eighteenth century and decayed physically from sheer neglect, new market areas emerged and the pattern of at least aristocratic residence changed considerably in a search for quiet and semi-rural living. Both tendencies perpetuated the city's historic westward drift, leaving behind a zone of discard characterised by poverty, decay and ruin.[78] In some relatively small towns, the number of residential quarters rose as population increased, but a more general stability was to be found in others. Some of the quarters were doubtless purely residential, but the more central ones seem to have been a mixture of shops, workshops, offices and housing sewn into the fabric of the town not only by shopping, service and employment needs but also by networks engendered by 'putting-out' systems of manufacturing, especially in textiles.[79] There may also have been a tendency in the cities towards greater physical differentiation of quarters through neglect of all but a few of the entrances to them and by the use of gates to bar access. This seems to reflect insecurity and a growing introversion amongst communities within towns.

A second tendency becomes clear during the twentieth century but probably originated much earlier. This was for the functions of such permanent structures as bazaars and caravanserais to change over time.[80] Paradoxically, the grouping of trades and crafts, which some have seen as a characteristic of the Islamic town, emerges clearly in the documentation of the period 1500 to 1900, and is doubtless associated with the administrative and fiscal control exerted through guilds.[81]

A third trend which also emerges in the period 1500 to 1900 is the deliberate planning of new urban developments. Physical planning itself was not new to the Islamic town for it had been found in some early Muslim creations, notably the Round City of Baghdād.[82] What was perhaps novel was its re-emergence after a long period of apparent neglect and the forms which it took. Ettinghausen has pointed to the degree of organisation involved in the laying out in sixteenth-century İstanbul of *külliyeh* complexes integrating large mosques, *medreses*, libraries, baths, kitchens and hospitals, a development seen earlier in İzmir and Bursa.[83] But the most striking planned developments before the intrusion of Western ideas into the region are associated with successive imperial capitals in Iran. Although to some extent anticipated, for example, at Tabrīz during the fifteenth century and at Qazvīn in the sixteenth century, as well as followed by a reorganisation of the north-eastern section of Shīrāz in the eighteenth century, the flowering of what might be called the Persian garden suburb came at Eşfahān under the direction of Shah Abbas I (1587 to 1630).[84] The heart of his new *ville de gouvernement*, 1.5 km south of the historic city, was a vast rectangular space (510 × 165 m) used for target shooting and polo. Close to it stood two large mosques, the imperial palace and a vast bazaar. Four wide streets led to the *maydān* or approached close to it. One of these, the famed Chahār Bāgh, was laid out in three lanes separated by hedges and trees. It formed the axis for an extensive gridiron plan integrating gardens and palaces into one vast and impressive unit, only part of which now, sadly, survives.

During the nineteenth century regular, planned suburbs became common features of at least the larger Middle Eastern towns, as the wealthy and their emulators moved out from congested city centres. In some cases, dual towns developed. One was Europeanised and characterised by widely spaced houses, set in wide gardens well back from the straight and often surfaced roads intersecting at right angles or radiating out from public gardens. The other town was Oriental, a crumbling and crowded version of the traditional Islamic town.[85] Even outside the areas of direct French control in the Maghreb, the influence of Baron von Haussmann can be detected, notably in the Cairo suburb of Ismāʿīlīyah, begun in 1867 to 1869, and the Khedive Ismāʿīl's plans which shaped the subsequent development of the city as massive immigration began to effect it towards the end of the century.[86] The hand of the ruler was thus crucial in these planned accretions to the Islamic town. It was also of fundamental importance in shaping not only the detail of earlier towns and cities in the region, but in giving them life. Relative locational advantage in the dynamic space-economy of the Middle East determined how long they flourished beyond the four-ruler span suggested by that shrewd observer of the human drama, Ibn Khaldûn.[87]

References

1. P. Wheatley, 'The concept of urbanism', in P.J. Ucko, R. Tringham and G.W. Dimbleby (eds.), *Man, Settlement and Urbanism* (Duckworth, London, 1972), pp. 601-37.

2. C.T. Smith, *An Historical Geography of Western Europe before 1800* (Longmans, London, 1967), p. 299, but derived from discussion in J.H. Mundy and P. Riesenberg, *The Medieval Town* (Van Nostrand, Princeton, 1958), pp. 9-15.

3. C.C. Lamberg-Karlovsky, 'Urban interaction on the Iranian plateau: excavations at Tepe Yahya, 1967-1973', *Proceedings of the British Academy*, vol. 59 (1973), 283-319.

4. K.M. Kenyon, *Digging Up Jericho* (Benn, London, 1957); J. Mellaart, *Çatal Hüyük. A Neolithic Town in Anatolia* (Thames and Hudson, London, 1967); R.J. Braidwood, 'Jericho and its setting in Near Eastern history', *Antiquity*, vol. 31 (1957) 73-81.

5. R.M. Adams, 'The origin of cities', *Scientific American*, vol. 203 (1960) 153-68; B.W. Blouet, 'Factors influencing the evolution of settlement patterns', in P.J. Ucko, R. Tringham and G.W. Dimbleby (eds.), *Man, Settlement and Urbanism*, pp. 3-15; K.V. Flannery, 'The origins of the village as a settlement type in Mesoamerica and the Near East: a comparative study', in Ucko, Tringham and Dimbleby, ibid., pp. 23-53; L. Mumford, *The City in History* (Penguin Books,

Harmondsworth, 1966), pp. 40-69; A.C. Renfrew, 'Trade as action at a distance: questions of integration and communication', in J.A. Sabloff and C.C. Lamberg-Karlovsky (eds.), *Ancient Civilisation and Trade* (Benjamin Cummings, Albuquerque, 1975), pp. 3-59; B. Trigger, 'Determinants of urban growth in pre-industrial societies', in Ucko, Tringham and Dimbleby, ibid., pp. 575-99; T.C. Young, 'Population densities and early Mesopotamian urbanism', in Ucko, Tringham and Dimbleby, ibid., pp. 827-42.

6. V.G. Childe, 'The urban revolution', *Town Planning Review*, vol. 21 (1950) 3-17.

7. R.M. Adams, 'Patterns of urbanization in early southern Mesopotamia', in Ucko, Tringham and Dimbleby, *Man, Settlement and Urbanism*, pp. 735-49; B.J. Kemp, 'The early development of towns in Egypt', *Antiquity*, vol. 51 (1977) 185-200; H.J. Nissen, 'The city wall of Uruk', in Ucko, Tringham and Dimbleby, *Man, Settlement and Urbanism*, pp. 793-8.

8. C.C. Lamberg-Karlovsky, 'Urban interaction on the Iranian plateau: excavations at Tepe Yahya, 1967-1973', pp. 283-319; J. Mellaart, 'The earliest settlements in western Asia from the ninth to the end of the fifth millennium B.C.', in *The Cambridge Ancient History*, 3rd edn., vol. 1, pt. 1 (Cambridge, 1970), pp. 248-326; M. Mallowan, 'The development of cities from Al-'Ubaid to the end of Uruk 5', in *The Cambridge Ancient History*, 3rd edn., vol. 1, pt. 1, pp. 326-462.

9. Kemp, 'The early development of towns'; P. Lampl, *Cities and Planning in the Ancient Near East* (Studio Vista, London, 1968), pp. 23-4; D. O'Connor, 'The geography of settlement in ancient Egypt', in Ucko, Tringham and Dimbleby, *Man, Settlement and Urbanism*, pp. 681-98; J.A. Wilson, 'Cities in ancient Egypt', *Economic Development and Cultural Change*, vol. 3 (1954) 74.

10. N.G.L. Hammond, *A History of Greece to 322 B.C.* (Oxford University Press, Oxford, 1959), p. 121; B.H. Warmington, *Carthage* (Hale, London, 1960), pp. 20-33.

11. Lampl, *Cities and Planning*, pp. 25-32; A.L. Oppenheim, *Ancient Mesopotamia: Portrait of a Dead Civilisation*, 4th impression (University of Chicago Press, Chicago and London, 1964), pp. 115-40. For some of the problems involved see P.J. Parr, 'Settlement patterns and urban planning in the ancient Levant: the nature of the evidence', in Ucko, Tringham and Dimbleby, *Man, Settlement and Urbanism*, pp. 805-10.

12. Lampl, *Cities and Planning*, pp. 21-2; Oppenheim, *Ancient Mesopotamia*, pp. 127-8.

13. In particular, Lampl, ibid., Figs. 25, 53, 55, 56.

14. Kemp, 'The early development of towns'.

15. R.M. Adams, 'Agriculture and urban life in early southwestern Iran', *Science*, vol. 136 (1962) 109-22; Adams, *Land Behind Baghdad. A History of Settlement on the Diyala Plains* (University of Chicago, Chicago and London, 1965), pp. 33-45 and Figure 2.

16. S. Lloyd, *Early Anatolia* (Penguin Books, Harmondsworth, 1956), pp. 112-18.

17. This is best demonstrated at the moment by Figures 2 to 6 in R.M. Adams, *Land Behind Baghdad*.

18. Lampl, *Cities and Planning*; Oppenheim, *Ancient Mesopotamia*, pp. 132-5; Parr, 'Settlement patterns and urban planning in the ancient Levant'.

19. As Parr, ibid., points out, the date is disputed and could be either 915 BC or 732 BC.

20. Kemp, 'The early development of towns'; Lampl, *Cities and Planning*, pp. 26-7.

21. Lampl, ibid., pp. 14-19; D. Oates, 'The development of Assyrian towns

and cities', in Ucko, Tringham and Dimbleby, *Man, Settlement and Urbanism*, pp. 799-804.

22. Lampl, *Cities and Planning*, pp. 43-4, Figure 131.

23. B.J. Kemp, 'Temple and town in ancient Egypt', in Ucko, Tringham and Dimbleby, *Man, Settlement and Urbanism*, pp. 657-80; Lampl, *Cities and Planning*, p. 31.

24. Oppenheim, *Ancient Mesopotamia*, p. 140; Lampl, *Cities and Planning*, p. 119.

25. Lampl, ibid., pp. 38-9, Figures 115, 116.

26. The major source for this section is A.H.M. Jones, *The Greek City from Alexander to Justinian* (Oxford University Press, Oxford, 1940).

27. G.E. von Grunebaum, 'Hellenistic and Muslim views on cities', *Economic Development and Cultural Change*, vol. 3 (1954) 75-6; von Grunebaum, 'The Muslim town and the Hellenistic town', *Scientia*, vol. 90 (1955) 364-70.

28. N.J.G. Pounds, 'The urbanisation of the Classical world', *Annals of the Association of American Geographers*, vol. 59 (1969) 135-57.

29. G.E. Bean and J.M. Cook, 'The Halicarnassus peninsula', *Annual of the British School at Athens*, vol. 50 (1955) 56-171.

30. R. Martin, *L'Urbanisme dans la Grèce Antique* (Picard, Paris, 1956); J.B. Ward-Perkins, *Cities of Greece and Italy: Planning in Classical Antiquity* (Sidgwick and Jackson, London, 1974).

31. Ward-Perkins, ibid., pp. 14-16, 31-2.

32. Ward-Perkins, ibid.; A. McNicoll, 'The development of urban defences in Hellenistic Asia Minor', in Ucko, Tringham and Dimbleby, *Man, Settlement and Urbanism*, pp. 787-91.

33. J.C. Russell, 'Late ancient and medieval population', *Transactions of the American Philosophical Society*, new series, vol. 48, pt. 3 (1958) 3-152.

34. Ward-Perkins, *Cities of Greece and Italy*, pp. 20-1, Figures 22-5.

35. J. Sauvaget, 'Esquisses d'une histoire de la ville de Damas', *Révue des Etudes Islamiques*, vol. 4 (1934) 422-80; 'Esquisse d'une histoire de la ville d'Alep', *Révue des Etudes Islamiques*, vol. 8 (1934) 421-80; *Alep: Essai sur le developpement d'une grande ville syrienne des origines au milieu du XIX siècle* (Librarie Orientaliste Paul Geuthner, Paris, 1941); see also N. Elisseeff, 'Damas à la lumière des théories de Jean Sauvaget', in A.H. Hourani and S.M. Stern (eds.), *The Islamic City: A Colloquium* (Bruno Cassirer, Oxford, 1970), pp. 157-77.

36. 'Life of St Joshua the Stylite' quoted in J.B. Segel, 'Mesopotamian communities from Julian to the rise of Islam', *Proceedings of the British Academy*, vol. 41 (1956) 109-39.

37. F. Benet, 'The ideology of Islamic urbanisation', *International Journal of Comparative Sociology*, vol. 4 (1963) 211-26; W.J. Fischel, 'The city in Islam', *Middle Eastern Affairs*, vol. 7 (1956) 227-32; G.E. von Grunebaum, 'The Muslim town and the Hellenistic town', pp. 363-70; von Grunebaum, *Islam: Essays in the Nature and Growth of a Cultural Tradition* (Routledge and Kegan Paul, London, 1955), pp. 141-58; G. Hamdan, 'The pattern of medieval urbanism in the Arab world', *Geography*, vol. 47 (1962) 121-34; X. de Planhol, *The World of Islam* (Cornell University Press, Ithaca, NY, 1959).

38. Benet, 'The ideology of Islamic urbanisation'; Hamdan, 'The pattern of medieval urbanisation in the Arab world'; E. Pauty, 'Villes spontanées et villes crées en Islam', *Annales de l'institut d'Etudes Orientales*, vol. 9 (1951) 52-75.

39. Ibn Khaldûn, *An Introduction to History. The Muqaddimah*, trans. F. Rosenthal, ed. N.J. Dawood (Routledge and Kegan Paul, London, 1967), pp. 263-9, 272-95.

40. Fischel, 'The city in Islam'; Hamdan, 'The pattern of medieval urbanism

in the Arab world'; Pauty, 'Villes spontanées'; R. le Tourneau, *Les Villes Musulmanes de l'Afrique du Nord* (Algiers, 1957).

41. L. Lassner, 'Massignon and Baghdad: the complexities of growth in an imperial city', *Journal of the Economic and Social History of the Orient*, vol. 9 (1966) 1-27; 'The Caliph's personal domain. The city plan of Baghdad re-examined', in A.H. Hourani and S.M. Stern (eds.), *The Islamic City: A Colloquium*, pp. 103-18; J.M. Rogers, 'Sāmarrā: A study in medieval town-planning', in Hourani and Stern, ibid., pp. 119-55.

42. A. Bourgay, 'Islam et géographie', *Révue de Géographie de Lyon*, vol. 45 (1970) 75-104; S. Landay, 'The ecology of Islamic cities: the case for the ethno-city', *Economic Geography*, vol. 47 (1971) 303-13; I.M. Lapidus, 'Muslim cities and Islamic societies', in I.M. Lapidus (ed.), *Middle Eastern Cities* (University of California Press, Berkeley and Los Angeles, 1969) 47-74; Lapidus, 'The evolution of Muslim urban society', *Comparative Studies in Society and History*, vol. 15 (1973) 21-50; R. Mantran, *L'Expansion Musulmane (VIIe-XIe siècles)* (PUF, Paris, 1969); D. et J. Sourdel, *La Civilisation de l'Islam classique* (Arthaud, Paris, 1968).

43. Le Tourneau, *Les villes musulmanes*; Pauty, 'Villes spontanées'.

44. I.M. Lapidus, 'The evolution of Muslim urban society', *Comparative Studies in Society and History*, vol. 15 (1973) 21-50

45. For example, Qur'ān, 9, 98.

46. I.M. Lapidus, 'The evolution of Muslim urban society'.

47. Bourgay, 'Islam et géographie'; K. Dettman, 'Zur Variationsbreite der Stadt in der Islamisch-Orientalischen Welt', *Geographische Zeitschrift*, vol. 58 (1970) 95-123; Fischel, 'The city in Islam'; von Grunebaum, 'The Muslim town and the Hellenistic town'; Hourani and Stern, *The Islamic City*, especially pp. 11-14; J. Gulick, 'Images of an Arab city', *Journal of the American Institute of Planners*, vol. 29 (1963) 179-98; A.A. Ismail, 'Origin, ideology and physical patterns of Arab urbanisation', *Ekistics*, vol. 33 (1972) 113-23.

48. I.M. Lapidus, 'The evolution of Muslim urban society'.

49. O. Grabar, 'The architecture of the Middle Eastern city', in I.M. Lapidus (ed.), *Middle Eastern Cities*, pp. 26-46.

50. I.M. Lapidus, 'Muslim cities and Islamic societies', pp. 47-74.

51. O.L. Barkan, 'Essai sur les données statistiques des registres de recensement dans l'Empire ottoman aux XVe et XVI siècles,' *Journal of the Economic and Social History of the Orient*, vol. 1 (1957) 9-35; I.M. Lapidus, *Muslim Cities in the Later Middle Ages* (Harvard University Press, Cambridge, Mass., 1967), p. 85.

52. Lapidus, ibid.

53. D.F. Eickelman, 'Is there an Islamic city? The making of a quarter in a Moroccan town', *International Journal of Middle East Studies*, vol. 4 (1974) 274-94.

54. Graber, 'The architecture of the Middle Eastern city'.

55. S.D. Goitein, 'Cairo: an Islamic city in the light of the Geniza documents', in Lapidus (ed.), *Middle Eastern Cities*, pp. 80-95.

56. Al-Mukaddasi, *Ahsan At-taqasīm*, ed. M.J. de Goeje, *Bibliotheca Geographorum Arabicorum* (Leiden, 1906), p. 47. See Ismail, 'Origin, ideology and physical patterns', Figure 2.

57. R.M. Adams, *Land Behind Baghdad. A History of Settlement on the Diyala Plains* (University of Chicago Press, Chicago and London, 1965), pp. 84-106, Figure 6.

58. Lassner, 'Massignon and Baghdad: the complexities of growth in an imperial city'.

59. Russell, 'Late ancient and medieval population', p. 99.

60. Lassner, 'Massignon and Baghdad: the complexities of growth in an imperial city'.

61. J.L. Abu-Lughod, *Cairo: 1001 Years of the City Victorious* (Princeton University Press, Princeton, 1971), pp. 32, 38, 131.

62. I. Tekeil, 'On institutionalised external relations of cities in the Ottoman Empire — a settlement models approach', *Etudes Balkaniques*, vol. 8 (1972) 49-72; 'Evolution of spatial organisation in the Ottoman Empire and Turkish Republic', in L.C. Brown (ed.), *From Madina to Metropolis: Heritage and Culture in the Near Eastern City* (Darwin Press, Princeton, 1973), pp. 244-73.

63. O.L. Barkan, 'Quelques observations sur l'organisation economique et sociale, des villes ottomanes, des XVIe et XVIIe siècles', *Recueils de la Société Jean Bodin*, vol. 7 (1955) 289-311; 'Essai sur les données statistiques des registres de recensement dans l'Empire ottoman aux XVe et XVIe siècles', *Journal of the Economic and Social History of the Orient*, vol. 1 (1957) 9-35.

64. R. Mantran, *Istanbul dans la seconde moitié du XVIIe siècle* (Adrien Maison-Neuve, Paris, 1962), p. 47; Naval Intelligence Division, *Geographical Handbooks Series, Turkey*, vol. 2 (London, 1943), p. 20; E. Wirth, 'Damaskus-Aleppo-Beirut; en geographischen Vergleich drier nahöstlicher Stadte im Spiegel ihrer sozial und wirtschaftlich tanangebenden Schichten', *Die Erde*, vol. 97 (1966) 96-137, 166-202, especially Figures 1 and 2.

65. Barkan, 'Quelques observations sur l'organisation' and 'Essai sur les données statistiques'; R.C. Jennings, 'Urban population in Anatolia in the sixteenth century: a study of Kayseri, Karaman, Amasya, Trabzon, and Erzerum', *International Journal of Middle East Studies*, 7 (1976) 21-57.

66. Barkan, 'Quelques observations sur l'organisation' and 'Essai sur les données statistiques'; Abu-Lughod, *Cairo*, pp. 37-79.

67. I. Tekeil, 'Evolution of spatial organisation in the Ottoman Empire and Turkish Republic', pp. 244-73.

68. J.H.G. Lebon, 'The Islamic city in the Near East. A comparative study of Cairo, Alexandria and Istanbul', *Town Planning Review*, vol. 40 (1970) 179-94; Wirth, 'Damaskus-Aleppo-Beirut'.

69. Z.Y. Hershlag, *Introduction to the Modern Economic History of the Middle East* (Brill, Leiden, 1964); C. Issawi (ed.), *The Economic History of the Middle East, 1800-1914* (University of Chicago Press, Chicago and London, 1966).

70. J. Bharier, 'The growth of towns and villages in Iran, 1900-66', *Middle Eastern Studies*, vol. 8 (1972) 51-62.

71. Idea derived from B.J.L. Berry, 'City size distributions and economic development', *Economic Development and Cultural Change*, vol. 9 (1961) 263-82.

72. F. Firoozi, 'Tehran — a demographic and economic analysis', *Middle Eastern Studies*, vol. 10 (1974) 60-76.

73. G.N. Curzon, *Persia and the Persian Question*, 1st edn. (Frank Cass, London, 1892); 2nd impression, 1966, vol. 1, pp. 210-11, 518-28; C. Issawi, 'The Tabriz-Trabzon trade, 1830-1900: the rise and decline of a route', *International Journal of Middle East Studies*, vol. 1 (1970) 18-27.

74. P. Beckett, 'The city of Kerman, Iran', *Erdkunde*, vol. 20 (1966) 119-25.

75. P.W. English, *City and Village in Iran: Settlement and Economy in the Kirman Basin* (University of Wisconsin Press, Madison, 1966).

76. V.F. Costello, *Kashan: A City and Region of Iran* (Centre for Middle Eastern Studies, Durham, 1976); E. Ehlers, 'Die Stadt Bam und ihr Oasen-Umland/Zentraliran', *Erdkunde*, vol. 29 (1975) 38-52.

77. For example, P. Benedict, 'The changing role of provincial towns: a case study from southwestern Turkey', in P. Benedict, E. Tümertekin and F. Mansur (eds.), *Turkey: Geographic and Social Perspectives* (Brill, Leiden, 1974), pp. 241-80.

78. Abu-Lughod, *Cairo*, pp. 56-79; A. Raymond, 'Essai de géographie des quartiers de résidence aristocratique au Caire au XVIIe siècle', *Journal of the Economic and Social History of the Orient*, vol. 6 (1963) 58-103.

79. V.F. Costello, 'The industrial structure of a traditional Islamic city', *Tijdschrift voor Economische en Sociale Geografie*, vol. 64 (1973) 108-20.

80. G. Schweizer, 'Tabriz (Nordwest-Iran) und der Tabrizer Bazar', *Erdkunde*, vol. 26 (1972) 32-46; E. Wirth, 'Strukturwandlungen und Entwicklungstendzen der orientalischen Stadt', *Erdkunde*, vol. 22 (1968) 101-28.

81. G. Baer, 'The administrative, economic and social functions of Turkish guilds', *International Journal of Middle East Studies*, vol. 1 (1970) 28-50.

82. K.A.C. Creswell, *A Short Account of Early Muslim Architecture* (Penguin Books, Harmondsworth, 1958), pp. 161-79; G. Le Strange, *Baghdad during the Abbasid Caliphate* (Oxford, 1900).

83. R. Ettinghausen, 'Muslim cities: old and new', in Brown, *From Madina to Metropolis*, pp. 290-318.

84. E.E. Beaudouin and A.U. Pope, 'City plans', in A.U. Pope (ed.), *A Survey of Persian Art* (Oxford University Press, Oxford, 1939), vol. 3, pp. 1391-410; J.I. Clarke, *The Iranian City of Shiraz*, Research Paper Series (Department of Geography, University of Durham, 1963), p. 15.

85. M. Berger (ed.), *The New Metropolis in the Arab World* (Allied Publishers, New Delhi, New York, 1963); C.L. Brown, 'Introduction' to Brown, *From Madina to Metropolis*, pp. 27-41; J. Gulick, *Tripoli: A Modern Arab City* (Harvard University Press, Cambridge, Mass., 1967), pp. 19-30; M. Seger, 'Strukturelemente der Stadt Teheran und das Modell der modernen orientalischen Stadt', *Erdkunde*, vol. 29 (1975) 21-38; E. Wirth, 'Strukturwandlungen und Entwicklungstendzen der orientalischen Stadt', *Erdkunde*, vol. 22 (1968) 101-28.

86. Abu-Lughod, *Cairo*, pp. 83-122.

87. Ibn Khaldûn, *An Introduction to History*, pp. 263-8, 283-4, 289-91; Benet, 'The ideology of Islamic urbanisation'.

2 CONTEMPORARY URBAN GROWTH

J. I. Clarke

Urban Growth in Less Developed Countries

Urban growth in the Middle East must be seen in the context of that in the world as a whole, which is even faster than the much more publicised population growth. While at the beginning of the nineteenth century only about 20 million people in the world lived in towns, say one in 40 of the total world population, by 1970 the number had risen to 1,500 million, two out of five,[1] with the highest proportions of town-dwellers in the most developed countries and the lowest proportions in the least developed countries. By the end of this century the number living in towns may reach 3,000 million, roughly half the world population, and most of these will be living in less developed countries, which account for at least 85 per cent of world population growth and for an increasing proportion of its urban growth. Moreover, much of this mercurial urban growth in the world is localised in large cities; between 1950 and 1970 the number of cities with a million inhabitants or more rose from 75 to 162, nearly half of which were in the Third World. During the 1960s alone the number of cities with 100,000 inhabitants or more increased more than threefold from 249 to 837.

So the world is experiencing an 'urban explosion' of enormous magnitude, triggered off by the industrial and agricultural revolutions in nineteenth-century Europe and their subsequent diffusion around the world, assisted by the spread of Europeans overseas, the widespread improvements in communications, and the ramifications of the world economy. The twentieth century has witnessed an acceleration of urbanisation through diverse processes such as increasing human mobility, rapid population growth, the dispersal of industrial locations, the rise of the service sector and the waves of political independence across the Third World. These varied processes have contributed differently to urbanisation in time and space, so that cities and towns vary enormously in size and spacing, in form and function, and in age and amenity, and consequently urban systems exhibit many contrasts. Even the terms 'town', 'city', 'urban' and 'rural' are difficult to define and delimit, and have particular connotations in different countries; and so does the process known as urbanisation or urban growth, which may be variously defined as: (i) the growth in the number of people living in urban centres; (ii) the growth in the proportion of people living in urban

Table 2.1: Urban Populations of Less Developed Countries

Countries	% of population in urban areas		% annual population growth		% annual urban population growth	
	1960	1975	1960-70	1970-5	1960-70	1970-5
1. Low income	8	13	2.4	2.4	5.4	5.5
2. Middle income	32	43	2.7	2.7	4.8	4.5
3. Industrialised	66	76	1.0	0.8	1.9	1.8
4. Capital-surplus oil exporters	23	31	4.0	4.2	6.6	6.3
5. Centrally planned economies	40	57	1.2	0.9	3.2	2.8

Source: The World Bank, *World Development Report 1978*, pp. 100-3.

centres; (iii) the growth in the number of urban centres; (iv) the socio-economic processes involving an increase in urban life; (v) the physical extension of urban land use; or (vi) combinations of the above. Obviously, any one of the five processes may occur without corresponding change in the other four. Generally the term is used without precision, especially with reference to less developed countries, where some of the most rapid rates of urban growth are found among the least urbanised countries. So although contemporary urban growth is undoubtedly rapid, it is notoriously difficult to measure and compare internationally.[2] Indeed, nowadays there are fewer efforts to attain precise statistical comparisons of urbanisation and city size, knowing that such attempts tend to be unsatisfactory.

Urbanisation in less developed countries has been particularly rapid since mid-century as the gap in economic opportunities between urban and rural areas has widened, and as government policies have favoured the localisation of most modern economic activities in cities rather than in rural areas. So although between 1950 and 1975 the total population of less developed countries increased at 2.4 per cent a year, their total urban population increased much faster, probably at about 6 per cent. However, 'less developed countries' is an all-embracing term which includes a wide variety of countries. In their fivefold classification, the World Bank categorises some as low-income countries, middle-income countries, capital-surplus oil exporters, or centrally planned economies, but none as industrialised countries. Table 2.1 reveals that these five categories have distinctive levels of urban population and rates of urban population growth, the most rapid rates being in the capital-surplus oil exporters and low-income countries, which are collectively the most feebly urbanised. Indeed, the five categories indicate almost an inverse relationship between the level of urban population and rate of urban population growth; a fact which will not surprise statisticians, but intensifies the problems of urban management in countries which can least afford to solve them.

Urban Growth in the Middle East

It is in these contexts that we observe contemporary urban growth in the Middle East, here defined as stretching from Morocco to Iran and from Turkey to Sudan. This region contains about 224 million people (1977 estimate) living on 8.75 million km^2 — 5.5 per cent of the world's population living on 6.5 per cent of its land area. Its average density of population of 25.6 per km^2 is therefore slightly less than the world average of 30.0 per km^2. Nowadays a facile physical explanation

Table 2.2: Population Estimates of North Africa and South-West Asia since the Time of Christ (in millions)

	AD 0	1000	1500	1750	1900	1975
North Africa	10-15	5-10	6-12	10-15	53-55	80-82
South-West Asia	25-45	20-30	20-30	25-35	40-45	115-125
Together	35-60	25-40	26-42	35-50	93-100	195-207
World total	270-330	275-345	440-540	735-805	1605-1710	3950-4050

Source: J.D. Durand, 'Historical estimates of world population: an evaluation', *Population and Development Review*, vol. 3, no. 3 (1977) 259.

can be easily propounded for this relatively low population density, but we should recall that 'Mesopotamia at the beginning of the Christian era was undoubtedly one of the world's most densely populated countries',[3] and that both North Africa and South-West Asia possibly had more people in ancient times than at the beginning of the modern period. Indeed, at the beginning of the Christian era they may well have contained 10 to 20 per cent of the total world population (Table 2.2), a situation which is unlikely to be retrieved in the foreseeable future, despite a recent upsurge in the average annual population growth rate to 2.6 per cent during the period 1950 to 1975, well in excess of the world average.

The long history of urban life in the Middle East must be seen within this setting of former numerical strength, which facilitated and even stimulated urban growth. Nowadays, this region is not one of the major demographic concentrations in the world. Although its population is growing rapidly in response to high fertility and markedly declining mortality, the Middle East and North Africa has about as many people as South America and a few million more than the United States, but fewer than the Soviet Union and less than half as many as Europe.

On the other hand, the Middle East, with many capital-surplus oil exporters and middle-income countries and few low-income countries, is one of the most urbanised regions of the Third World, exceeded only by Middle and Tropical South America. It is also one of the most rapidly urbanising regions. Precise figures are unobtainable, but Population Reference Bureau[4] estimates for 1977 suggest that some 44 per cent of the population of South-West Asia and 39 per cent of Northern Africa live in towns (as defined by each country), and that these are higher percentages than those of other regions in Asia and Africa. A

United Nations survey,[5] however, suggested that in 1975 the urban population of North Africa and the Middle East as a whole accounted for 44 per cent of the total population (cf. 32 per cent in 1960), and that the average annual growth rate of the urban population during 1960 to 1975 was 5.0 per cent.

Urban Populations of the Middle East

For a variety of reasons the estimates of the urban populations of individual countries in the region (Table 2.3) are not very reliable, particularly for international comparisons. First, census data are distinctly uneven in quantity and quality; while countries like Algeria, Tunisia, Egypt and Turkey have had a long run of censuses, others like Lebanon, Oman and Qatar, have never held a full census, Jordan has not held one since 1961 and Saudi Arabia never officially accepted the results of its only censuses. So Table 2.4, which lists censuses held in the Middle East since 1945, is more impressive than the reality, for the censuses vary greatly in detail and accuracy. Another major difficulty for international comparability is the variation in definition of urban status, from country to country and from time to time. Table 2.5 reveals that even the criteria for definition vary, and it should be noted that Lebanon, Oman, Qatar, Saudi Arabia and Yemen AR have no official definitions at all.

Perhaps one of the most important reasons for low international comparability of levels and rates of urban population growth is the wide range of population sizes of states from 0.1 million to 41.9 million inhabitants (1977 estimates). This results from the intense political fragmentation of the Middle East, one of the world's shatter belts. At the bottom end of the demographic scale are some small countries (e.g. Qatar, United Arab Emirates and Bahrain) which are little more than city states, while at the top of the scale the large countries (Turkey, Egypt, Iran) have complex urban systems and well developed urban hierarchies including regional capitals. However, there are no clear relationships between the areas and populations of countries on the one hand and percentage urban populations on the other (Figures 2.1, 2.2). It would appear that state boundaries are not very significant divides between urban systems. Some of the largest states (e.g. Saudi Arabia, Algeria, Sudan, Iran, Libya) contain several urban subsystems, while some of the smallest states (e.g. the Gulf states) form part of multinational urban systems. Indeed, most of the largest cities in the Middle East, like Cairo, Tehrān, İstanbul, Baghdād, Casablanca and Beirūt, have an international significance far surpassing the boundaries of the

Table 2.3: Urban Populations of Middle Eastern Countries

	Total population (millions)	GNP per capita (US dollars)	Area (thousand sq. km)	Percentage urban population		Percentage annual growth rate of urban population	
	1976	1976		1960	1975	1960-70	1970-5
Turkey	41.2	990	781	30	43	5.2	4.2
Egypt	38.1	280	1,001	38	48	4.3	3.9
Iran	34.3	1,930	1,648	33	44	5.0	4.7
Morocco	17.2	540	447	30	38	4.2	5.1
Algeria	16.2	990	2,382	31	50	3.2	3.2
Sudan	15.9	290	2,506	9	13	6.2	5.5
Iraq	11.5	1,390	435	43	62	6.3	5.0
Saudi Arabia	8.6	4,480	2,150	12	21	6.6	6.3
Syria	7.7	780	185	37	46	4.8	4.2
Yemen AR	6.0	250	195	4	9	9.0	8.0
Tunisia	5.7	840	164	32	47	4.9	4.2
Israel	3.6	3,920	21	78	84	4.0	3.4
Lebanon	3.2	1,070	10	35	60	7.4	5.4
Jordan	2.8	610	98	43	56	5.1	4.9
Libya	2.5	6,310	1,760	23	31	5.8	5.0
PDR Yemen	1.7	280	330	20	29	5.5	5.4
Kuwait	1.1	15,480	18	69	89	13.0	8.2
Oman	0.8	2,680	213		5[a]		
United Arab Emirates	0.7	13,990	84		84[b]		
Cyprus	0.6	1,480	9		42[a]		
Bahrain	0.3	2,140	1		80[a]		
Qatar	0.2	11,400	11		88[a]		

a. United Nations Economic Commission for Western Asia, *Demographic and Related Socio-Economic Indicators for Countries of the ECWA Region* (1975).
b. Population Reference Bureau, *World Population Data Sheet 1977.*

Source: The World Bank, *World Development Report* (1978).

Table 2.4: Population Censuses of Countries of the Middle East since 1945

Algeria	1948, 1954, 1966, 1977
Bahrain	1950, 1959, 1965, 1971
Cyprus	1946, 1960, 1973
Egypt	1947, 1960, 1966, 1976
Iran	1956, 1966, 1976
Iraq	1947, 1957, 1965, 1977
Israel	1948, 1960, 1972
Jordan	1952, 1961
Kuwait	1957, 1961, 1965, 1970, 1975
Lebanon	
Libya	1954, 1964, 1973
Morocco	1950, 1960, 1971
Oman	
PDR Yemen	1973
Qatar	1970[a]
Saudi Arabia	1962-3[a], 1974[b]
Sudan	1955-6, 1973
Syria	1960, 1970
Tunisia	1946, 1956, 1966, 1975
Turkey	1950, 1955, 1960, 1965, 1970, 1975
United Arab Emirates	1968, 1971[a], 1975
Yemen AR	1946, 1955 (Aden colony), 1975

a. Enumeration considered largely incomplete.
b. Only total population figures published.

countries in which they are situated. Cairo and Tehrān each has more inhabitants than over half of the countries in the region, including Israel, Lebanon, Jordan and Libya; Baghdād has as many as Lebanon and İstanbul has as many as Libya.

In these circumstances statistical analyses of urban populations, however defined, are not particularly enlightening except in the broadest terms. Then it is apparent that there is a fairly marked north-south contrast between the more urbanised, longer settled countries of the Northern Tier, the Fertile Crescent and the Atlas lands of the Maghreb, and the less urbanised, traditionally more nomadic countries of the Arabian peninsula, Libya and Sudan (Table 2.3). In nearly all the more urbanised countries at least 40 per cent of the population live in localities

Table 2.5: Definitions of Urban Population in Middle Eastern Countries

Morocco	:	All municipalities, *Centres autonomes* and other urban centres
Algeria	:	Centres of communes with 1,000 or more population and at least 50 per cent or more of them in non-agricultural sectors. More than 75 per cent: urban; between 50 and 75 per cent: semi-urban
Tunisia	:	Population living in all communes
Libya	:	No specific definition. After the census is taken, population of Tripoli and Benghazi *Muhafadat* and the urban parts of the *Mutassarifias* of Beida and Derna are treated as urban
Egypt	:	The governorates of Cairo, Alexandria, Suez, Ismâ'ilyâ and Port Said and the chief towns of provinces and districts
Sudan	:	Centres with 5,000 or more population having some urban characteristics
Jordan	:	Urban includes the population resident in all localities of 10,000 or more population (excluding localities inhabited only by Palestinian refugees), all district capitals regardless of size, all localities of 5,000 to 10,000 inhabitants in which two-thirds or more of the economically active males were reported in non-agricultural occupations and those suburbs of Jerusalem and Amman cities with at least two-thirds of males in non-agricultural pursuits
Israel	:	All settlements with more than 2,000 inhabitants, except those where at least one-third of the heads of households, participating in the civilian labour force, earn their living from agriculture
Syria	:	Cities, district (*Mohafaza*) centres and subdistrict (*Mantika*) centres
Cyprus	:	Six district towns and Nicosia suburbs
Turkey	:	Population of the localities within the municipality limits of administrative centres of provinces and districts
Iraq	:	Population living within the boundaries of municipality councils
Iran	:	All *Shahrestan* centres, regardless of size and all places of 5,000 or more inhabitants
Kuwait	:	Kuwait city (Dasman Sharq/1, Sharq/2, Murgab, Salihia and Qibla) and Labourer's City
Bahrain	:	Towns of Al Manamah, Al Muharraq (including Al Muharraq suburbs), Hedd, Jiddhafs, Sitrah, Rifa'a and Awālī
PDR Yemen	:	The entire former colony of Aden excluding the oil refinery and villages of Bureika and Fugum

Source: UN, *Demographic Yearbooks.*

defined as urban by each country, while in Israel and most of the Gulf states over 80 per cent live in such localities. On the other hand, in the less urbanised countries less than 40 per cent live in towns, and in two countries, Yemen AR and Oman, probably less than 10 per cent.

We should remind ourselves, however, that the percentage living in urban localities is a rapidly changing statistic. The oil-rich countries of the southern zone, like Oman, Saudi Arabia and Libya, are undergoing very rapid urbanisation and will not be permanently at the base of the league table of urban populations. Certainly high GNP per capita is not closely correlated with high urban population levels, but in time the correlation will be closer.

Figure 2.1: Relationship between Areas of Middle Eastern Countries and their Percentage Urban Populations, 1975

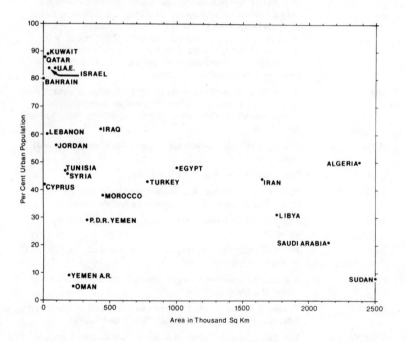

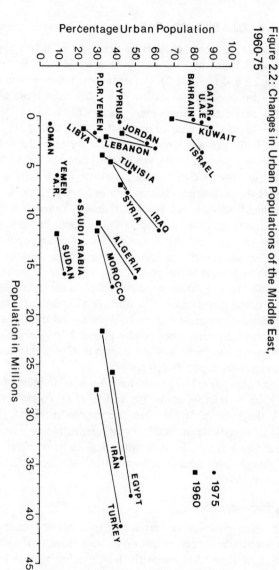

Figure 2.2: Changes in Urban Populations of the Middle East, 1960-75

Urban Growth Rates in the Middle East

Some indication of recent changes in the levels of urban population may be gleaned from the estimates by the World Bank for 1960 and 1975 (Table 2.3 and Figure 2.2). Unfortunately, urban growth rates are not available for some of the smaller states, but from those which are available it is clear that in almost every country of the region the annual rate of urban growth was quicker during the 1960s than during the first half of the 1970s, and was rarely less than 4 per cent, the only major exception being Algeria. The average national rate of 1960 to 1970 was 5.9 per cent, and for 1970 to 1975 5.1 per cent, which in more realistic terms implies that urban populations doubled every 12 to 14 years. In highly urbanised Kuwait and feebly urbanised Yemen AR the rates were even more spectacular, exceeding 8.0 per cent, but in Kuwait the total population was small and in Yemen AR the urban population was small, so absolute growth is less impressive than relative growth. Perhaps more impressive is the powerful growth (over 6 per cent annually) of Saudi Arabia's urban population from a previously low level, and of the urban populations of a number of countries which were already moderately urbanised: Algeria, Tunisia, Lebanon, Jordan and Iraq. Here political events have usually played an important role, sustaining the snowballing urbanisation, though in Algeria this was in spite of more modest overall population growth.

In contrast, Egypt's urban growth has been more impressive in absolute terms than in relative terms, for with that in Turkey and Iran it constitutes the bulk of Middle East urban growth. Urban growth is also slower than average in Israel, partly a reflection of planning; but only Cyprus has seen very little recent change in its numbers of town-dwellers, though considerable redistribution occurred after Turkish intervention in 1974.

Large City Populations

One of the most noteworthy features of urban growth in the Middle East is its overwhelming concentration in large cities. In the mid-1970s there were more than 140 cities with 100,000 inhabitants or more, but over half of them were in Egypt, Iran or Turkey, the most populous countries. In a number of countries (Egypt, Iran, Syria, Lebanon, Israel and Kuwait) these cities comprise at least one-third of the total populations. In contrast, middle-sized towns with 50,000 to 100,000 inhabitants are only numerous in the most populous countries, though the Middle East is not unusual in this respect.

Cities with over one million inhabitants are becoming much more

Figure 2.3: Recent Growth of Some Large Cities of the Middle East

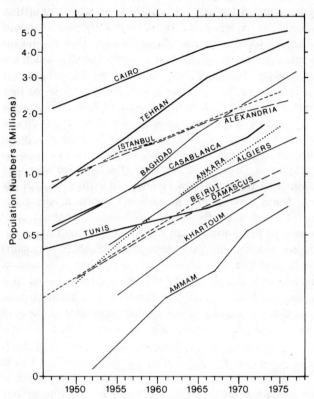

numerous. By the late 1970s there were at least a dozen: Cairo, Tehrān, İstanbul, Alexandria, Baghdād, Casablanca, Ankara, Algiers, Beirūt, Damascus, Greater Khartoum and Tunis. In addition, the agglomeration of Tel Aviv-Yafo contains more than a million, and it cannot be long before the list is joined by Riyadh and 'Amman. Moreover, by 1976 Cairo had over five million inhabitants, Tehrān 4.5 million and Baghdād over three million, so all three were well into the ranks of major world cities. Figure 2.3, which is based upon census data, depicts the growth of most of the actual and near 'million-cities' of the region, and is perhaps more effective than a table of growth rates giving a spurious indication of accuracy. It may, however, give a false impression of smooth growth, when the reality, especially where in-migration is voluminous (e.g. Baghdād, 'Amman), is less even. Particularly striking growth may be observed for Tehrān, Baghdād and Ankara, all interior capitals of highly centralised states, and therefore somewhat unusual among the less developed countries (though Mexico City and Bogota are other examples). Tehrān's population doubled from 1.5 million to three million between 1956 and 1966, and another 1.5 million were added by 1976. Even more remarkable was the growth of Ankara, which multiplied nearly six times in the 25 years 1950 to 1975 to reach a total of 1.7 million, while the formerly very much larger city of İstanbul multiplied just under three times to attain 2.5 million. Baghdād also multiplied six times during the 30 years 1947 to 1977. Lesser cities like Beirūt, Khartoum, Riyadh and 'Amman – the last three again with inland locations – have also grown rapidly, faster than most of the major cities of North Africa (Cairo, Alexandria, Casablanca, Algiers and Tunis), some of which were affected by decolonisation. Capital status is also important to the growth of large cities, and all but three of the million-cities are capitals, the exceptions being İstanbul, Alexandria and Casablanca, the first two curiously similar in size and rates of growth. İstanbul and Casablanca are still the largest cities in their respective countries, but the fact that there are two major cities in Turkey means that İstanbul contains a smaller percentage of the total population than most of the largest cities in countries of the Middle East.

City-size Hierarchies

In most countries the largest city is incorporating an increasing proportion of the total population. Excluding the micro-states with less than one million inhabitants, the largest cities of most of the remaining countries comprise at least one-tenth of the total populations, but in Saudi Arabia and PDR Yemen they contain a fifth, in Iraq, Jordan and Libya a quarter, in Israel a third, and in Lebanon nearly a half (Table 2.6). Obviously, there is a tendency for greater concentration in the largest cities of the less populous countries and more highly urbanised countries, but the correlation is not very clear. Apart from İstanbul, the two cities of Greater Khartoum and San'a stand out as containing only small proportions of the total populations of their respective countries, both of which are feebly urbanised.

On the other hand, analysis of two- and four-city indices (Table 2.6) shows that Greater Khartoum is very dominant in the urban hierarchy of Sudan, as Tehrān, Baghdād and Beirūt are in Iran, Iraq and Lebanon. All these cities are more than five times larger than their nearest rivals,

Table 2.6: Urban Primacy in Middle Eastern Countries

	Population of largest city (thousands)		Percentage of total population	Urban primacy Two-city index	Four-city index
Turkey	2,547	(1975)	6	1.50	0.91
Egypt	5,084	(1976)	14	2.19	1.33
Iran	4,496	(1976)	14	6.69	2.44
Morocco	1,753	(1973)	11	2.93	1.20
Algeria	1,523	(1977)	9	3.10	1.42
Sudan	800	(1973-4)	6	5.92	2.26
Iraq	3,206	(1977)	26	5.58*	2.41
Saudi Arabia	669	(1974)	18	1.19	0.59
Syria	1,042	(1975)	14	1.34	0.86
Yemen AR	139	(1975)	3	1.68	0.75
Tunisia	900	(1975)	16	3.46	2.12
Israel	1,181	(1975)	35	3.28	1.97
Lebanon	1,173	(1975)	46	5.97**	4.16
Jordan	691	(1976)	23	2.66	—
Libya	552	(1973)	24	1.96	—
PDR Yemen	285	(1973)	18	—	—
Kuwait	277	(1975)	28	—	—
Oman	—		—	—	—
United Arab Emirates	141	(1975)	25	—	—
Cyprus	116	(1973)	18	1.45	0.84
Bahrain	111	(1975)	43	—	—
Qatar	145	(1975)	85	—	—

Notes:
* 1965.
** 1970.

Two-city index = P_1/P_2 and four city index = $P_1/(P_2 + P_3 + P_4)$ where P_1 is the population of the first city, P_2 is the population of the second city, etc.

and more than twice as large as the combined populations of the second, third and fourth cities. Tunis also exhibits marked primacy, and city-size distributions of these five countries (Figure 2.4) clearly differ from those of most other countries in the Middle East, though Iran and Morocco have many more cities with at least 100,000 inhabitants than Iraq, Tunisia or Sudan.

Figure 2.4: City-size Distributions of Countries of the Middle East with at least Five Million Inhabitants

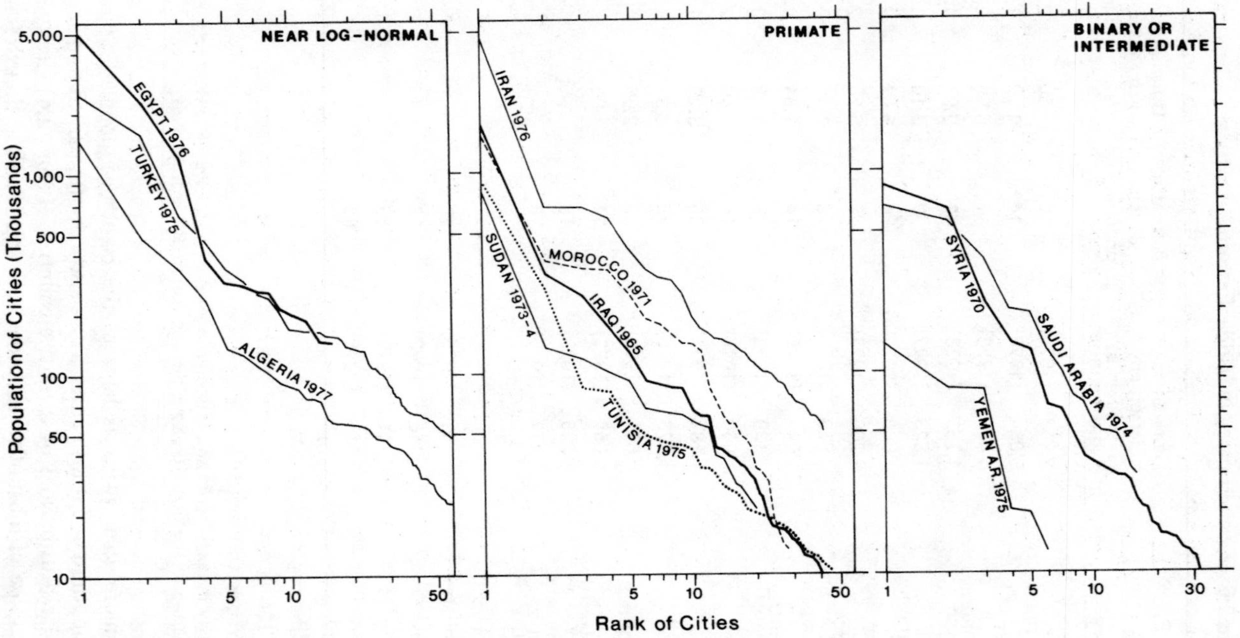

The city-size hierarchies[6] of Egypt, Turkey and Algeria approximate to log-normal (i.e. $P_n = P_1/N$, where P_n = the population of the nth city, P_1 = the population of the first city and N = the number of cities in the array), a reflection perhaps of factors such as their large size, long history of urban life and economic diversity. Turkey, however, has a tendency towards a binary (or intermediate) city-size distribution with two main cities, a pattern manifested by Syria, Saudi Arabia and Yemen AR (Figure 2.4) where no single city has achieved overwhelming preponderance.

These city-size distributions are not immutable; the growth of Ankara to offset the formerly strong primacy of İstanbul is indicative of the way that city-size distributions can change, as is the growing primacy of Tripoli in Libya. On the other hand, the evidence suggests that where the largest city is the capital the tendency for growing concentration is very strong, even when it is far from the sea. When it is also the major port (Algiers, Tripoli, Tunis, Beirūt, Tel Aviv, Aden), primacy is often intensified. Casablanca is the only primate city which is a port but not a capital.

Components of City Growth

Rapid city growth results from high natural increase, net in-migration and incorporation of surrounding villages. Natural increase averages 2.8 to 2.9 per cent per annum for the region as a whole, and is only substantially lower in Cyprus (1.5 per cent) and Israel (2.1 per cent) and substantially higher in Kuwait (4.2 per cent) and Syria (4.1 per cent). High rates are caused by sustained high fertility and declining mortality. In cities they are even higher because the difference between urban and rural mortality is greater than that for fertility; frequently natural increase rates of cities exceed 4.0 per cent, which means a doubling time of less than 18 years.

In the period 1970 to 1975 death rates of many countries were 14 to 16 per thousand, but higher (about 20) in Egypt, Sudan, Saudi Arabia, Yemen AR, PDR Yemen, Oman and Qatar, and much lower (below 10) in Cyprus, Lebanon, Kuwait, Bahrain and Israel. For many reasons, mortality has declined more rapidly in cities than fertility. Although Middle Eastern cities were formerly extremely unhealthy, and that is still the case in shanty-towns and refugee camps, there have been great improvements in sanitation, hygiene, nutrition and in medical and pharmaceutical services, raising the life expectancies of city-dwellers. Naturally, the degree of mortality decline varies considerably in time and space, and is less in San'a than Sousse, in Muscat than Meknès; but feebly populated oil-rich countries are able to effect more rapid declines than most other countries.

The situation is quite different as far as human fertility is concerned, as in this predominantly Islamic region the fertility levels of many countries are amongst the highest in the world, with birth-rates of 45 to 50 per thousand (1970 to 1975) and total fertility rates (TFRs) of about 7.0[7] — i.e. a woman would have seven children if she gave birth at the prevailing age-specific fertility rates and survived to the end of her reproductive years. The major exceptions are Cyprus and Israel, with TFRs of 2.8 and 3.7 respectively, but some fertility decline has been experienced in Egypt (TFR of 5.2), Turkey (5.8) and Tunisia (5.9), especially in urban areas, and the partly Christian Lebanon has a lower level of fertility (TFR of 6.3) than most Islamic Arab countries. But even in countries with high total fertility rates there are distinct signs that fertility is beginning to fall among some city-dwellers, as in Tehrān,[8] and that improved living standards, increased education and other aspects of socio-economic development are related to lower fertility.[9] Family planning is making limited progress among urban elites, and more widespread progress in Egypt, Turkey and Tunisia.

There still seems to be more immediate prospect of further mortality decline in cities than there is of fertility decline. Some of the oil states, for example, are not interested in family planning schemes, partly because they have experienced so much immigration of workers that they see their own nationals being outnumbered; yet they are able to establish the most modern of medical services. So high natural increase is likely to be the major and most persistent component of urban growth for some time to come.

Migration, on the other hand, is the cause of much spectacular growth of Middle Eastern cities, and accounts for many of the differences between growth rates of large cities. It is a more spasmodic and less general component of urban growth than natural increase, partly because net migration is the balance of in-migration and out-migration. Generally it leads to spurts of growth, as in the case of 'Amman, a city of migrants and refugees. Cities in oil-rich states have been particularly attractive to migrants, not merely the capitals but others like Benghazi, Jiddah, Damman and Abādān. But perhaps most impressive is the huge volume of migrants into the major Middle Eastern cities — Cairo, Tehrān, Baghdād — where net in-migration frequently exceeds 2 per cent per annum,[10] despite their size.

Population Concentration and Redistribution

By 1985, 37 per cent of the world's urban inhabitants may live in million-cities, and there may be 15 cities with 10 million inhabitants, most of them in less developed countries. The Middle East is no exception to this growing concentration; Greater Cairo is expected to be one of these 10 million-cities, and there could well be 15 million-cities by 1985. This mercurial metropolitan expansion poses urgent problems of many kinds, not least of which is the formulation of policies to cope with the spatial concentration of population.

Most modernisation in the Middle East has been highly polarised and strongly linked with 'the world economy'. It has thus contributed substantially to urbanisation, which has increased through initial advantage and cumulative causation. The often harsh conditions of the physical environment have made rural development expensive and difficult, and the huge revenues of the oil industry, the epitome of capitalistic multinational enterprise, are more easily spent in cities than in deserts or steppes. Industrialisation, the panacea of the 1960s, was also urban-orientated, so the contrast between cities and their rural surrounds was intensified. The cities attracted rural labour, but their links with the world economy meant that many of the traditional urban industries suffered from external competition, except where tourism enabled their survival, as in Tunisia.

There has been much discussion over whether these metropolitan cities are parasitic or generative, whether they drain their countries' lifeblood or whether they are centres of innovation and diffusion. In fact, it is unwise to generalise, as the situation varies from country to country, but there can be little doubt that many large cities have developed an enclave type of economy, especially in poor countries which suddenly acquire wealth. On the whole, the spread effects of large cities are greater in middle-income countries, where there is less spatial inequality than in low-income countries, and where there are stronger links between rural areas and major cities.

Despite much discussion over the economies and diseconomies of large cities in less developed countries, there is a growing consensus that the diseconomies are excessive and may culminate in 'ecodisasters'.[11] Many favour intermediate or middle-sized cities as potential growth centres.[12] Unfortunately, few population policies in less developed countries, and the Middle East is no exception, have paid much attention to spatial distribution or redistribution of population, but have focused on population growth.[13] The main policy approach to this question has been through urban and regional planning, which has mostly aimed at decentralisation but has met with mixed fortunes. Israel is, of course, an unusual case, but a prime aspect of policy has been to limit the growth of the three largest cities and encourage the growth of new towns; but in Jerusalem this policy has succumbed to the desire for a Jewish majority. Algeria, on the other hand, applied growth-centre concepts to restrict concentration of development and to spread it to lagging regions, but success has been limited because much development has been based upon industrialisation as the propulsive factor, thus causing further urban concentration even if in lesser cities. In Iran also, development plans have contributed to the evolution of regional capitals,[14] but without slowing down appreciably the massive growth of Tehrān. We shall have to see whether de-Westernisation in Iran will lead to changes in the urban system; so far de-colonisation of the Maghreb has had no significant effect.

Growth-centre policies have tended to reinforce economic dependency and existing urban spatial patterns. Time will tell whether political changes in the Middle East will provoke new approaches to regional and urban planning. These will not and should not be alike, because each country presents different historical and geographical conditions of urbanisation; but it is very doubtful if population measures to arrest migration or control fertility will do anything in the first instance except effect initial slowing down of metropolitan expansion. The real solution must be found in more effective spatial economic planning of each country as a whole. So far, planners' dreams have done little to change the spatial patterns of urban growth.

References

1. S. Goldstein, 'An overview of world urbanization, 1950-2000', *International Union for the Scientific Study of Population, International Population Conference, Liege 1973*, vol. 1 (1973) 177-90.

2. K. Davis, *World Urbanization 1950-1970*, Population Monograph Series (University of California, Berkeley, 2 vols., 1969 and 1972).

3. J.D. Durand, 'Historical estimates of world population: an evaluation', *Population and Development Review*, vol. 3, no. 3 (1977) 276.

4. Population Reference Bureau, World Population Data Sheet.

5. UN, *Selected World Demographic Indicators by Countries, 1950-2000* (New York, 1975).

6. J.I. Clarke and J.L. Murray, 'Population dynamics of large Middle Eastern cities', *International Union for the Scientific Study of Population, International Population Conference, Liege 1973*, vol. 1 (1973) 271-86; and J.I. Clarke, 'Primate cities of the World and the Middle East', in *The Population Framework: Data Collection, Demographic Analysis, Population and Development* (UN Economic Commission for Western Asia, 1978), pp. 290-7.

7. R.H. Cassen, 'Current trends in population change and their causes', *Population and Development Review*, vol. 4, no. 2 (1978) 332.

8. M. Amani, 'La population de L'Iran', *Population*, vol. 27, no. 3 (1972) 411-18.

9. J.F. Audroing *et al.*, 'Recherche des correlations entre des variables démographiques, sociologiques et economiques dans les pays Arabes', *Population*, vol. 30, no. 1 (1975) 61-80.

10. Cairo Demographic Centre, *Urbanization and Migration in Some Arab and African Countries*, Research Monograph Series, no. 4 (Cairo, 1973).

11. J.C. Elizaga, 'The demography of metropolitan growth and planning', *International Union for the Scientific Study of Population, International Population Conference, Mexico 1977, Proceedings*, pp. 289-300.

12. N.M. Hansen, *Intermediate-sized Cities as Growth Centres* (Praeger, New York, 1971).

13. A. Bose, 'Population policies and metropolitan growth', *International Union for the Scientific Study of Population, International Population Conference, Mexico 1977*, vol. 2 (1977) 225-40.

14. D. Behnam and M. Aman, *La Population de L'Iran* (CICRED, 1974).

3 MIGRATION IN SPACE: IMMOBILITY IN SOCIETY

A.M. Findlay

Introduction

Migration matters. Population flux is an all pervasive element of life in Middle Eastern cities. Migration from rural to urban areas has dual significance. First, it reflects the physical needs of migrants, many of whom could not secure a satisfactory standard of living in rural areas. Second, it demonstrates the increasing urge felt by many Arabs, Turks and Iranians to adopt urban life-styles, and to achieve occupational and social mobility within the urban community, commensurate with the levels of spatial mobility which they have already experienced in moving from village to metropolis.[1]

The significance of rural-urban migration lies in the quality as well as in the quantity of newcomers entering the city. This chapter demonstrates that the location of migrant activities and the behaviour of migrant populations are functions of the distinctly different demographic, educational and occupational characteristics of migrant communities. The most serious problems facing urban and regional planners in the near future will arise from the widening gap between the high social aspirations of migrants and the severely constrained occupational and societal roles available to them. Under optimal conditions spatial and social mobility should complement one another, the city operating effectively and equitably as the chief focus of population interchange in space and society.

Power, Peripheries and Migration Patterns

Just as the legitimacy of academic comparisons between disparate cities is hard to determine,[2] so also it is hazardous to generalise about immigration to cities in a region as diverse in its geographical and historical character as the Middle East.[3]

A wide spectrum of studies has identified different aspects of rural deprivation which encourage emigration. For example, Adibi describes three interrelated problems stimulating emigration from the Iranian countryside — increasing population pressure in village society, increasing mechanisation of agriculture, and environmental problems (such as drought, soil erosion and inefficient land tenure systems).[4]

54

The accumulation of wealth in the largest cities of the Middle East, partly as a spin-off from rising oil revenues, and more fundamentally as a result of changes in the scales and modes of production, has widened the gap between rural and urban incomes at the national scale and has increased the attraction of the city for the rural population. Within the city disparities of wealth have also increased.[5] In Kuwait, for example, 15 families and 5,000 merchants dominate the state's commercial life.[6] A recent study of urbanisation in the Arabian peninsula states that 'this concentration of economic power in key groups has tended to express itself spatially in the growth of core regions and corresponding areas of relative underdevelopment'.[7] The cores coincide with the large urban centres and have become the termini for massive migration flows of workers from the underdeveloped peripheries. Urban growth does not therefore equate with modernisation, but rather with a particular distribution of economic power which favours the use of land, labour and capital in certain modes of production.[8]

Core-periphery relationships are mirrored in the migration patterns of many Arab countries such as Tunisia and Syria (Figure 3.1).[9] The core-periphery concept can also be extended to the international scale. Friedman and Wulff suggest that the true core urban areas for North Africa lie in Western Europe.[10] There is considerable evidence to support the theory that Tunis, Algiers and Casablanca were major departure points for international labour migration to Europe up until the economic recession of 1973.[11]

Within the Middle East two core regions of international significance have emerged, one in Libya and the other in the Gulf and Saudi Arabia. It seems probable that international labour migration within the Arab world will become a potent force in encouraging further urbanisation, and that in the Middle East as in other world regions, the most critical planning problems of the future will be of an international rather than national nature.

It is surprising within the gamut of core-periphery studies that more attention has not been given to the dual role of small and medium-sized cities. They have traditionally served as urban foci for surrounding rural hinterlands and have attracted migrants from nearby villages. Simultaneously they are often peripheral points relative to the primate city or to the national development axis. In relation to these national cores the small cities are points of emigration. As both core and periphery, it is interesting to ask whether small towns are truly termini to one migration system and source to another, or whether they serve as intermediary points in a more complex step-migration process.

Figure 3.1: Regional Migration Patterns

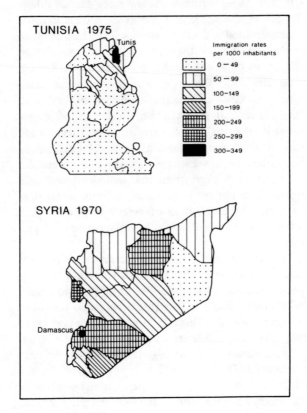

It is peculiarly difficult from reviewing micro-studies of migration in the Middle East either to support or refute the geographical concept of step migration.[12] The process suggests that population transfer initially occurs from village to provincial town and later from town to metropolis. Where the urban hierarchy is undeveloped as in the case of the Omani settlement structure, migrants pass directly from village to metropolis. In Oman, large villages such as Ibri hold little attraction to inhabitants of smaller villages, who depart directly for foreign employment or for residence in the Muscat-Mutrah conurbation.[13] Where the urban hierarchy exhibits a structure which is more of a continuum in size and in spacing as in the case of Syria, it appears that rural areas do send migrants first to small towns and later to larger centres. Munro claims that movement of this kind was operative in Turkey in the

Figure 3.2: Destination of Primary Migration Flows from each Délegation of Tunisia, 1966

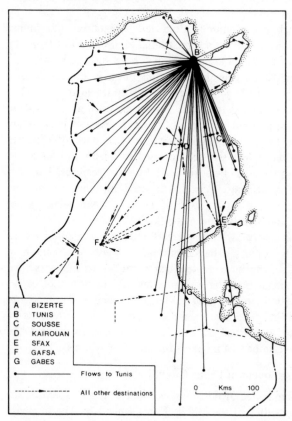

A	BIZERTE
B	TUNIS
C	SOUSSE
D	KAIROUAN
E	SFAX
F	GAFSA
G	GABES

Flows to Tunis

All other destinations

0   Kms   100

intercensal period 1960-5,[14] while Blake with reference to Morocco suggests that small market towns were used as steps in the migration process.[15] In the Tunisian case the dominance of Tunis over the mountain region of the Tell and over the central steppelands of the country, as demonstrated in Figure 3.2, precludes the possibility of step migration in much of the country.[16] Signoles in a study of internal migration in Tunisia asserts that most population moves are single step either to Tunis or to a local city.[17] Further evidence against step migration in Tunisia comes from Bchir's study of immigration to Sousse.[18] Only 6 per cent of immigrants wanted to move on to Tunis. It may tentatively be inferred that the persons who did migrate from Sousse to Tunis were native to the city and were not rural persons who had previously moved to Sousse. The city is therefore a terminus as well as a source to migrant flows; Sousse is not a relay centre in the migration process.

The balance between immigration and emigration determines whether population mobility is a force adding to or detracting from the natural increase of city populations. Many centres such as Kairouan,[19] Fès and Taza[20] make net gains by migration, but high levels of emigration from these cities to larger centres has greatly lessened the level of urban growth. In Iran the growth of Tehrān has been at the expense of provincial cities, particularly those of the north-west.[21] Polarisation of population in larger cities is in part a consequence of effective national integration. Local services provided by medium-sized towns have been undermined by those offered by larger centres. Benedict suggests that this is the major cause for the economic and demographic malaise of many of the small towns of Turkey,[22] particularly those along the Aegean and Mediterranean coastlands.[23]

In summary, urban sprawl of the largest cities in the Middle East is a function not only of rural-urban migration, but also of urban-urban migration. Small towns have proved less attractive to migrants than large towns and small towns have themselves become points of departure for migrant flows to the larger cities. Both rural and urban communities located in peripheral zones of national and international economic and socio-political systems appear unable to prevent the departure of large numbers of migrants towards core regions.

Migration as a Component of Urban Growth

The numerical dominance of migrants over natives is a frequent occurrence in the large cities of the Middle East (Table 3.1). The immense numbers of migrants resident in these conurbations have triggered complex changes in urban form and life-style. Meaningful planning of the great metropolis must therefore consider migrants as an essential component of the urban populace. The magnitude of the migration influx would be still more dramatic if the children of migrants were also registered as newcomers to the city.

The percentage of urban growth attributed to the migration component is in many cities closely related to the overall rate of urban expansion. Long-established urban centres such as the cities of the Maghreb and of the Levant have grown less rapidly than those of the Gulf, and migration has been a less important component of their growth than in the new oil cities.[24] The cities with the most rapid rates of increase are coincident with those attracting the largest numbers of

Table 3.1: Migrants in Selected Arab Cities

City or city state		Year	Population surveyed	Percentage Migrant	Non-migrant
Dammam and Al Khubar	(b)	1972	144,000	93.5	6.5
Jiddah	(b)	1972	381,000	88.2	11.8
Riyadh	(b)	1974	667,000	84.9	15.1
Tä'if	(b)	1972	106,000	83.9	16.1
Oran	(b)	1974	78,000[a]	79.7[a]	20.3[a]
Abu Dhabi	(n)	1975	236,000	78.5	21.5
Dubai	(n)	1975	209,000	69.4	30.6
Qatar	(n)	1975	170,000	68.9	31.1
Medina	(b)	1975	100,000	64.2	35.8
Mecca	(b)	1972	274,000	58.6	41.4
Kuwait	(n)	1975	990,000	52.6	47.4
Salé	(b)	1970	332,000	51.8	48.2
Meknès	(b)	1970	233,000	50.9	49.1
Kénitra	(b)	1970	129,000	47.2	52.8
Safi	(b)	1970	122,000	45.2	54.8
Casablanca	(b)	1970	1,363,000	44.8	55.2
Tangier	(b)	1970	168,000	38.4	61.6
Tunis	(b)	1975	940,000	35.6	64.4
Marrakech	(b)	1970	317,000	29.0	71.0
Damascus	(r)	1970	836,000	26.8	73.2
Homs	(r)	1970	216,000	26.1	73.9
Sousse	(r)	1966	85,000	23.3	76.4
Cairo	(b)	1966	2,076,000	21.3	78.7
Al Hufuf	(b)	1972	74,000	21.1	78.9
Bahrain	(n)	1971	216,000	21.0	79.0
Aleppo	(r)	1970	639,000	19.6	80.4
Alexandria	(b)	1966	884,000	16.4	83.6
Sfax	(r)	1966	252,000	10.8	89.2

(b) Migrants from place of birth
(r) Migrants from place of last residence
(n) Migrants by nationality

a. Considers only heads of households.

Source: Compilsed from Tunisian Census, 1966; Moroccan Census, 1970; Syrian Census, 1970; Tunisian Census, 1975. Other sources: AARDES, *Etude Nationale sur les migrations* (Secrétariat d'Etat, Algiers, 1975); W. Abd el Aal, 'Spatial patterns of population dynamics in Egypt, 1947-1970', unpublished PhD thesis (University of Durham, 1977), p. 170; T. Baddou, 'Les migrations internes'; Grill, *Urbanization in the Arabian Peninsula*, pp. 69, 99; G. Schweizer, *Saudi Arabien*, ed. H. Blume (Tubingen, 1976), Chap. 3.

both international and internal migrants. For example, in Riyadh 23 per cent and in Jiddah 42 per cent of the labour force is foreign.[25]

The impact of migration varies with the passage of time. In Tehrān migrants increased as a percentage of the total population from 46 per cent in 1956 to 49 per cent in 1966.[26] In North Africa the contribution of migration to urban expansion is also believed to have grown from 45 per cent of population increase between 1950 and 1960 to 58 per cent of urban growth between 1970 and 1975.[27] By contrast Baghdād is typical of the Arab East where the migration component has become of less importance. It accounted for 61 per cent of the urban growth of Baghdād between 1957 and 1965 but only 46 per cent of growth between 1965 and 1970.[28]

Some cities have experienced migration surges because of sudden forced migrations. For example, 63 per cent of urban growth in 'Amman city between 1967 and 1971 resulted from refugee migration. Prior to the 1967 Israeli conflict only 44 per cent of urban growth was migration induced.

The migrant contribution to city growth is not *necessarily* a function of changes in the magnitude of migration flows. If rates of increase in migration flows are lower than rates of increase by natural growth, then the migrant contribution to city expansion will decline, even though the number of migrants arriving in the city may be greater than at any previous time. Shorter and Tecke's lucid study of Turkish urbanisation, examines the complex relation between migration and urban development.[29] In Turkey divergent trends have emerged between the absolute and relative contributions of migrants to urban growth. While the absolute number of migrants to Turkish cities consistently grew between 1945 and 1970, migration as a percentage of urban population increase was of peak importance in two separate time periods — 1950 to 1955 and 1965 to 1970.

As in Turkey, so also throughout the Middle East, the absolute number of migrants arriving in the city can be expected to continue to grow. The importance of migration as a component of urban growth is less predictable. It seems possible in the next few decades that the adoption of family planning measures may result in a declining rate of natural increase in some of the more mature urban economies of the Middle East, while rural population pressure in peripheral regions will continue to sustain large rural-urban migration flows.

In summary, the increase or decrease of the migration component of urban growth is not *necessarily* mirrored by a growth or decline in the absolute numbers of rural-urban migrants. In the Middle East the absolute number of migrants living in cities is and will continue to be a very high proportion of the populations of large cities.

Migration Behaviour and Time

The presence of so many newcomers in the Middle Eastern city is important but not surprising. Higher ratios of migrants to natives have been recorded over longer periods in South American cities.[30] Arab cities do not belong to the top league of the world's fastest growing cities.[31] Movement from village to city is no more than the inevitable spatial manifestation of a much more deeply rooted transformation of human values and aspirations.

The impact of migration in the Arab world cannot be adequately measured in terms of the numbers of rural bred persons now living in urban areas. It cannot even be understood in terms of the changing shape and form of the city. Migration matters because it involves the concentration of people of different abilities, hopes and beliefs. Migration necessitates change in human relationships, and the new order of urban life requires the adaptation of human resources to new economic and social structures. This involves change in the behaviour patterns both of migrants and of native urbanites. Migrants who have not adapted to or do not intend to adapt to urban life have an entirely different impact on the city from those who are committed to a metropolitan existence.

This distinction in behaviour can conveniently be described by the terms 'temporary' and 'permanent' migration. There is a tradition of temporary migration[32] in the Middle East.[33] In some cases migrants have developed very distinctive trades. From the Berber village of Chenini migrants to Tunis have traditionally become newspaper vendors.[34] The Libyan mountain village of Takul sends bakers to Tripoli, while in Egypt the Nubian peoples have often emigrated to Cairo to become domestic servants.[35] Shi'a Persians operate as merchants in Dubai, Kojas as salesmen in Mutrah[36] and the Shleuh as grocers throughout the cities of Morocco.[37] Shleuh brothers and cousins take turns to work the family grocery in the city. By this means they can corporately supplement the family income and simultaneously assure the right of the individual to return periodically to participate in tribal and family life in the village.[38]

Temporary participation of persons from traditional subsistence societies in an urban money economy is often associated with the pendular migration of young unmarried men who cannot find full employment in the village economy throughout the year.[39] Short-term city employment as labourers, service workers or small entrepreneurs can increase their income and provide cash, surplus to subsistence requirements. This they may save with the subsequent intention of buying village land or property. Attachment to the village is very strong and many temporary migrants strive to do well in the city with the sole intention of financing the village economy and of furthering the development of the rural and not the urban community. The pervasive nature of temporary migration of one or two members of a family is illustrated by a Turkish village survey (1968) which revealed that one fifth of families had at least one person working away from home.[40]

Throughout the Middle East the tendency for migrants to stay more permanently in the city has been observed. Karpat notes an increase in migrant permanency in Turkey in the 1950s,[41] Amersfoot proposes 1960 as the turning point in the migration of the Shleuh of Morocco,[42] while Birks describes the economic and political circumstances which altered the frequency of migration from Omani villages after 1970.[43]

Rising population pressure in the country and higher urban unemployment in the city have inhibited the periodic return of less well-organised migrant groups from city to village. It has become increasingly difficult to obtain secure urban employment and the growing gap between rural and urban incomes[44] has discouraged temporary migrants from giving up city jobs.

In short, one of the most critical aspects of contemporary migration in the Middle East is the increasing permanence of migrant residence in the city. Even fewer migrants view themselves as sojourners; many have come to the city to stay; and by the increasing permanence of their presence they have transformed the character of the Arab city.

Migrant Housing

The degree of migrant commitment to permanent residence is reflected in the social patterns of each city. Each urban area has a unique mix of temporary and permanent migrants. Families in the old *gecekondu* of İstanbul and Ankara represent a much more permanent migration influence on the infrastructure of these cities,[45] than do the large numbers of male migrant workers in the Gulf cities. The latter group remit a large proportion of their earnings to their families in Baluchistan,[46] Oman or the Yemen AR and they intend to return home after a short period of urban employment.

The unaccompanied and often unskilled male migrant, who wishes to earn a fixed sum of money or achieve a particular goal — such as saving to pay a bride price — will wish to minimise expenditure and effort in finding city accommodation.[47] Central lodging houses and hostels are often full of young rural migrants willing to rent cheap and often communal accommodation. Many migrants are employed on a daily basis and perform menial manual jobs in the service industries, in small, owner-operated firms or in peddling and street vending.

The medinas of many cities have been invaded by rural populations, and the fine houses of the old urban families have been sublet room by room. Rents here are lower than in the modern commercial zones of the metropolis. A survey of Tunis medina revealed that 76 per cent of the inhabitants are now immigrants and of these two-thirds are of rural origin.[48] Micaud reports that the secularisation of the *habous* properties of Tunis, as of many Maghreb cities, has led to the abandonment of fine palaces and old houses.[49] The former occupants of the *madrasas* and *zāwiyas* have subdivided their properties, rented them to the newcomers, and departed to villas in the new elitist suburbs.

Some migrants, usually those who are accompanied by their families and who have a moderate commitment to participating in urban life, build small houses or huts on the city periphery. These squatter suburbs are described as *hillas* in Saudi Arabia,[50] *sarīfas* in Baghdād, *gecekondu* in Turkey, *bidonvilles* in Libya and *gourbivilles* in Tunisia, and are identifiable not only by their flimsy fabric but also by the demographic characteristics of the residents, which are transitional between those of rural and urban populations.

The types of social relationships formed by temporary and permanent migrants are quite distinct. Abu-Lughod has described the myriad of village societies which have developed to meet the social and economic needs of migrants in Cairo.[51] Temporary migrants seldom make friends outside the migrant community. They are reluctant to join urban-based organisations or even to be affiliated with workers' unions. A relatively high degree of migrant integration in city life was found by Karpat in a study of migrant contact patterns in İstanbul.[52] It was found that although a large number of persons considered their primary contacts to be with relatives (32 per cent) or with co-villagers (19 per cent) many of them had made new friends (37 per cent) since arriving in the city.

In the City But Not of the City

There is nothing inherently evil or unsatisfactory about the progressive concentration of population in an increasingly permanent fashion in cities, either in the Middle East or in any other part of the world. Permanent settlement of migrants in the city brings a potential for fruitful interaction of disparate human resources. Regrettably nearly every migration study in the Middle East records or implies unsatisfactory interaction between migrants and native town-dwellers, and even between migrants and other migrants.

A number of characteristics of migrant and native urban populations can be identified which favour segregation rather than integration in the city. Barriers to integration are twofold – first, some migrants are ill-equipped in terms of their educational and occupational skills to adapt to the urban system. Secondly, the structures and social processes of urban systems do not necessarily operate in favour of migrant integration.

The desire of many migrants to become accepted urbanites is very great. Migrants who have made the city their permanent home wish to adopt new behaviour patterns. They often search for more satisfactory accommodation. Nelson comments that migrants who are successful in their city job, subsequently invest some of their earnings in improving their homes,[53] and in certain cities squatter settlements become respectable suburbs (e.g. the Caglayin quarter of İstanbul)[54] despite their initially unplanned and ill-serviced character.

Just as the housing chosen by migrants indicates their intentions to stay or depart from the city, so too does the demographic structure of migrant populations. Highly imbalanced sex ratios are symptomatic of the presence of temporary migrants. In İstanbul the migrant male/female ratio of 143:100 is high compared with the ratio of 117 men to 100 women for the population as a whole. In Cairo families from the Delta have balanced sex ratios, while migrants from upper Egypt are male dominated with 129 men for every 100 women.[55]

One of the most interesting findings of Birks' and Sinclair's demographic study of Kuwait is the tendency for the immigrant Jordanian population to develop increasingly balanced sex ratios through time, as migrants are joined by their wives.[56] It is possible that the same trend will occur amongst other migrant groups in the Gulf cities, a trend which has important ramifications with regard to the provision of housing and services for the migrant community.

Time spent in the city does not in itself result in migrant assimilation. Specific characteristics both at the level of the individual and of the group favour rapid assimilation. In two independent studies, one in Riyadh,[57] the other in Tripoli (Libya),[58] research has shown that high educational attainment and high socio-economic status amongst migrants are key variables encouraging assimilation. In both cases it was recognised that these characteristics favour the integration of migrants who already have some urban experience or who were born or bred in small urban communities.

Levine, in a study of male migrants in Ankara, has shown that the number of personal contacts made by a migrant is a function of the migrant's contact patterns in his previous environment.[59] Regardless of the extent of a migrant's new contact network, a positive correlation remained between his education and his perceived adjustment to city life.

The spatial location of migrants within the structure of the city also influences assimilation. Residents of the medina of Tripoli were more deeply involved in urban life than those who lived in peripheral shanty-towns.[60] The integrative force of the medina in the social life of the city has fortunately been recognised by some town planners and in certain cases it survives as the living core of the Arab city and not merely as a mausoleum of Islamic monuments for the tourist industry.

While squatter settlements and suburban migrant villages do not favour the rapid assimilation of newcomers, it can be argued that they play a necessary role in providing structural and social units which aid in the adjustment of migrants to city life. In the longer term the nurtur-ing of rural values in migrant suburbs reduces the need for temporary workers to return to their own villages to experience and share in tradi-tions familiar to them. By encouraging more permanent residence in the city, these concentrations of migrant dwellings introduce an opportunity for newcomers to imitate the urban life-styles adopted by earlier migrants.

Nagi, in a study of a rural-urban migration in Egypt, makes the important distinction between urbanisation and urbanism.[61] The former describes the physical expansion of the city in terms of area and population, the latter refers to a mode of behaviour characteristic of life in the city but not necessarily characteristic of all residents of the city. That rural life-styles persist in the city is manifestly clear in cases such as Cairo, but the long-term survival of rural values within the city is by no means assured. Migrant communities foster a cultural lag which follows the physical attrition of migrants to the urban population and precedes their social integration in city life. Abu-Lughod argues that rural values are as active in transforming the city as is the urban system in remoulding migrant characteristics.[62] While this is true, it should be noted that migrants adopt at an early stage the urban innovations which they can afford, and those who are successful in finding modern sector employment experience the profound change in life-style which follows from observing regular hours of work in a factory or in service employment in the modern sector.

Many migrants are not and may never be assimilated within the modern sector, in the sense that they may maintain characteristics distinctive from those of the native population. Nevertheless involvement in the 'informal' sector involves change in the life-styles of migrant workers so that they begin to lose their rural characteristics. Their limited contact with the complex economic systems of the city acts as a physical catalyst bringing changes in their life-style which distinguish them irrevocably from rural people. They are in the city, they are part of the city, yet they remain distinct from those who are native to the city.

Ultimately the most important factor restricting the integration of migrants and influencing the attitude of rural persons towards the urban environment, is the ability of migrants to find suitable employment. The long-term satisfaction or dissatisfaction of migrants with city life will be a function of the levels of occupational and social mobility which they experience.

Occupational and Social Mobility

The occupational status of a migrant first describes his ability to earn a living for himself and his family, and secondly serves as a surrogate measure of his social status relative to persons born in the city and relative to other migrants.

Migration is not only associated with the selective demographic transfer of the rural population to the city, but it is also linked with the selective channelling of population into specific occupational and social categories. Of migrants from Amarah province interviewed in Baghdād, 64 per cent were found to be manual workers.[63] In Kuwait, in 1975, 57 per cent of immigrants were employed in social and transport services,[64] while in Riyadh the proportion was lower being only 17 per cent of migrants from villages.[65] Some migrants succeed in establishing themselves as small merchants. In Baghdād 10 per cent of migrants were greengrocers and mobile shopkeepers, in Kuwait 16 per cent were in commerce and in Tunis 10 per cent of actively employed migrants were merchants or traders.[66]

With only a few notable exceptions[67] modern sector employment is dominated by urban born persons. For example, Fakhfakh reports that new industrial developments such as the treatment of phosphates at Sfax have offered employment only to skilled workers of urban origin. Few if any of the rural migrants from the hinterland of Sfax have entered modern employment.[68]

Most demographic and economic surveys record high rates of urban unemployment, but often such surveys are unable to uncover or fail to classify the diversity and irregularity of 'informal' employment opportunities adopted by migrants. Underemployment, rather than unemployment, is the typical experience of migrants during their first few months in the city. This distinction is recognised by Hay, who found in a micro-study that only 17 per cent of newcomers did not find some form of employment in the first month, and only 9 per cent were still unemployed after three months.[69] Initially, 49.8 per cent of migrants worked in the 'informal' or traditional sector of the city economy, but with the passage of time this percentage dropped to 28 per cent of the total, as migrants found more secure employment in the modern sector.

This rosy picture is not mirrored throughout the Middle East. Bartsch estimates that 71 per cent of residents in the immigrant Ku-ye 9 Aban district of Tehran were unemployed, underemployed or irregularly employed.[70] In the Egyptian case Birks and Sinclair report urban unemployment in 1976 running at one and a half million persons, and suggest that transfer of labour from the traditional to the modern sector was minimal.[71] This substantiates Abu-Lughod's claim that the 'urban villagers' of Cairo are occupationally concentrated in the lowest tiers of the service sector mostly in unproductive and often highly dubious employment.[72]

While one may assume, from the continued presence of large numbers of migrants in cities throughout the Middle East, that most of them discover some means of earning a living, equally one may infer from the poverty of migrant communities that the newcomers are failing to experience the full benefits of an urban economy. As has already been demonstrated with regard to the housing market, it is not a lack of desire on the part of migrants that is the cause of blockages. Rather it is the immobility of the employment market. Rigidity is reinforced by certain institutional processes which foster occupational segregation. Cne may safely assert that the majority of migrants have their hopes dashed as they move from a situation of underemployment in the agricultural sector to one of underemployment in the urban economy. Migration may have relocated them in physical proximity to the national core, but in economic terms their transfer has been from the periphery of the rural economy to the periphery of the urban economy.

Malik, in a survey of the actively employed migrants of Riyadh, reports that their occupational status was highly dependent on their environment of origin.[73] In general, migrants from other Saudi cities had achieved better jobs than the native population of Riyadh. By contrast, nomads and villagers were forced to take menial jobs and had failed to achieve any significant social or occupational mobility within the city. While rural migrants may have been frustrated in their attempts to rise to higher positions, Malik reports that they have been willing to maintain their lowly position in the urban hierarchy. Even working at the lowest occupational levels, these migrants consider themselves to be better off than had they remained in the villages of origin or pursued a nomadic existence.

The introduction of migrants to urban society in Saudi Arabia has been facilitated by the polarity of immense oil wealth, fuelling upward mobility amongst the native urban populations, and of extreme rural poverty, encouraging the exodus of persons from village and nomadic society. The model of occupational mobility in the Saudi city proposed by Malik and reformulated by Grill (Figure 3.3, A)[74] indicates that current social and economic conditions permit entry of migrants to the social structure of the city at several different levels. Whether the status of the migrant labourer at the base of the urban employment pyramid will remain tenable in the future, depends first on whether the economic system will sustain the aforementioned spectrum of employment opportunities, and secondly on whether the consciousness of the urban poor remains fragmented and their aspirations of upward mobility continue to be thwarted.

While Malik's model is valid for most of the oil-rich states of the Arab East, the problems and potentials for the urban labour market in the Maghreb and the countries of the Northern Tier of the Middle East are rather different. In Turkey international emigration has diverted some of the demand for city jobs in the lower occupational categories to the European labour market. By comparison with other countries of the Middle East several of Turkey's towns have relatively advanced urban economies. Savan has attempted to measure the occupational mobility of some of İstanbul's migrants.[75] A number of her interviewees had been settled in the city for 40 years and were well integrated in the urban system. Of these, 73 per cent came from households where the migrant's father had worked in agriculture, while 14 per cent came from families who were involved in private businesses. By contrast 44 per cent of migrants were now employed in the industrial sector, 17 per cent worked for private enterprises and 13 per cent were employed by government offices.

In the Maghreb the high levels of occupational mobility which followed decolonisation added an extra dimension to the urban occupation

Figure 3.3: Flow of Migrants into the Urban Employment Hierarchy

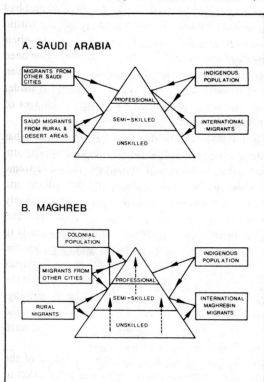

structure. Vacancies released by the departure of Europeans in the largest cities affected not only town-dwellers, but also villagers from prosperous agricultural zones. At the lowest occupational levels, landless labourers entered urban employment at the 'informal' sector on a par with unskilled city-bred workers. A sample survey of employment opportunities revealed that the earnings of migrants arriving in Tunis between 1962 and 1972 were greater than those of persons born in the city.[76]

The moderate occupational mobility of Maghreb populations has not been typical of other countries. For example, the highly segmented character of the Egyptian labour market has discouraged all upward occupational mobility.[77] Government domination of the economy has reduced opportunities for self-employment and reinforced rigidities in labour transfer between sectors. This has been greatly to the detriment of unskilled less educated persons who are caught in a 'poverty trap'.[78] They are too poor financially to emigrate to the oil-boom cities of the Gulf and too poorly skilled to rise to better positions within the Egyptian employment hierarchy.

Now that the initial post-independence restructuring of the Maghreb economies has occurred it seems likely that lower occupational mobility will be experienced. Nevertheless the higher educational attainment of rural populations in the Maghreb will continue to militate in favour of higher occupational mobility than in the Arab East.[79] The continuing trend towards international emigration of Maghrebian workers from the lower portion of the urban employment pyramid[80] has also temporarily reduced the pressure on the labour market. In the light of the fundamentally different relationships in labour supply and demand in the Maghreb, a separate model is proposed (Figure 3.3, B). A dearth of research makes difficult further generalisation concerning the critical interaction between social and spatial mobility in the Middle East.

Future Migration

Despite Ibrahim's claim that overurbanisation exists in many Arab states[81] sustained emigration from rural areas seems to imply the existence of the inverse condition of rural overpopulation. As Abu-Lughod has stated, the majority of migrants make higher marginal contributions to the economy of the city than to the economy of the village.[82] Empirical examination suggests that population redistribution towards cities is inevitable. Therefore the problem is not to decide whether rural-urban migration is economically desirable, but rather to find the optimal ethical, ecological and economic distribution of population between cities of different sizes.

The majority of inhabitants of large cities have developed aspirations far beyond their current standards of living. Despite the gap between the desires of the populace and their real-life experience, return migration from cities to villages is low and attests to the absence of any inclination to revert to former rural life-styles. Alternative opportunities in other cities and foreign labour markets is a more attractive option for dissatisfied migrants. The massive emigration of workers from many cities of the Middle East in search of more lucrative employment abroad indicates that standards of living and opportunities for self-improvement in many of the cities of countries such as Turkey, Jordan, Yemen AR and Oman are inadequate. Studies of the occupational expectations of the current student populations in the Maghreb and in

Iran, Turkey and Lebanon, also reveal the extremely high hopes held by the youthful populations of these countries, despite the rigidity of current occupational structures.[83] It seems likely that international migration will in the future serve as a mechanism for both the skilled and unskilled to help match occupational ambitions and the realities of the international labour market. For the less well qualified worker, underemployment in the 'informal' sector of a large city in one of the poorer nations, may be a first step towards subsequent upward mobility as an international migrant worker in modern sector employment in Libya or the Gulf. Simultaneously the availability of international workers willing to enter the urban employment market at the most menial levels, has facilitated the upward mobility of city-dwellers native to the richer countries, who would in other circumstances have been required to perform lower status functions. It is predicted that spatial mobility will operate on an increasingly large scale permitting occupational mobility at the international scale which cannot be achieved at national, regional or city levels.

High rates of natural population growth in many Middle Eastern countries are likely to continue over the next few decades. In order to avoid chronic unemployment and underemployment in regions where economic expansion is slow, emigration must continue to operate as a vital mechanism of population redistribution both in spatial and economic dimensions. Far from being prevented, migration must be projected and planned.

Attempts to improve rural life and to hold population on the land by agricultural reforms have not met with great success in the Middle East. Land reform in Iran is considered to be one of the most important contributory causes to rural-urban migration. Two strategies currently hold promises as viable alternatives to the further polarisation of migrants in a few large cities.[84] Abu-Lughod proposes that rural-urban population drift could, in many Middle Eastern countries, be redirected from existing urban cores towards settlements and industrial poles located on intermetropolitan axes.[85] Such a policy permits continued regional concentration of population, but by encouraging the development of linear conurbations avoids the structural problems of enormous unicentric cities. A second alternative is to attract migrants to entirely new growth poles, as in the development of the Egyptian Canal Zone, thus decentralising existing urban patterns. One of the great imponderables of Turkish geography must surely be the impact which relocation of the capital in Ankara has had on the diversion of at least some migrants away from İstanbul.

Important as is the debate over the optimum spatial redistribution of population in cities of particular shapes and sizes, more critical is discussion of the values and criteria by which planners should select economic and social structures appropriate for national development. As the renaissance of Islam has led to a redirection of educational policy in many Arab states, so it may also succeed in infusing city and regional planning with integrative religious values. Migrant resources can only be unlocked for the benefit of the entire urban community when contact, communication and ultimately integration occur between the new arrivals and the settled population.[86] The planner's job is to understand and to overcome the undesirable forces maintaining the spatial, social and economic segregation of migrants.

In the past planners have succeeded in identifying, but not in solving, the ecological problems associated with the attrition of migrant settlements around Middle Eastern cities. More difficult to isolate and cure will be the social pathologies which may be expected to arise if the increasing spatial mobility of Middle Eastern populations is not accompanied by strategies which facilitate greater occupational and social mobility.

References

1. Bibliographic reviews of rural-urban migration in the Middle East include M.E. Bonine, 'Urban studies in the Middle East', *Middle East Studies Association Bulletin*, vol. 10, no. 3 (1976) 1-37; V. Costello, *Urbanization in the Middle East* (Cambridge University Press, Cambridge, 1977), Ch. 4; K.S. Seetharam, *et al.*, 'Urbanization and migration in Arab countries: an overview', *Urbanization and Migration in some Arab and African Countries*, Cairo Demographic Centre, Research Monograph 4 (Cairo, 1973) 473-504. Recent studies of national migration systems include: J.S. Birks, 'The development of a tradition of migrant labour movements from the Sultanate of Oman, and some aspects of its modern significance', *Human Resource Development in the Middle East*, ed. J. Socknat (Olympus, Utah, 1979); C. Dobbs, 'Rural-urban migration in Turkey', unpublished MA thesis (University of Durham, 1975); M.V. George and R. Al Sa'adi, 'Population change and internal migration in Iraq, 1947-65', *Urbanization and Migration in some Arab and African Countries*, Cairo Demographic Centre, Research Monograph 4 (Cairo, 1973) 331-58; N. Grill, 'Urbanization in the Arabian peninsula', unpublished MA thesis (University of Durham, 1977); M.J. Hay, 'An economic analysis of rural-urban migration in Tunisia', unpublished PhD thesis (University of Minnesota, 1974); M. Hemmassi, 'Migration and problems of development; the case of Iran', *The Social Sciences and Problems of Development*, ed. K. Farmanfarmaian (Studies on the Near East, Princeton University Press, Princeton, 1976), pp. 208-25; K. Karpat, *Rural Migration and Urbanization in Turkey: the Gecekondu* (Cambridge University Press, Cambridge, 1976); R. Koelstra and H. Tieleman, *Developpement ou migration* (Remplod, The Hague, 1977); M.T. Mertaugh, 'The causes and effects of rural-urban migration

in Morocco, 1960-1970', unpublished PhD thesis (University of Michigan, 1976); M.H. Nagi, 'Internal migration and structural change in Egypt', *Middle East Journal*, vol. 28, no. 3 (1974) 261-82; M. Shadman-Valavi, 'An analysis of the determinants of migration in Iran', unpublished PhD thesis (Northwestern University, 1974); C. Sinclair and J. Socknat, 'Choosing a development and employment strategy with migration a critical variable', *Human Resources Development in the Middle East*, ed. J. Socknat (Olympus, Utah, 1979); K.E. Vaidyanathan and M.L. Fanes, 'Population redistribution in Algeria, 1954-1966', *Urbanization and Migration in Some Arab and African Countries*, Cairo Demographic Centre, Research Monograph 4 (Cairo, 1973), pp. 31-72; K.E. Vaidyanathan and M. Ghannam, 'Urbanization and internal migration in Syria, 1960-1970', *Urbanization and Migration in Some Arab and African Countries*, Cairo Demographic Centre, Research Monograph 4 (Cairo, 1973), pp. 305-30.

2. J. Abu-Lughod, 'The legitimacy of comparisons in comparative urban studies: a theoretical position and an application to North African cities', *Urban Affairs Quarterly*, vol. 11, no. 2 (1975) 13-35.

3. K.S. Seetharam, *et al.*, 'Urbanization and migration in Arab countries'.

4. H. Adibi, 'Rural-urban migration in Iran, research notes', *Australian and New Zealand Journal of Sociology*, vol. 13, no. 2 (1977) 175-8.

5. See F. Halliday, *Arabia without Sultans* (Penguin, Harmondsworth, 1974).

6. D. Harris, *The Times*, 'Special report on Kuwait', 4 November 1976, p. 1.

7. N. Grill, *Urbanization in the Arabian Peninsula*, p. 56.

8. F. Stambouli, 'Systeme social et urbanisation', *Revue Tunisienne des Sciences Sociales*, vol. 27 (1971) 39-68.

9. Sources: Tunisian Population Census, 8 May 1975: Population by Place of Residence and Place of Birth; Syrian Population Census, 1970: Population by Place of Current and Previous Residence.

10. J. Friedman and R. Wulff, 'The urban transition: comparative studies of newly industrializing societies', *Progress in Geography*, vol. 8 (1976) 26.

11. G. Simon, *Etat et perspectives de l'emigration Tunisienne* (BIT, Tunis, 1977).

12. For discussion of the concept see: J.B. Riddell and M.E. Harvey, 'The urban system in the migration process: an evaluation of stepwise movement in Sierra Leone', *Economic Geography*, vol. 48 (1972) 270-83.

13. W. Donaldson, personal communication, 1978. Distinction between international and internal migration in Oman is artificial in view of the recency of the state boundaries which cut across traditional migration paths.

14. J.M. Munro, 'Migration in Turkey', *Economic Development and Cultural Change*, vol. 22, no. 4 (1974) 634-53.

15. G.H. Blake, 'Urbanization in North Africa', *Tijdschrift voor Economische en Sociale Geografie*, vol. 62 (1971) 191.

16. Calculated from the Tunisia population census, 3 May 1966.

17. P. Signoles, 'Migrations interieures et villes en Tunisie', *Cahiers de Tunisie*, tome 20, nos. 79-80 (1972) 207-40.

18. M. Bchir, 'Les migrations dans une métropole regionale: Sousse', *Revue Tunisienne des Sciences Sociales*, vol. 26 (1971) 107.

19. M. Trabelsi, 'L'exode rural et son impact sur le développement des villes régionales; l'example de Kairouan', *Revue Tunisienne des Sciences Sociales*, vol. 44 (1976) 141-71.

20. T. Baddou, 'Les migrations internes: enquête à Fez et à Taza', *2 éme Colloque de Demographie Maghrebienne, 21-26 April 1975* (INSEA, Maroc, 1975).

21. J.I. Clarke, *The Iranian city of Shiraz*, Department of Geography, Research Paper 7 (University of Durham, 1963), p. 7.

22. Towns of 2,000 to 20,000.

23. P. Benedict, 'The changing role of provincial towns', *Turkey, Geographic and Social Perspectives*, ed. P. Benedict *et al.* (Brill, Leiden, 1974), pp. 241-80.

24. See J. Abu-Lughod, 'Problems and policy implications of Middle Eastern urbanization', *Studies in Development Problems in Selected Countries of the Middle East* (UNESOB, 1973), p. 47.

25. N. Grill, *Urbanization in the Arabian Peninsula*.

26. F. Firoozi, 'Tehran: a demographic and economic analysis', *Middle Eastern Studies*, vol. 10, no. 1 (1974) 66.

27. US Bureau of Census, *Planning for Internal Migration* (US Government Printing Office, Washington, 1977), p. 36.

28. J. Abu-Lughod, 'Problems and policy implications', p. 47.

29. P. Shorter and B. Tecke, 'The demographic determinants of urbanization in Turkey, 1935-1970', *Turkey: Geographical and Social Perspectives*, ed. P. Benedict *et al.* (Brill, Leiden, 1974), pp. 281-94.

30. D.J. Hogan and M.T. Berlinck, 'Conditions of migration', *Internal Migration, the New World and the Third World*, eds. A.H. Richmond *et al.* (Sage, California, 1976), p. 226.

31. D.J. Dwyer, 'The third world city', *Geographical Magazine*, vol. 50, no. 8 (1978) 520.

32. Sometimes termed 'pendular migration'.

33. K. Karpat, *Rural Migration*; R. Antoun and I. Harik, *Rural Politics and Social Change in the Middle East* (Bloomington, Indiana, 1972).

34. D.E. Stephenson, 'Migration and community', *Change in Tunisia*, ed. R. Stone *et al.* (State University of New York Press, Albany, 1976), pp. 107-19.

35. M.H. Nagi, 'International migration and structural change in Egypt'.

36. W. Donaldson, personal communication, 1978.

37. A. Adam, 'Berber migrants in Casablanca', *Arabs and Berbers*, ed. E. Gellner *et al.* (Lexington, London, 1972).

38. J.M. Amersfoot, 'Migrant workers, circular migration and development', *Tijdscrift voor Economische en Sociale Geographie*, vol. 69, nos. 1 and 2 (1978) 17-26.

39. J.M. Amersfoot, ibid.

40. E. Ozburdun, *Social Change and Participation in Turkey* (Princeton University Press, Princeton, 1976).

41. K. Karpat, *Rural Migration*.

42. J.M. Amersfoot, 'Migrant workers'.

43. J.S. Birks, 'The development of a tradition of migrant worker movements'.

44. The increasing gap between rural and urban incomes has been studied in Tunisia by R. Koelstra, *Au travail dans la peripherie* (Remplod, The Hague, 1978) and reported in Iran by F. Vakil, 'Iran's basic macro-economic problems', *Economic Development and Cultural Change*, vol. 25, no. 4 (1977) 713-30.

45. N. Savan, 'Squatter settlement problems in Istanbul', *Turkey: Geographical and Social Perspectives*, ed. P. Benedict *et al.* (Leiden, Brill, 1974), pp. 327-62.

46. T.A. Brun *et al.*, 'Le Baloutchistan Iranien, un reservoir de travailleurs sous alimentés pour les Emirats', *Revue Tiers Monde*, vol. 18 (1977) 131-8.

47. D. Darwent, 'Urban growth in relation to socio-economic development and Westernization', unpublished PhD thesis (University of Durham, 1966).

48. F. Stambouli, 'Systeme social'.

49. E. Micaud, 'Urban planning in Tunis', *Change in Tunisia*, ed. R. Stone *et al.* (State University of New York Press, Albany, 1976), pp. 137-58.

50. A.A. Shamekh, 'Spatial patterns of bedouin settlement in Al-Qasim region, Saudi Arabia', unpublished PhD thesis (University of Kentucky, 1975).

51. J. Abu-Lughod, 'Migrant adjustment to city life: the Egyptian case',

American Journal of Sociology, vol. 67 (1961) 22-32.

52. K. Karpat, *Rural Migration*.

53. J. Nelson, 'Sojourners versus new urbanites', *Economic Development and Cultural Change*, vol. 24, no. 4 (1976) 721-58.

54. N. Savan, 'Squatter settlement problems'.

55. J. Nelson, 'Sojourners versus new urbanites', 726.

56. J.S. Birks and C. Sinclair, 'Kuwait', *International Migration Project Working Paper* (University of Durham, 1977), pp. 26-7.

57. S.A. Malik, 'Rural migration and urban growth in Riyadh, Saudi Arabia', unpublished PhD thesis (Michigan State University, 1973).

58. Y.A. El Kabir, 'Assimilation of rural migrants in Tripoli, Libya', unpublished PhD thesis (Case Western University, 1977).

59. N. Levine, 'Value orientation among migrants in Ankara, Turkey', *Journal of Asian and African Studies*, vol. 8, nos. 1 and 2 (1973) 50-68.

60. Y.A. El Kabir, 'Assimilation of rural migrants'.

61. M.H. Nagi, 'Internal migration'.

62. J. Abu-Lughod, 'Migrant adjustment'.

63. M.M. Azeez, 'Geographical aspects of rural migration from Amara province, Iraq, 1955-1964', unpublished PhD thesis (University of Durham, 1968), p. 284.

64. J.S. Birks and C. Sinclair, 'Kuwait'.

65. S.A. Malik, 'Rural migration and urban growth'.

66. Republique Tunisienne, *Enquête Nationale Demographique 1968-1969* (INS, Tunis, 1974).

67. K. Peterson, 'Villagers in Cairo: hypothesis versus data', *American Journal of Sociology*, vol. 77 (1971) 565.

68. M. Fakhfakh, 'Evolution des relations de Sfax et de sa région', *Revue Tunisienne des Sciences Sociales*, vol. 15 (1968) 263-73.

69. M.J. Hay, 'An economic analysis'.

70. W.H. Bartsch, 'Unemployment in less developed countries: a case study of a poor district of Tehran', *International Development Review, 1971*, vol. 13, 19-22.

71. J.S. Birks and C. Sinclair, 'Egypt', *International Migration Project Working Paper* (University of Durham, 1978).

72. J. Abu-Lughod, 'Varieties of urban experience; contrasts, coexistence and coalescence in Cairo', *Middle Eastern Cities*, ed. I. Lapidus (University of California Press, Los Angeles, 1969), pp. 159-87.

73. S.A. Malik, 'Rural migration and urban growth'.

74. Source: S.A. Malik, ibid., p. 22 and N. Grill, *Urbanization in the Arabian Peninsula*, p. 86.

75. N. Savan, 'Squatter settlement problems', 342-3.

76. Republique Tunisienne, *Enquête migration et emploi, Tunis 1972-1973* (INS, Tunis, 1974).

77. J.S. Birks and C. Sinclair, 'Kuwait'.

78. J.S. Birks and C. Sinclair, ibid.

79. R. Stone, 'Anticipated mobility to elite status among Middle Eastern university students', *International Review of History and Political Science*, vol. 10, no. 4 (1973) 1-17.

80. G. Simon, *Etat et perspectives*.

81. S. Ibrahim, 'Overurbanization and underurbanism: the case of the Arab world', *International Journal of Middle East Studies*, vol. 6, (1975) 29-45.

82. J. Abu-Lughod, 'Problems and policy implications', 48.

83. R. Stone, 'Anticipated mobility to elite status'.

84. Strategies for migration planning are discussed in greater depth by the US

Bureau of Census', *Planning for Internal Migration*.
    85. J. Abu-Lughod, 'Problems and policy implications', 57.
    86. Methods of achieving social cohesion are discussed by J. Abu-Lughod, ibid., 61.

4 ASPECTS OF URBAN EMPLOYMENT

J.S. Birks and C.A. Sinclair

Introduction

Types of urban employment structure and the nature of their growth differ widely in the Arab world.[1] These variations can be attributed to the unequal resource endowment prevailing in the area, compounded by the vagaries of planned and spontaneous political, social and economic development.[2] This chapter examines the pattern of employment in selected Arab countries, and finds that, despite overt differences, analysis can demonstrate some important underlying relationships between urban employment patterns of various nations in the Middle East.

In the argument, distinction is made between 'capital-rich' and 'poor' nations upon the basis of GNP per capita.[3] Although this indicator embodies a series of serious shortcomings when used as an index of economic development, it does serve to illustrate the distinction that is necessary for this analysis. The difference in GNP between the two groups of countries is illustrated in Table 4.1.

For purposes of exemplification, the capital-rich countries are here illustrated by Kuwait, Bahrain, Qatar and the United Arab Emirates. The capital-poor countries under discussion comprise Egypt, Yemen AR and Sudan. The difference in GNP per capita between these particular nations is substantial; the former group, the capital-rich countries, have per capita incomes averaging US $9,949. In contrast, the group less well endowed with resources averages US $180 per head.

Urban Employment in Capital-rich Countries

It is as a result of their unusual resource endowment, together with relatively small populations, that the striking urban employment pattern of the capital-rich states is found.[4]

Several factors are influential in making their urban labour markets very distinctive, not only within the Middle East, but also in the Third World as a whole. These states are small in population terms, with almost all inhabitants living in the major urban areas; they are city states.[5] Secondly, agriculture is virtually non-existent. The climatic and soil conditions of the Gulf region are well known and virtually preclude a sizeable rural agricultural labour force. Fishing is now hardly

Table 4.1: Gross National Product, for Selected 'Capital-rich' and 'Capital-poor' countries

	US Dollars GNP/Capita	Year
Capital-rich states		
Kuwait	11,600	1972
Bahrain	1,672	1976
Qatar	11,343	1977
United Arab Emirates	10,800	1977
Capital-poor states		
Egypt	145	1975
Sudan	307	1973
Yemen AR	120	1975

Note: This table is intended to be indicative rather than exact. Sources are official figures except when these are unavailable, in which case an estimate is made by the authors.

a significant source of employment in the upper Gulf, though it was before modern economic development a major source of livelihood for many.[6] With the exception of this now small sector, the urban labour markets of these capital-rich states comprise their entire labour force. The same is true, though the details differ, of that much larger capital-rich state, Saudi Arabia.[7]

The populations of the Gulf are small, as are their work forces.[8] Table 4.2 shows the limited sizes of the labour forces of the Gulf states, which are not on the same scale as those in Egypt, Sudan or Yemen AR (shown in Table 4.7).

Kuwait, Qatar and the United Arab Emirates together have a total work force of only about three-quarters of a million workers.

The concentration of these small labour forces into the urban areas in the capital-rich states is associated with the fact that virtually all employment falls within the 'modern sector'. This is shown by Table 4.3 for each of the capital-rich nations under consideration. These countries share the common features of small and declining employment in agricultural pursuits and fishing, the preserve of traditional non-wage employment.

It is under 'community, social and personal services' that an inordinately large proportion of employment falls in these states. This sector

Table 4.2: Total Population and Work Force of Capital-rich States

State	Population	Work force	Year
Kuwait	994,837	304,582	1975
Bahrain	290,342	76,998	1975
Qatar	158,000	66,205	1975
United Arab Emirates	655,937	296,516	1975

Source: Kuwait: 1975 Census; Bahrain: estimated from 1971 Census and from information supplied by the government of Bahrain; Qatar: estimated from 1970 Census and information supplied by official agencies and government institutions; United Arab Emirates: 1975 Census.

alone accounts for over one half of total employment in Kuwait, and only in the United Arab Emirates does it fall to less than 30 per cent of the total (this is largely a consequence of the construction boom).

If these employment data are summarised into 'primary', 'secondary' and 'tertiary' sectors as in Table 4.4, the dominance of the latter is even more obvious.

Only in the United Arab Emirates does the proportion of the urban labour force engaged in the tertiary sector fall below 60 per cent; in 1975, in the United Arab Emirates, 53.6 per cent of the labour force were in service sectors. Even this is a remarkably high value, but in Kuwait almost 75 per cent of those employed are within the tertiary sector.

That such high proportions of the labour force are employed in tertiary activities is surprising. It represents not only an unusual pattern of development, but also an absolute reversal of the normal evolution of the structure of labour force.[9] Generally a rapid expansion of tertiary employment in relative and absolute terms follows an industrial phase: the enlarged provision of services is normally a post-industrial phenomenon. In this case, however, tertiary developments, together with urbanisation, have taken place *before* the industrial phase, and not as a consequence of the growth of manufacturing and other secondary activities, as is vividly demonstrated in Table 4.3.

The key to why the structure of these urban labour forces has not appeared to obey the normal patterns of development lies in the approach to distributing oil wealth taken by these states. These are societies in which the leader of the community had traditionally borne responsibility for his followers.

Table 4.3: Employment in the 'Capital-rich' Countries of Kuwait, Qatar, United Arab Emirates and Bahrain (per cent)

	Kuwait				Qatar	United Arab Emirates		Bahrain		
	1957	1965	1970	1975	1970	1968	1975	1959	1965	1971
Agriculture and fishing	1.2	1.1	1.7	1.5	4.3	17.6	4.5	9.5	8.7	6.6
Mining and quarrying	6.3	3.9	3.1	1.6	4.6	–	2.3	1.0	–	–
Manufacturing	7.7	13.9	16.8	10.6	10.8	7.8	7.9	21.2	13.8	14.0
Construction	9.9	16.1	14.4	10.8	16.1	25.8	31.7	10.1	15.6	17.2
Electricity	–	–	–	–	–	–	–	–	–	–
Wholesale	9.6	12.9	14.1	13.3	16.9	11.4	14.8	10.7	14.6	14.6
Transport	4.2	5.6	5.2	5.3	6.7	11.1	8.0	3.5	10.3	12.8
Community, social and personal services	51.3	46.0	44.4	55.9	40.6	26.3	29.3	42.9	36.7	34.8
NAD	9.8	6.5	0.3	–	–	–	11.5	1.1	0.3	–
Total	100.0	100.0	100.0	100.0	100.0	100.0	100.0	100.0	100.0	100.0
Total number	85,555	179,284	234,354	298,415	48,390	78,071	296,516	46,955	53,274	59,590

Source: Census data in appropriate years.

Table 4.4: Employment in the Capital-rich Countries Summarised
by Primary, Secondary and Tertiary Sectors in Selected Years (per cent)

	Kuwait (1975)	Qatar (1971)	United Arab Emirates (1975)	Bahrain (1970)
Primary	4.1	9.2	6.8	6.6
Secondary	21.4	26.9	39.6	31.2
Tertiary	74.5	63.9	53.6	62.2

Source: Summarised from relevant censuses, establishment and employment surveys.

The now customary approach to the distribution of oil revenues is to establish provision of social services on what is, in Western eyes, a lavish scale. The early provision of unlimited fresh water, electricity, subsidised housing and the general advent of medical care and education not only satisfied local demand but created a greater one. In fact, the scale of provision, initially seen as fabulous, was rapidly perceived as inadequate, and with the justification that the ruler was fabulously wealthy, citizens of Gulf states have progressively demanded a wider provision of social services and an improved quality.[10]

The development of the requisite government administration to provide services has facilitated the distribution of the oil wealth without destroying the existing political order and hierarchies; nationals were enlisted in positions in the civil service at levels commensurate with their traditional status, and so could be paid a salary which included an element of social security payment. By this means, the continuation of traditional loyalties under new economic conditions was assured.

The impact of this modern interpretation of a traditional relationship has been to swell inordinately the ranks of government employees. Many government jobs exist solely as sinecures for nationals, who contribute little to the provision of services.[11] Consequently an appropriate number of expatriates are employed to discharge the duties of government. Hence the number of civil servants in total is far greater than is strictly necessary.

The procedure of the creation of public sector posts for nationals has resulted in a fundamental distortion of urban labour markets in the capital-rich countries. At least, it is this strategy, together with the extremely rapid economic growth of recent years that has resulted in a very small, virtually non-existent informal sector.

The lack of informal sector employment in these countries is the result of nobody being obliged or able to remain at low rates of remuneration or in occasional employment. Nationals who might, in less wealthy countries, be obliged to work in the informal sector can, in these capital-rich economies, acquire a substantial income by taking a post in the public sector. Wealth has transformed the employment of nationals from their traditional activities — fishing, date farming and even earlier, pearling — into the modern and wage sector of the economy.

Moreover, the poor sections of the expatriate communities who, in many cases, have moved to the capital-rich countries from, say, Cairo, 'Amman or Damascus, are not able to survive as informal petty traders and providers of services for three reasons. One is that the cost of basic necessities is high compared to most countries, and the income from petty trading is inadequate. Secondly, residence visas are normally given only when a work permit is held. To obtain a work permit requires a sponsor, normally a recognised 'employer'. Even if a potential informal sector worker were able to find a sponsor, the fee required by the sponsor would be prohibitive. Thirdly, the more successful informal sector activities are typically taken over by private entrepreneurs — usually nationals — who are seeking investment opportunities. Thus formal employment expands by absorbing activities which would elsewhere form the core of the informal sector. The result is that the generally ubiquitous subsistence existence in the Third World countries is almost non-existent in Gulf states. None the less, this explanation is not quite complete: more fundamental causes for the absence of the informal sector in the capital-rich countries will be developed after consideration of the capital-poor countries.

The degree to which policies in capital-rich countries treat government employment as a means of distribution of income rather than performing essential services and generating wealth can be best evidenced by Kuwait. The Kuwaiti economy and society can, in many respects, be considered a pointer towards the future development of the other capital-rich states. From 1970 to 1975 there has been a marked reduction of numbers of Kuwaiti nationals working in the private sector, and an increase in their number working in the public sector.

This absorption of national labour by the government, at the expense of the private sector, in these rapidly growing economies is only made possible by the immigration of foreign labour.[12] The degree to which non-national labour has come to feature in the work forces of these capital-rich nations is illustrated by Table 4.5. Only in Bahrain does the expatriate component of the work force comprise less than one half of the total number of economically active. In Kuwait, Qatar and the United Arab Emirates, over 75 per cent of the work force are non-national.

Table 4.5: Work Forces of the Capital-rich States by Nationality

State	Total work force	Nationals	Per cent	Non-nationals	Per cent	Year
Kuwait	298,415	86,971	29.1	211,444	70.9	1975
Bahrain	76,998	46,816	66.8	30,182	39.2	1975
Qatar	66,205	12,500	18.8	53,705	81.2	1975
United Arab Emirates	296,516	45,000	15.1	251,516	84.9	1975

Source: See Table 4.2.

How this non-national labour is distributed by sector can again be illustrated by reference to Kuwait. Table 4.6 shows that in no urban sector does the non-national labour force comprise less than 60 per cent of the total number of employees (even in agriculture and fishing, a small, semi-traditional non-urban sector employing only 7,500 people, almost one half are non-Kuwaiti). In certain critical sectors, such as manufacturing and construction, the non-Kuwaiti sections of the labour force rises to over 90 per cent of the total. The patterns illustrated here are again similar to those prevailing in the remaining capital-rich states.

One question needing answer at some point is the degree to which this trend of transfers of national labour from the private to the public sector can continue. When will the drain of national labour on the private sector cease? Could the ranks of government swell to accommodate all nationals over the course of time, leaving the private sector employees entirely non-national?

Essentially, the trend will only reverse when government aims and philosophies change. Whilst public sector employment is seen as an extension of the traditional duty of a ruler to provide for his people, the superior conditions of service attaching to public sector posts are likely to continue to attract nationals.

Table 4.6: Kuwaiti and Non-Kuwaiti Share of Employment by
Economic Sector 1975

	Kuwaiti		Non-Kuwaiti		
	Number	Share of total (per cent)	Number	Share of total (per cent)	Total number
Agriculture and fishing	3,983	53.1	3,531	46.9	7,514
Mining and quarrying	1,779	36.6	3,080	63.4	4,859
Manufacturing	2,258	9.4	22,209	90.6	24,467
Construction	1,756	5.5	30,500	94.5	32,256
Electricity, gas and water	2,034	28.0	5,237	72.0	7,271
Wholesale and retail trade	6,327	16.0	33,232	84.0	39,559
Transport, storage and communication	4,567	29.2	11,118	70.8	15,685
Community and personal services	4,265	38.6	102,537	61.4	166,802
Activities NAD	2	—	—	—	2
Total	86,971	29.2	211,444	70.8	298,415

Source: Census 1975.

The Urban Employment Pattern in the Capital-poor Countries

Egypt, Sudan and Yemen AR all share the same characteristics: a large
work force by Middle Eastern standards; a considerable proportion of
this work force being employed in the agricultural sector; limited
modern sector employment; a sizeable 'informal' sector; a large number
and, in the case of Yemen AR, a large proportion of their populations
working abroad. These features are summarised for the countries
chosen in Table 4.7. All contrast markedly in these characteristics with
the capital-rich states.

It is particularly important in this analysis to note the small proportion of employment in the modern sector in these countries, even in
Egypt, often thought of as a relatively well-developed Middle Eastern
state, where only some 33 per cent of employment is in the modern
sector.[13] Over one half of employment is in agriculture. In the Yemen
AR the proportion of the labour force involved in the modern sector is
as low as 7 per cent; almost six Yemeni workers out of ten are employed
on the land. A large majority, virtually all, of this modern sector

Table 4.7: Employment Distribution in Egypt, Sudan and Yemen AR

Employment category	Egypt (1976) per cent	Sudan (1973) per cent	Yemen AR (1975) per cent
Agricultural workers	50.7	55.2	57.9
Informal sector	11.5	14.5	14.5
Modern sector	33.1	28.6	6.6
(of which government)	(25.7)	(8.6)	(2.8)
(of which private sector)	(7.4)	(20.0)	(3.9)
Workers abroad	4.7	1.7	20.9
Total	100.0	100.0	100.0
Total number	12,811,500	513,236	355,085

Source: Egypt: Ministry of Planning, *Five Year Plan, 1978-82*, and J.S. Birks and C.A. Sinclair, *International Labour Migration Project. Country Case Study, Arab Republic of Egypt* (Durham, 1978); Sudan: Census 1973; Yemen AR: Census 1975.

employment is found in the urban centres. This is evident in Egypt, Sudan and in Yemen AR, where the modern sector is almost non-existent outside San'a.[14]

If the urban employment patterns prevailing in these poorer countries are examined in greater detail, a common feature becomes apparent. In each case, the majority of job opportunities are again found in the sector loosely called the 'service' or 'tertiary' sector.

In this characteristic, it would seem that the capital-poor countries resemble the capital-rich. This is, perhaps, unexpected. As noted, the factors explaining the predominance of the tertiary sector in the capital-rich countries are very particular, and do not pertain to capital-poor countries of the Middle East.[15] So here is an instance of a group of demonstrably poor countries, which are certainly not in post-industrial phase (and so which have not followed the expected evolution of the labour market from primary through secondary to tertiary expansion), and yet which have a disproportionately large share of employment in the tertiary sector.

There are two major factors behind this distribution of urban employment. First, in the capital-poor countries of the Middle East the manufacturing sector has failed to provide either the wealth or the

Table 4.8: Modern Sector Non-farm Employment Distribution

	Yemen AR per cent	Egypt per cent	Sudan per cent
Primary	0.2	0.8	21.4
Secondary	18.2	29.5	12.1
Tertiary	81.6	69.7	56.5
Total	100.0	100.0	100.0
Total number	90,180	404,300	1,003,834

Source: See Table 4.7.

employment that was anticipated would follow attempts to develop manufacturing in the 1950s and early 1960s. The investment that took place then was similar in kind to that which prevails in the developed world: a large investment was made in capital-intensive processes requiring a small number of highly skilled workers.

The failure of such programmes to create either wealth, or a large number of productive jobs, is well evidenced in urban Egypt and the towns of Sudan. In neither of these countries has industry proved able to create anything approaching the scale of employment or to sustain the levels of growth in real terms that were hoped for. The capability of the manufacturing sectors to create wealth has remained very limited.

In the case of Yemen AR, the brief recent period of modern economic development with only limited resource endowment is in itself reason for the limited extent of industrial employment. Yet this same limited period of development has witnessed the emergence of sizeable government employment.

Closer examination of Table 4.7 reveals that the Yemen AR 'government' alone accounts for 25.7 per cent of total employment. This gives the second facet of the explanation for the predominance of tertiary sector employment in these capital-poor economies: economic development and the establishment of 'modern sector' wage employment began here too with the setting up of a government administration.

Not only does the government account for a large proportion of urban employment in Yemen AR, it does so also in Egypt and Sudan, despite the difference in scale of their economies.[16] In Egypt, the nationalisations of the 1950s and 1960s, together with the creation of public corporations, enlarged the sphere of government activity to include most of industry and service provision. This increase in the public sector has subsequently been reinforced by a policy of graduate employment that has guaranteed every graduate a position in the ministries or public corporations.

Table 4.9: Modern Sector Employment in the Yemen AR

Economic sector	Numbers employed	Per cent
Agriculture	200	6.2
Mining and quarrying	51	–
Manufacturing	8,473	9.4
Electricity, gas and water	870	1.0
Construction	7,950	8.8
Wholesale and retail trade, restaurants and hotels	27,570	30.6
Transport, storage and communications	1,047	1.2
Finance, insurance, real estate and business services	1,126	1.2
Community, social and personal services	42,893	47.6
Total	90,180	100.0

Source: C.A. Sinclair and J. Socknat, *Assessment of Manpower Development and Policy and Programme Suggestions for the Yemen Arab Republic* (San'a, 1976), Table 1.1, p. 1.3.

Apart from an increasing proportion of Sudanese investment being government in origin, a similar employment policy between 1966 and 1970 served to stimulate government employment artificially. Modern sector employment in Sudan has now reached the stage that some 35 per cent is public sector, and much of this (85 per cent) is concentrated in Khartoum, despite the large area of the country and the dispersed nature of the population.[17] This is, then, an instance of a similarity of labour policy effected by both the capital-rich and the capital-poor Arab states despite the vast differences in economies which prevail but the coincidence of policy stems from contrasting motives.

The tertiary sectors in the urban centres of these capital-poor Arab countries are not only enlarged by government employment. Almost as significant are the burgeoning ranks of the petty traders – informal sector workers — who have emerged with the development of urban conglomerations. In fact the informal sector is growing rapidly in importance as the area where an increasing number of individuals gain a livelihood. Here is a major difference between the capital-rich and the capital-poor countries: whilst there is no informal sector in the capital-rich nations, it is of growing significance in employment terms in the capital-poor countries.

Table 4.10: Employment in Urban Formal and Informal Sectors in Egypt, Sudan and Yemen AR

Country	Year	Urban formal sector		Urban informal sector	
		No. of workers	Proportion of total work force per cent	No. of workers	Proportion of total work force per cent
Egypt[a]	1976	3,900,000	33.3	1,500,000	12.8
Sudan[b]	1973	120,000	2.6	713,000	15.3
Yemen AR[c]	1975	90,180	6.6	196,727	14.5

Sources: (a) Egypt, Ministry of Planning, *Five Year Plan, 1978-82*, vol. II, p. 200 (Arabic); (b) derived from J.S. Birks and C.A. Sinclair, *Country Case Study: International Labour Migration Project. Democratic Republic of the Sudan* (Durham, 1977); (c) calculated from 1975 Census figures and cited in J. Socknat and C.A. Sinclair, *Migration for Employment Abroad and Its Impact on the Development of the Yemen Arab Republic* (US Department of Labor Research Monograph Series, 1978), Table 10.

Table 4.10 illustrates the extent of the informal sector employment in the Yemen AR, Sudan and Egypt. In Yemen AR, informal employment actually amounts to more than double the number of those involved in the formal sector, and outweighs considerably the numbers in government employment. In Sudan the proportion of employment accounted for by the informal sector is smaller, but the numbers, of course, are substantially greater.

In Egypt, the position seems rather different. The informal sector is smaller in proportional terms than in either Sudan or Yemen AR. This is a result of the past nationalisations and heavy government control by which the economy has been shaped in the past. However, one unexpected side effect of the 'open-door' policy, reinforced by the most recent five-year plan, 1978-82, has been that the informal sector is now increasing very rapidly.

In terms of the labour market, one side effect of the rapid urbanisation which has occurred in Egypt, Sudan and Syria, in particular, has
been a growing number of persons seeking work in towns. The inability
of the productive sectors of the economy to generate sufficient employment to meet the supply of labour has resulted in the growth of the
informal sector. This sector is characterised typically by persons deriving
a living from such activities as selling matchboxes, state lottery tickets,
and street stall vendors. Their livelihood yields a subsistence income.
Thus, in these capital-poor countries, a fairly large informal sector is
only to be expected.

The Significance of the Urban Informal Sector

The existence of the urban informal sector in the capital-poor countries
is an important element in a consideration of one of the most important interrelationships between the capital-poor and capital-rich states
of the Middle East: the export of labour from the former to the latter.
It is suggested here that the process of migration of workers from the
capital-poor to the capital-rich nations engenders further development
of the large informal sector in the capital-poor countries, whilst militating against its growth in the capital-rich nations.

Migration abroad for employment is a common experience amongst
populations of capital-poor countries.[18] It is argued that it contributes
to urban growth, and hence, that of the informal sector, for three
reasons. First, it is thought that migrants who have worked abroad tend
to acquire skills that are useful in towns and cities, rather than rural
areas. Consequently they tend to return to urban areas after migrating
rather than returning to their villages. Moreover, they are thought to
acquire attitudes and aspirations that can only be fulfilled in cities.

Secondly, the process of international migration tends to occur in
the Middle East as a series of steps, migrants moving from hamlets to
towns and cities, with the ultimate aim of international migration. A
chain of migration steps is thus established, that ends abroad, though
a residue of unsuccessful migrants is left in the urban centres. Potential
migrants join the queue to travel abroad, and end up successfully or
otherwise in the city, probably depending for their livelihood on the
informal sector. Those who have failed to migrate internationally
remain in the city, depending for their livelihood on a subsistence
existence in the informal sector.

A third factor contributing to the size of the informal sector is
the essential selectivity of international migration. As a result of the

migration of the more skilled, the productive sectors of the economy, which might otherwise have developed, are starved of their most essential labour. Hence, the growth of wealth-creating sectors is slowed. Moreover the reduced expansion of wealth-creating sectors leaves a greater residue of unemployed who eventually fall into the informal sector. Therefore, despite the apparent advantages of international labour migration, the result is an enlarged informal sector at the expense of a productive sector in the capital-poor nations.

Future Evolution of Employment Patterns

It would appear that in both the capital-rich and capital-poor states there has been, associated with urbanisation, not only the development of a larger tertiary sector, but also an apparently odd reversal of the normal pattern of evolution of the economy and labour market.

Although the process of the creation of a service sector has been comparable in both capital-rich and capital-poor economies, the motives behind the stimulation of what is arguably 'false' employment or even underemployment have been widely different. As has been noted, government employment in the capital-rich countries has been seen largely as a means of distribution of wealth accruing to the rulers of the states. In the capital-poor countries, the stimulation of government employment has been a conscious move to mop up unemployment by expansion of its own cadres. In both cases, this process is better described as generation of underemployment, rather than employment.

It is thus possible to conceive of these two types of urban economies, so different in scale of population, resource endowment, national wealth, and macro-economic patterns, evolving on broadly similar lines in terms of urban employment patterns. At least, this is so but for one important aspect of the urban labour market, the informal sector. Informal employment is likely to grow rapidly in the urban economies of the capital-poor countries, whilst remaining virtually absent from the more wealthy Arab states.

International flow of labour from the capital-poor to the capital-rich countries is, in every respect, likely to increase the size and rate of expansion of the informal sector in the capital-poor countries. As a corollary, these processes will militate against the development of informal employment in the capital-rich states.

References

1. I.M. Lapidus (ed.), *Middle Eastern Cities* (University of California Press, Berkeley and Los Angeles, 1969).

2. See, for example, the essays in: International Labour Office, *Manpower and Employment in Arab Countries: Some Critical Issues*, Selected papers and reports of the ILO/ECWA Seminar on Manpower and Employment Planning (Beirut, May 1975).

3. See also, R.E. Mabro, 'Employment, choice of technology. Sectoral priorities', in *Manpower and Employment in Arab Countries: Some Critical Issues* (ILO, Geneva, 1975), pp. 16-31 for a similar classification.

4. A.K. Al Kuwari, 'Oil revenues of the Arabian Gulf emirates: pattern of allocation and impact upon economic development', unpublished PhD thesis (University of Durham, 1975).

5. See, in the case of the United Arab Emirates, for example, K.G. Fenelon, *The United Arab Emirates, An Economic and Social Survey* (Longman, London, 1976).

6. W.J. Donaldson, 'Fisheries of the Arabian Peninsula', *Change and Development in the Middle East: Geographical Essays in Honour of W.B. Fisher* (forthcoming, London); 'Fisheries of the Arabian Peninsula', report of a Tour of Arabian Peninsula Countries, December 1977 (unpublished typescript), Centre for Middle Eastern and Islamic Studies (University of Durham, 1977).

7. A.M. Al Shuaiby, 'The development of the eastern province with special reference to urban settlement and evolution in Eastern Saudi Arabia', unpublished PhD thesis (University of Durham, 1976).

8. G. Fischer and A.M. Muzaffar, *Some Basic Characteristics of the Labour Force in Bahrain, Qatar, United Arab Emirates, and Oman* (Kuwait, 1975), mimeograph.

9. For a discussion of the 'normal evolution' of the labour force in the Third World, see for example, R. Jolly *et al.*, *Third World Employment, Problems and Strategy* (Penguin, Harmondsworth, 1973); and P. Baroch, *Urban Employment in Developing Countries* (International Labour Office, Geneva, 1973).

10. Y.A. Sayigh, *The Economies of the Arab World* (Croom Helm, London, 1978).

11. J.S. Birks and C.A. Sinclair, *Country Case Study: Kuwait*, International Migration Project, Department of Economics (Durham University, 1977).

12. J.S. Birks and C.A. Sinclair, *A Preliminary Assessment of Labour Movement in the Arab Region: Background Perspectives and Prospects*, Migration for Employment Project, World Employment Programme Research (International Labour Office, Geneva, 1977).

13. Middle East Economic Digest, *Special Report on Egypt* (May 1978).

14. C.A. Sinclair and J. Socknat, *Assessment of Manpower Development and Policy and Programme Suggestions for the Yemen Arab Republic* (San'a, 1976).

15. For a summary of this process related to Bahrain see: M.G. Rumaihi, *Bahrain: Social and Political Change since World War I*, Centre for Middle Eastern Studies (University of Durham, Bowker Press, London, 1977).

16. For detail in the case of the Sudan, see International Labour Office, *Growth, Employment and Equity, A Comprehensive Strategy for Sudan* (ILO, Geneva, 1976).

17. Estimates derived from J.S. Birks and C.A. Sinclair, *Country Case Study: The Democratic Republic of the Sudan*, International Migration Project, Department of Economics (Durham University, 1978).

18. M. Todaro, *International Migration in Developing Countries: A Survey*, Ms. for conference on Population and Economic Change in Less Developed Countries (National Bureau of Economic Research, September 1976).

5 SOCIO-ECONOMIC PROBLEMS – THE ROLE OF THE INFORMAL SECTOR

D.W. Drakakis-Smith

Introduction

Rapid urban growth in the Middle East has put the city, as a physical and functional entity, under severe pressures. Resources and opportunities have proved inadequate to cope with the population influx and serious socio-economic problems have emerged. In the eyes of most planners and administrators the essence of the problem is the inability of the city to meet, *in conventional terms*, the need for employment and shelter. The large numbers employed in the tertiary or service sector, and housed in squatter settlements, are frequently cited in support of this argument. Almost inevitably, such problems are associated with migrants who are commonly considered to be marginal urban residents in all senses of the word – physically located on the city periphery, and tenuously linked to its economy and culture. As a consequence migrant communities are viewed with some suspicion by the authorities as politically unpredictable and unstable groups.

Such points of view are essentially Eurocentric in nature, measuring Middle Eastern cities against the 'norms' of the First World. The very size of the problems involved has turned administrators away from direct attention and action, towards broader 'solutions' of increased economic growth based on modern industrialisation programmes in the hope that the associated gains will eventually percolate down to the urban poor. However, overall expansion in gross national product does not necessarily bring benefits for the community as a whole and in many countries economic growth has been accompanied or followed by greater inequalities in income distribution and high levels of unemployment (Table 5.1).

One *caveat* to such observations is that unemployment *per se*, in the sense of persons out of work and actively seeking jobs, is again a Western concept. Stambouli,[1] for example, has noted that the concepts of unemployment and underemployment were, until recently, totally unknown in the Maghreb and that the etymological origin of the French word *chomâge* refers simply to abstaining from work during the heat of the day. Observations such as these make the wholesale application of Western analytical concepts of dubious value and raise the issue of

Table 5.1: Economic Growth and Selected Inequality Indicators

	GNP 1974 (US dollars)	GNP percentage annual growth 1965-74	Gini coefficient	Percentage of GNP held by poorest 40 per cent households (various years)	Percentage urban unemployed
Algeria	730	4.5			26.6
Bahrain	2,350	21.2			
Egypt	280	1.0	0.4129		
Iran	1,250	7.7	0.4728	12.5	5.5
Iraq	1,110	4.8	0.6068	8.5	
Israel	3,460	5.8			
Jordan	430	− 2.5			
Kuwait	10,030	− 2.3			
Lebanon	1,070	3.7	0.5175	9.5	
Libya	4,440	6.5	0.2575		
Morocco	430	2.8			20.5
Oman	1,660	19.2			
PDR Yemen	220	− 4.3			
Qatar	7,240	8.1			
Saudi Arabia	2,830	9.2			
Syria	560	4.2			7.3
Tunisia	650	5.4	0.4859	11.4	
Turkey	750	4.3	0.5443	9.3	
UAE	11,060	10.4			
Yemen AR	180	−			

Sources: S. Jain, 'Size distribution of income', IBRD Staff Working Paper No. 190 (Washington, 1974); *World Bank Atlas* (Washington, 1976); O.F. Grimes, *Housing for Low Income Families* (Johns Hopkins University Press, Baltimore, 1976).

what, for better or worse,[2] has come to be known as the 'informal sector' and its role in urban societies in the Middle East.

In recent years the concept of the informal sector has become an important analytical tool in Third World urban studies generating considerable debate on its content, character and on the implications it raises *vis-à-vis* policy issues. In general, it would be true to say that this discussion has by-passed the Middle East, at least as far as the social sciences is concerned, being based primarily on studies which have taken place in Latin America, Africa or Asia. This is not to say that the principal features of the informal sector have gone unrecognised, but that they have not been examined in any holistic sense. Thus, although the importance of tertiary employment has been noted (Figure 5.1) discussion of future employment strategies often occurs without the informal sector receiving more than a passing mention.[3] In the light of these comments, it is worth reiterating the nature and development of informal sector theory.

Figure 5.1: Distribution of Active Population by Industry in the Major Cities of Jordan and Syria (1960-1)

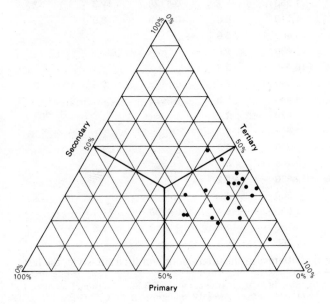

The Characteristics of the Informal Sector

Development of the Informal Sector Concept

There are two distinct lines of interest which have fused into what may be termed the concept of the informal sector. The first is related to the rapid numerical growth of the urban poor in Third World cities. For many years there was very little concern with the plight of these people, except from political commentators such as Fanon[4] who saw a vast revolutionary potential in the apparent misery and degradation. Most development scientists favoured the similar path thesis[5] which suggested that the lag between the growth of population and modern employment would soon close once the mythical take-off point was reached. Within this context, the urban poor were considered to be traditional, representing 'a static homogeneous culture with a consistent body of norms and values which are opposed and antithetical to modernisation'.[6] These prejudices were maintained by data-collection systems which were geared to the modern, industrial sector of the urban economy, so that there was, and still is, very little information with which accurately to assess the nature of the informal sector.

Interest in this large group of urban poor, neither peasant nor proletariat,[7] has grown rapidly over the last decade with the realisation that economic growth has not diminished urban poverty but in many instances has contributed to it because of distributive inequalities. Attention has been drawn to this phenomenon by a wide range of social and political scientists; in the Middle East and North Africa, the work of Amin[8] and Bennoune[9] has been particularly important in this respect.

These trends have been reinforced, at least for Western researchers, by the growing concern with the impersonal, large-scale, corporate nature of the development process; an attitude which has been reflected in a wide range of reactions, from an interest in small-scale technology to an increase in urban squatting in Western Europe.[10] As Abu-Lughod[11] has noted 'increasingly sociologists have come to understand and appreciate the indispensable role played by small systems . . . in mediating between the individual and the large scale society . . .'

Paralleling this interest in the urban poor and their life-style, the last decade has also witnessed a rapid development of conceptual theory on the urbanisation process in the Third World. This initially emerged from historical studies of pre-industrial, colonial and neo-colonial urban patterns.[12] The dichotomous nature of these patterns – the distinction between pre-industrial and modern, or exploiters and exploited – was fused with the more individualistic studies of the urban poor *per se* by Geertz[13] who was the first to emphasise the important difference between firm-centred and bazaar elements in the urban economy. As Jackson[14] has pointed out, Geertz did not construct a bipolar model, emphasising instead the continuum of activities which existed between these two extremes. Nevertheless, later work based on Geertz' initial postulations has ignored this fact and has concentrated on the production of more refined bipolar models in which the attributes of each sector are detailed at great length.[15] A varied nomenclature has arisen to describe these dualistic models but the most simple description of their respective characteristics is that of the International Labour Office[16] given in Table 5.2.

Table 5.2: Characteristics of the Urban Informal and Formal Sectors

Informal	Formal
1. ease of entry	difficult entry
2. reliance on indigenous resources	frequent reliance on overseas resources
3. family ownership	corporate ownership
4. small-scale operation	large-scale operation
5. labour-intensive and adapted technology	capital-intensive and imported technology
6. skills acquired outside formal education system	formally acquired skills — often expatriate
7. unregulated and competitive market	protected markets

Source: ILO, *Employment, Incomes and Equality.*

Over recent years the informal-formal concept has been subject to increasing criticism, largely because it fails to approximate to reality. On the one hand, its characteristic features have been shown to vary markedly from country to country and the mix does not always coincide with the typological models put forward. The hypothesised ease of entry, for example, has proven to be uncharacteristic of much of the informal sector and several studies[17] have indicated that entry into occupations such as hawking or construction labouring is very selective and formalised. Other observers have noted that bipolar conditions seldom exist in reality and that broad transitional continuums are more characteristic of activities such as food distribution and the construction of squatter housing.[18]

Few models are intended to reproduce reality and the informal-formal concept is no exception. It is simply an aid to understanding the real world and as such has stimulated much useful work. On the other hand, it is basically a descriptive model and offers little explanation of the dynamic features of the informal sector, particularly its links with the formal sector, and with the wider urban, national and international settings of which it is part.

Dick[19] has suggested that these criticisms may be overcome by a reorganisation of informal sector characteristics into three sets focusing on technology, market structure and behaviour, and access to resources. He argues that the last of these categories should be widened to incorporate general features of organisation. This theme has been developed by Dick and Rimmer[20] into a useful model which modifies the bipolarisation of earlier constructs by allowing for intermediate forms of organisation.

At present, therefore, informal sector theory is in a healthy state of critical flux, at least with regard to its role in conceptual methodology. In contrast, the main features of the informal sector are now fairly well established, even if their implications have not yet been fully explored. The organisation, scale and redistributive aspects of economic activities have received the most comprehensive coverage since this has formed the kernel of previous work. However, the informal sector overlaps into many other aspects of the development process, from social grouping to political organisation. In the latter context, for example, there has been contentious discussion on the revolutionary potential of the urban poor in the informal sector. Early protagonists[21] argued, often with more emotion than reason, that the inequalities and alienation experienced by the urban poor would lead to frustrations that could only be solved by resorting to violence. This view has been attacked by both Marxist theorists and social scientists[22] who argue that the lumpenproletariat are basically conservative and have no revolutionary class consciousness. This may be true of the present generation but might not apply to the next, despite Oscar Lewis's theories on the persistence of poverty.[23]

The expenditure patterns of the urban poor obviously extend to the physical framework of their life. Elements such as housing and transportation are therefore closely linked to incomes and give rise to a related set of informal sector features designed to satisfy minimum needs at minimum cost. For the urban poor, therefore, accommodation is inextricably linked to other aspects of their daily existence — place and type of work, regularity and size of income. In short, housing provision and acquisition is part of the overall development process of the individual, the group and the city, and should be treated as such. However, in the past this has seldom been the case and most work on housing has been divorced from the mainstream of development studies and dealt with simply as an extension of land-use planning. The corollary is that general conceptual change in relation to the urban poor and the informal sector has failed to penetrate all but a few of the investigations on housing provision. Most studies have, therefore, been characterised by a descriptive rather than analytical approach, and have sought for a panacea to what is regarded as a homogeneous problem. The remainder of this chapter will re-examine the problem of housing the urban poor as part of the general development process in the Middle East.

Housing the Lower-income Groups in the Middle East

The Nature of the Housing Problem

It is customary to commence any discussion of Third World housing with some form of statistical assessment of the overall needs. The calculation of such needs usually involves demographic data on population growth rates and household formation, together with an assessment of current dwelling units in terms of their number, condition, size and facilities. However, international comparison of national statistics is bedevilled by the wide variety of definitions and comparisons used, and most global or regional collations rely on some form of surrogate criteria, such as density or overcrowding indicators, which ostensibly have some common basis of comparison. But here again definitions vary enormously so that a 'room' in Ankara, Cairo or Casablanca will differ both within and between cities.

This criticism is particularly apposite in relation to estimates of slum and squatter housing which tend to be widely used as indicators of overall urban housing conditions. Apart from the basic lack of distinction between two very different types of low-income housing, such data also incorporate and conceal wide-ranging local idiosyncrasies. In Cairo,[24] for example, the estimates of 'slum and squatter' populations do not include the large numbers living in the tombs and mausoleums of the 'city of the dead'. On the other hand, in Ankara[25] the *gecekondu* totals include many dwellings which, whilst originally of squatter origin, have been granted legal or semi-legal status over the years. In most Middle Eastern cities, there have been even fewer serious attempts to assess the real extent of substandard housing but the vague estimates which are produced have, by their eventual incorporation into international collations, been given a legitimacy far beyond their real value.

Within individual countries the assessment of housing needs is a more useful exercise designed to assist in development planning programmes. Unfortunately the urban housing shortage in the Middle East is such that massive deficit figures are produced. Not untypical, in this respect, is Cairo where estimates put the annual housing need in the region of 62,000, in the face of residential construction rates, for both private and public sectors, of less than 14,000.[26] Similarly in Syria, 20,000 additional dwelling units are needed each year to keep pace with population growth and physical deterioration, but only 7,000 are constructed. Shortfalls of such magnitude serve only to discourage rather than encourage government investment.

In an effort to overcome situations such as these, there has been a tendency in recent years to plan on the basis of housing 'demand' rather than housing 'need'. Effective housing demand differs primarily in its relationship to an ability to pay for the commodity offered, and is determined by factors such as household income, expenditure patterns, housing prices and construction rates. Aside from the fact that the calculations require a greater input of unreliable data, housing demand does provide a good basis for differentiating policies aimed at specific income groups. Unfortunately this is seldom the case and in most countries is used simply to direct programmes towards those groups less likely to fall into rental arrears.

As later sections of this chapter will illustrate, bias against the lowest income groups is common to most housing programmes within development planning, either by design or default. Investment in low-cost housing is commonly considered to be a waste of scarce resources bringing in few immediate returns, particularly in comparison with investment in manufacturing. In short, housing investment is seen as a social overhead which is wholly resource-absorbing rather than resource-producing. The limited government investment in housing for the urban poor is almost inevitably spent on prestige projects — high rise, high density apartment blocks based on Western standards, techniques and materials which are intended to be visible evidence of the government's concern with the plight of the poor rather than catering for any of their real needs.

Issues such as these are crucial in attempting to understand the nature of the housing situation in the Middle East, much more so than the collection and statistical analysis of dubious data. What is perceived as a 'problem' by housing administrators, may be considered quite adequate by its inhabitants. The real problems lie in resolving the attitudinal conflicts of what Turner[27] has termed 'the rule makers and the game players', but in order to do this it is necessary to establish the structural setting within which the game is to take place.

Housing Provision for the Urban Poor

A simple model of the major sources of housing provision open to the urban poor has been outlined elsewhere.[28] Basically it comprises two sectors, the conventional and non-conventional, which are distinguished by their relationship with the institutions of production in terms of such factors as credit, materials, labour supply and observation of legislation and regulations. Each sector has two main components: slum and squatter housing in the non-conventional sector, and private and government housing in the conventional. None of these categorisations are intended to be rigid or complete, and overlap frequently occurs. It would be inappropriate to discuss the conceptual background to this framework in this chapter, but it will be useful to describe the principal features of each component together with the role each plays in government policy formation on the one hand, and in actually housing the poor on the other. Each component will be described first in terms of general definitional characteristics, and second in the way that Middle Eastern conditions relate to them.

Squatter Housing. The most appropriate definition of a squatter is juridical, viz. a person who occupies land without the permission of the owner, or who occupies a dwelling in contravention of existing legislation. This approach is more accurate than recent neologisms, such as spontaneous or uncontrolled, because it clearly establishes the relationship of the squatter community to the urban authorities. If basic shelter is illegal, there is little reason for the squatter to abide by other laws and conventions so that most squatter settlements conceal numerous illegal economic activities. No matter how tolerant an urban government may appear to be, by intent or default, this legal situation gives the squatter no security whatsoever, and provides the authorities with complete justification for any punitive or clearance action they choose to take.

It is worth noting at this point that juridical criteria do not always correlate with physical appearance, which is more directly related to the degree of tolerance shown and the age of the settlements. More recently there have been attempts to define squatters by the mode of production involved in construction. Burgess,[29] for example, has identified squatters with an artisanal or self-built approach. However, there is as yet insufficient evidence to confirm this and petty capitalist production may be more prominent than is realised.

There has been no comprehensive survey of squatter settlements in the Middle East and North Africa.[30] Perhaps, as Abu-Lughod has suggested, this is because the circumstances which have given rise to such communities vary so greatly from country to country. In juridical terms, the Islamic pattern of land ownership is certainly very different from elsewhere in the Third World, particularly regarding the extent of religious holdings. Historical factors also play an important role, so that in the directly colonised nations of North Africa the ethnic segregation which characterised most cities forced the continuing stream of migrants to settle outside the ring of European suburbs in the urban periphery.

Squatting began as long ago as the 1920s in some cities, such as Rabat-Salé and Baghdād. In the latter, the proportion living in *sarīfa* settlements reached almost one-third of the total population by the late 1950s. As in most cities, however, the main period of growth has been during the third quarter of the present century.

The immediate origins of Middle Eastern squatters vary markedly, in many cities step migration through the urban hierarchy still predominates but in others there is increasing evidence of direct migration from villages, as well as movements from the crowded central areas of the city.[31] In addition, of course, there have been the war refugees and Palestinian migrants who have added to the squatter populations in Beirūt, Damascus and 'Ammān.[32] Overall, living conditions in squatter settlements are poor although, as the case study of Ankara will indicate, there are notable exceptions. Makeshift and impermanent materials are used to construct small huts which are generally overcrowded and poorly serviced.

It would be incorrect, however, to assume that all squatter settlements are self-built, and that their inhabitants are marginal to the conventional or formal sectors of urban life. Many surveys indicate that large numbers of squatters rent their dwellings from squatter landlords or purchase complete units built by petty entrepreneurs. One survey in 'Ammān,[33] for example, indicated that one-third of the squatters purchased their dwellings and that a substantial proportion of the remainder hired brick-layers to help them construct their homes. The same survey showed that considerable numbers of squatters worked in formal sector activities, such as factory or white-collar occupations. This has been confirmed for Baghdād[34] where in 1957, squatters apparently constituted 57 per cent of the industrial work force of the city.

Slums. These are units of housing which have been rendered substandard (in local terms) by virtue of age, neglect or internal subdivision.

They differ from squatter settlements in that their creation occurs within permanent, legal structures. Subdivision or physical deterioration may both occur with or without the knowledge of the property-owner, as in squatting, but the mode of production is much less likely to be of a petty capitalist nature. In some instances, however, deterioration or subdivision may be a deliberate act by the owner to increase income *vis-à-vis* costs.

Compared to squatter settlements, the slums in most Third World cities are a less visible feature of the urban landscape, so that information is scarce and unreliable. In the Middle East, however, the greater age of the cities has given rise to slum areas which are coincident with the old quarters or *medinas* – the *sūqs*, *bazaars*, *haras* and narrow, twisting lanes which were the heart of the medieval Islamic city. Colonialism saw the designation of the *medinas* as 'native' quarters, often separated by a *cordon sanitaire* from the newer suburbs of the foreign elites.

The overcrowding of the *medinas* soon caused population movement outwards to other parts of the city. The families who found it easiest to relocate were those linked to the alien power structure, such as the Cairene Copts or Maghribian Jews. Their places were taken by newer and poorer arrivals to the city so that by the 1920s what Abu-Lughod[35] has called the 'proletarianisation' of the *medinas* was virtually complete.

The effect on the physical fabric of the old cities was devastating – as the more affluent residents moved away their houses were increasingly subdivided in a process of *taudification*. In the *medina* of Tunis 28,000 households occupy 15,000 houses and the ground population densities are fourfold those of the city as a whole.[36] In some cities, but not all, this residential overcrowding has been exacerbated by the extension of commercial and industrial activity within the *medina* – a natural growth of the informal sector in the search for, and creation of, income-earning opportunities.

The extent to which commercialisation and the consequent physical erosion of the *medina* has taken place has varied enormously throughout the Middle East. In Saudi Arabia and parts of the Maghreb the old walled cities still exist as before, albeit somewhat shabbier. In contrast, the *medinas* of the large cities of Egypt and the Levant have all but disappeared beneath burgeoning central business districts. Over recent years there has developed a growing concern with the fate of the old quarters and therefore the slums which they contain, as tourism has emerged as a major source of income.[37] However, the problems inherent in the improvement and restoration of the old cities, together with the need to keep as much low-cost accommodation as possible, have yet to be resolved.

Private Housing. Conventional private housing is that which is constructed by private individuals or firms through normal institutional channels in compliance with existing legislation and standards. The units are then offered for sale or rent on the open market. It is widely assumed that because of the profit margins demanded by commercial firms, the private sector plays a minor role in housing the urban poor. To a large extent this is true, but under certain conditions low-cost housing does provide 'acceptable' profits and the private sector has responded accordingly.

This has occurred in Cairo as a result of the massive influx of urban refugees from cities in the canal zone. The private sector has responded by producing twice as many low-cost housing units as the government — at lower prices. This situation has not been repeated in all cities affected by refugee migration. In Beirūt, for example, the private sector continued to build in excess for the profitable luxury housing market, so that by 1971 it was estimated that more than 20,000 expensive apartments lay vacant whilst the urban poor suffered chronic shortages.[38]

It is difficult to assess the potential of the private sector for increased production of low-cost units because so little is known about its composition and the factors which induce change. Although most of the residential output of the private sector is produced by large firms — what neo-Marxists would call the dominant capitalist sector — such firms tend to form a relatively small proportion of the total number of producers. Many of the smaller firms are located outside the capital cities in provincial centres; they operate on smaller profit margins, are more labour-intensive, and given the right kind of encouragement and assistance offer considerable potential for the construction of *relatively* low-cost housing.[39] As yet, however, few positive measures can be taken until more information is known.

Government Housing. With few exceptions most governments pay little attention to low-cost housing, preferring instead to invest in industrial projects and hoping to reap relatively quick returns. Housing is considered to be only one of many problems involved in general urban growth and is usually the responsibility of physical planners. Most municipal planning, however, is linked to stereotyped master plans, usually formulated by overseas consultants and related more to Western urban development than to the specific needs of the Middle East.[40] Planning for housing development therefore tends to be in the negative form of controls, restrictions and zoning.

Positive, as opposed to indifferent, housing policies may be loosely classified into three categories — reactionary, alien and indigenous. Reactionary responses are those which aim at eradication of slum and squatter settlements because they disfigure and disrupt the city. This attitude is very common amongst the administrative hierarchy in the Middle East but wholesale demolition and clearance involve political risks so that only on a few occasions have such actions occurred on a large scale. However, small-scale clearances take place frequently as a consequence of various municipal projects such as road improvements or the construction of public buildings. Alternative accommodation or compensation is rarely offered to the affected families who are reabsorbed in the remaining slum or squatter communities.

This undercurrent of reaction towards the urban poor was well illustrated in Morocco during the years of economic depression which followed the withdrawal of the French in 1956. Johnson[41] has described the situation in relation to subsequent development planning as follows:

The policy of deliberate neglect of urban problems that emerges from the development plans for 1965-67 and for 1968-72 was accompanied by an increasingly harsh policy of repression in the cities. Speeches and private statements of high government officials talked increasingly of the need to eliminate the *bidonvilles*. These growing communities were seen not only as a threat to security, but as a blot on the national character and an unmitigated evil. The *bidonvilles* were literally fenced in, and further expansion or alteration of existing shacks was strictly forbidden; in some places the *bidonvilles* were actually demolished, though they invariably sprang up again, on the same site or nearby.

In speeches and radio broadcasts, the unemployed were repeatedly urged or warned to go back where they belonged, to their farms. There were a number of instances where jobless men were actually rounded up and shipped back to the country in trucks. There was talk at one time of requiring work permits and thus forcing 'vagrants' to leave the cities. These activities were never combined into an effective or determined drive actually to eliminate *bidonvilles* from the face of Morocco or to banish the unemployed from the cities.

They do, however, indicate that there were many officials who would have liked to do so. These attitudes and the piecemeal activities that arose from them illustrate very clearly the negative cast of official thought on the problems of the cities.

More progressive policies are those which attempt to accompany clearances with alternative provision of public housing, but city governments in most Middle Eastern countries are hampered by the limited amount of land they hold, and the complicated and costly procedures needed to acquire large tracts for housing schemes. Of the large cities in the region only Baghdād, and to a certain extent Damascus, currently has large areas of land under government control and it is not surprising that some of the major attempts at clearance and relocation have occured there. In 1963 many *sarīfa* dwellers were relocated outside the city at Madinat al-Thawra and their huts were destroyed.[42] Since then the government has carried out other resettlement programmes and most of the *sarīfas* have now disappeared.

Large-scale resettlement is not necessarily the answer to the housing problems of the Middle East, particularly as many of the schemes are alien in nature. The massive, high-rise estates that characterise such projects not only create cultural stress but are also very expensive. Heavy subsidies are required for rents to remain within the reach of the urban poor, and only the oil-rich states such as Kuwait can afford to do this. Elsewhere the newer schemes tend to be very quickly taken over by middle-income families for whom serious housing shortages also exist.

Another fault of relocation is that it tends to break up established and functionally efficient communities in the older sections of the city. The movement of families to peripheral urban areas not only means loss of employment for the individual but the loss of productive enterprises to the city. The new estates are rarely built in conjunction with nearby employment opportunities and the overall result is decreased family income during a period when rental demands increase and become regularised. The *trames sanitaires* of Morocco probably epitomise this feature most clearly, and it is significant that these were largely conceived, if not built, during the French colonial period immediately prior to independence.[43]

However, in most cities the authorities have had neither the inclination nor the finance to engage in large-scale housing programmes. Housing improvement programmes have therefore been oriented around the upgrading of facilities and services where this is possible, although even in this context the improvements have rarely been the result of philanthropic or welfare motivation as much as political gestures. Another form of government assistance has been to encourage the formation of housing co-operatives, particularly by the offer of favourable credit terms for loans. Such co-operatives have proven very popular in several Middle Eastern countries, such as Iraq and Turkey, but in few instances have they brought direct benefits to the urban poor. Indeed, the great majority of housing co-operatives involve government or military personnel for whom cheaper credits are usually available.

In recent years, in the face of continued urban population growth, it has become apparent even to the most conservative governments that slum and squatter settlements cannot be eradicated or replaced. Attitudes towards their inhabitants have also changed[44] and their positive attributes have become more appreciated. Considerable effort and investment have obviously been put into such housing and it has become clear that a cheaper, more practical and more satisfactory way to improve the living standards of the urban poor is to use their own energies in aided self-help schemes.

The aided self-help concept, or indigenous approach, has become very popular during the present decade in the wake of increasing financial aid, specifically tied to this type of project, from the multinational organisations, such as the World Bank.[45] Despite its populist origins, therefore, aided self-help housing has become a highly organised government-sponsored and supervised activity. This is particularly true of site-and-service schemes which are now as rigidly institutionalised as any other type of conventional public housing and are just as firmly controlled by the urban capitalist sector.

It is perhaps fortunate, therefore, that aided self-help projects in their present form have not yet made much headway in the Middle East. Such schemes are not the panacea their protagonists claim, particularly when undertaken for motives of political expediency as seems to be the case in many Third World countries. It is therefore not atypical to find in Morocco that the ambitious clearance and improvement schemes put forward by the research unit of the Department for Urban Planning and Housing are largely the work of expatriate French planners.[46] Seldom are the urban poor themselves asked to participate in the process. It is very significant that in 'Amman, on one of the rare occasions that squatters were asked if they wanted to participate in a self-help programme, the idea was totally rejected by more than three-quarters of the heads of household.[47]

Ankara: A Case Study of Non-conventional Housing

Since 1945 in Turkey there has been extensive population movement from the rural areas in to the large cities. Whilst the bulk of this movement has been to İstanbul, the largest city, the effects have been most marked in the smaller capital city of Ankara where the population increased by over 400 per cent between 1950 and 1970 and now stands at 1.5 million. This rapid growth has brought great pressure to bear on housing supply and the limited resources of the conventional sector have largely been utilised in the construction of high-rise apartment blocks for the middle- and upper-income groups. Little attention has been paid to the needs of the urban poor either by the private or public components of the conventional sector.[48]

Only 3.6 per cent of GNP is invested in housing and of this only 3 per cent is direct government investment in residential construction. The Turkish government prefers to foster house purchase indirectly by supporting credit agencies but the type of housing built and financed through these institutions is too expensive for most families. One scheme involves the Social Insurance Agency which draws funds

Figure 5.2: Distribution of Housing Types in Ankara 1970

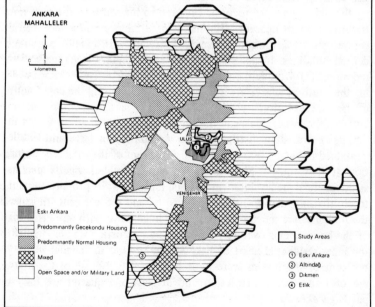

from a wide range of employees but only lends to those who are low risk. In effect, the poor subsidise the middle-income groups.

The response from the urban poor to situations such as these, has been to create their own housing. First, there has been subdivision of the old houses in Eski Ankara, the original pre-republic settlement clustered around the citadel. Second, there has been extensive *gecekondu* squatter settlement both on the inner hills and on the outskirts of the city (Figure 5.2). The slum and squatter settlements differ markedly in their characteristics and these contrasts have important implications for future housing policy.[49]

Eski Ankara

Eski Ankara comprises the original town prior to its selection as the national capital in 1923. Its focal point is the *kale* or citadel, the steep surrounding slopes of which were covered with small, predominantly wooden houses built in village style. With the rapid growth of population in Ankara the dwellings in the old city experienced a process of subdivision or extension but the small areal extent of Eski Ankara prevented the emergence of a large slum district.

Eski Ankara is not the only slum district in Ankara, nor does it consist entirely of dilapidated housing. To the north-west it is bounded by the old commercial focus of Ulus and to the south by the even more traditional Samanpazaar (Haymarket). Both of these commercial centres still flourish and infuse Eski Ankara with extensive non-residential buildings. In addition the western boundary is gradually being redeveloped for modern commercial and administrative buildings whilst in the south extensive areas have been cleared during the construction of Hacettepe University and its associated park, a *cordon sanitaire* between the intellectuals and the slum residents.

The central slum district of Eski Ankara is not large and in 1965 contained about 58,000 people or 6.5 per cent of the total city population at that time.[50] Since then the population has slightly declined as commercial redevelopment has taken place but its proportion of the total urban population has dropped to around 4.5 per cent. In general the buildings are much older than their inhabitants with more than half of the houses being over 45 years old. The proportion is much higher in the inner residential heart of Eski Ankara around the citadel where 76 per cent of the houses were built before 1930. Not all of the houses are of traditional construction and at least one quarter are fully or partly *gecekondu*.

Whilst ground densities are reasonably high at 8,500 per km^2 (Table

Table 5.3: Physical Characteristics of Eski Ankara Housing

Size of living area under 30 m^2	29.1 per cent
Households living in one or two rooms	41.7 per cent
Two or more households per unit	40.9 per cent
Average number of persons per room	1.7
Average number of persons per km^2	8.454
Without own water supply	33.3 per cent
Without own inside WC	70.9 per cent
Without separate kitchen	27.8 per cent
Without separate washroom	53.1 per cent
Owner-occupiers	22.6 per cent
Total sample size	536

Source: Fieldwork, 1974.

5.3), they are in no way comparable to those which occur in Asian or Latin American slums. With 40 per cent of the dwelling units containing two or more families and over one-third of all households living in one or two rooms, Eski Ankara would seem to be overcrowded, but in comparison with either the old or the new *gecekondu* districts Eski Ankara offers a much better living environment since rooms and houses are generally larger whilst families are smaller. Thus only 49 per cent of the slum households have less than 10 m^2 per person compared to 65 per cent and 74 per cent in the new and old *gecekondu* districts respectively.

The great majority of the families who live in Eski Ankara rent their accommodation and the proportion of owner-occupiers has been dropping steadily since migration pressures began to increase during the 1950s. Most of the residents of Eski Ankara initially settled there because of the proximity to work and low rents but rents are currently cheaper in the squatter areas. Whilst the cost of housing in Eski Ankara is not low in absolute terms, its proximity to employment opportunities in both the old and the new commercial districts has made it acceptably low to the residents. Moreover there is a higher proportion of rentable accommodation in Eski Ankara and this is an additional attraction for newcomers to the city. Keleş[51] has shown that considerable movement occurs between houses within the slum district; this indicates the range of accommodation which exists both in size and the cost, enabling households to adjust relatively easily to changes in their social and economic circumstances.

There is a wide range of occupations represented in Eski Ankara (Table 5.4) with white-collar administrative jobs being just as important as the more traditional informal sector employment, such as carpentry or carpetry, usually associated with slums. The single most important source of employment is in commerce, with relatively wealthy merchants and shopkeepers being as numerous as the more informal occupations such as street peddling. Because of the nature of employment in Eski Ankara there is a tendency here for people to live near their work-place and to work for much longer hours than in the formal occupational sectors such as the public service or manufacturing.

Table 5.4: Socio-economic Characteristics of Eski Ankara Residents

Occupational structure	
formal	49.1 per cent
informal	50.9 per cent
Monthly household income	
under 1,000 T. Lira	17.4 per cent
1,000–1,599	44.3 per cent
over 1,600	32.8 per cent
no data	5.5 per cent
mode	1,374 T. Lira
Working more than 10 hours per day	42.6 per cent
Journey to work of 15 minutes or less	37.5 per cent
Resident in Ankara over 10 years	64.2 per cent
Total sample size	536

Source: Fieldwork, 1974.

The range and the diversity of occupations found in Eski Ankara is indicative that slum residence is not confined to the poorest elements in the capital. The incomes commensurate with these jobs are also wide-ranging and in general are much higher than those found in the adjacent *gecekondu* district of Altındağ. It is the proximity to remunerative employment that makes Eski Ankara so attractive for its residents despite the congested environment, of which most of them are very much aware.

This does not mean to say that the residents of Eski Ankara are completely satisfied with their living conditions or that they have not considered moving away from the slums. In fact, their awareness of, and attitudes towards, housing improvements are far more positive than those of the squatters in Ankara. Almost half have considered a residential change and a similar number would like to see an extended government housing programme to help realise their ambitions. However, in addition to being ambitious they are also practical and the great majority feel that the only way to improve their housing situation is to obtain accommodation in the private sector with the help of improved credit facilities.

Such features offer strong support for de Planhol's[52] observation that 'la vieille ville d'Ankara n'est pas une zone de dégradation'. Whilst the evidence does not deny the existence both of social and physical *malaise*, the diversity of socio-economic character in Eski Ankara suggests that there is a dynamic living environment with many positive attributes which should be incorporated into any future redevelopment programme.

Gecekondu Settlements

Squatter housing has always been of considerable importance in housing migrants to Ankara because the small pre-republican town had relatively few dwellings which could be converted into slums. With the development of the new capital there was a considerable movement of middle- and upper-income groups away from the old central areas to new suburbs in the south and west. Migration into the new capital was high from the outset, with refugees flooding into Turkey from the ceded areas of the defunct Ottoman empire. In the post-war period this was replaced by a heavy movement from the rural areas of Anatolia, a process which was greatly accelerated by the premature mechanisation brought about by Marshall Aid tractors.

In spite of the initial intention to plan the development of Ankara, population growth has been so rapid that no real attempts have been made to control the sprawl of construction until the last ten years. Most newcomers were unable to find or afford housing through the semi-official agencies which existed and so built their own housing on any available land, whether it was private or public. These squatter houses are described in Turkish as *gecekondu*, which literally means 'built overnight', and once established they were legally difficult to remove.

The initial *gecekondu* settlements were around the centre of the old town, Eski Ankara, on the steep sided hills which surround the medieval citadel. As squatter momentum grew, so the *gecekondu* settlements spread to the more open, rolling slopes around the city proper. Many of these outer areas had the additional advantage of being beyond municipal jurisdiction so that no planning controls existed in relation to the location or quality of the building. The first real attempt to control the spread of *gecekondu* settlement came in 1966 during the first five-year plan which empowered municipalities throughout Turkey to clear or improve squatter areas, or to prepare special 'prevention sites' in which self-help schemes would be promoted for the benefit of evicted or newly-arrived households. In Ankara, however, the cost of pursuing these objectives and the sheer scale of squatter settlement has resulted in little positive action. Almost 50,000 new *gecekondu* houses have been built since 1966 although the law expressly forbids such construction.

As a result of the uncontrolled settlement pattern, almost two-thirds of Ankara's population is estimated to live in *gecekondu* housing. In collated international statistics this is inaccurately translated into slum or squatter populations but the reality of the situation is very different. None of the *gecekondu* residents live in slums, which are located almost entirely in Eski Ankara and comprise less than 2 per cent of the city's population. Of the remaining *gecekondu* houses few are completely illegal in the sense that they occupy land without permission and fail to meet building regulations. It has been an increasing practice in Ankara to give *de jure* or *de facto* recognition to *gecekondu* areas by granting land rights, imposing taxes or constructing roads. These activities have tended to occur prior to elections, notably during the last ten years when the two major political parties in Turkey became evenly balanced in the national parliament.

Important differences exist in the nature of this recognition particularly between the old central settlements and the newer peripheral ones. The central *gecekondu* districts around the citadel received their rights as a by-product of an enactment of 1953 relating to general land use. As a result of this law the inhabitants became legal occupants of the land on which their houses were situated but were prevented by other laws from improving the properties themselves. The effect has been to freeze most of the central *gecekondu* houses in a state of dilapidation. In contrast, there were few laws which affected peripheral squatters and many had legally bought plots in the area in which they settled. Unfortunately the absence of detailed cadastral maps has meant that precise location and therefore complete legality has been difficult to establish. Nevertheless, most of the newer *gecekondu* units in the peripheral areas have been built as near to legal standards as possible and constitute very different housing units from those in the central areas. A more detailed examination of the contrasts which exist in

Table 5.5: Physical Characteristics of Gecekondu Residents in Ankara

	Inner areas per cent	Outer areas per cent
Size of living area under 30 m^2	50.6	20.8
Households living in 1 or 2 rooms	53.0	17.1
Two or more households per unit	34.3	11.9
Average number of persons per room	1.9	1.8
Average number of persons per km^2	9,516	1,147
Without own water supply	58.8	50.3
Without own inside WC	89.8	70.4
Without separate kitchen	50.2	25.4
Without separate washroom	80.7	50.3
Owner-occupiers	48.9	78.2
Total sample size	571	582

Source: Fieldwork, 1974.

Table 5.6: Socio-economic Characteristics of Gecekondu Residents in Ankara

	Inner areas per cent	Outer areas per cent
Occupational structure		
formal	47.4	62.4
informal	52.5	37.6
Monthly household income		
under 1,000 T. Lira	28.5	18.1
1,000–1,599	37.1	48.1
over 1,600	32.0	30.4
no data	2.4	3.4
mode[a]	1,265	1,310
Working more than 10 hours per day	31.1	17.9
Journey to work of 15 minutes or less	25.1	17.8
Resident in Ankara over 10 years	70.1	51.2
Total sample size	571	582

a. In Turkish Lira. Source: Fieldwork, 1974.

Ankara will emphasise the wide ranging problems that 'squatter' settlements can pose for planners in the Third World (Tables 5.5 and 5.6).

One of the older districts in central Ankara is Altındağ, which somewhat ironically means 'golden hill', a steep-sided area to the north of the citadel which contains over 50,000 people, two-thirds of whom live in wooden *gecekondu* units. The remainder live in equally old, but more legal, wooden houses. Living conditions within the area are very crowded in terms of both ground and housing densities whilst the majority of households lack adequate water supply, toilet, cooking and washing facilities. Although there is a sizeable minority of more recent arrivals, most of the families are long-term residents of Ankara, more than half having lived in Altındağ for over ten years. The low rents in the area and the proximity to job opportunities in the city centre were the main attractions for the residents. This is borne out by the occupational structure which emphasises employment in petty commerce, such as hawking, and in service activities such as *dolmuş* (shared taxi) driving.

Very different conditions are found in Dikmen and Etlik, two of the extensive peripheral squatter areas. Almost 90 per cent of the accommodation in these districts is solidly constructed from stone or brick and is much more spacious, internally and environmentally, than that in Altındağ, despite the fact that families in Dikmen and Etlik are larger. In addition, the great majority of these units are self-contained with regard to washing, toilet and cooking facilities. The deficiencies in the outer districts are mainly infrastructural as a result of both their relative newness and distance from the city proper; a large number of houses therefore have no electricity, sewage or water connections and arrangements for rubbish disposal are poor. Despite these defects areas such as Dikmen and Etlik are obviously popular with new migrants. Almost half of the residents had lived in Ankara for less than ten years, most of these coming directly from villages located outside Ankara province. In contrast, the older migrants of Altındağ were more likely to have come from towns nearer to Ankara. This indicates an important shift in migration patterns over recent years as improved communications have facilitated both the diffusion of news and the movement of people.

Although Dikmen and Etlik are districts of relatively recent settlement, their occupational structures are atypical of 'normal' squatter communities. Almost all of the household heads are in regular, full-time employment in either factories or offices. Many of these jobs involve considerable travel and almost one-third of the workers face

(top) The Traditional Islamic Townscape Shows Aesthetic and
Functional Harmony: San'a, Yemen AR (S. Richmond)

(bottom) Urban Sprawl Reflecting Western Planning Ideas and the
Needs of Modern Transport: Ahmadī, Kuwait in 1968 — the
Headquarters of the Kuwait Oil Company (Kuwait Oil Company Ltd)

Traditional Streets are Picturesque but Today Present Problems of
Access and Provision of Services: Ghardaïa in the Algerian Sahara
(G.H. Blake)

(top) Architectural Contrasts: Grim Concrete Apartment Blocks in Tehrān, Iran (B.D. Clark)

(bottom) City Development Shows Marked Social Contrasts: Planned Middle-class Housing in Tehrān, Iran (B.D. Clark)

Architectural Contrasts: Ornate Multi-storied Mud-brick Houses in San'a, Yemen AR (S. Richmond)

(top) City Development Shows Marked Social Contrasts: Shanty Town in Bandar-e-Shāhpūr, Iran, the Home of the Urban Poor (B.D. Clark)

(bottom) Contrasting Approaches to the Provision of New Public Space: Qom, Iran — Small-scale Design Can Be of a High Quality (B.D. Clark)

(above) Contrasting
Approaches to the Provision
of New Public Space: the
Expansive Central Shopping
Area of the New Town of El
Merj, Libya, Is Drab and
Characterless (R.I. Lawless)

(right) Development and
Change Within Traditional
Urban Quarters: Traditional
Bazaar Truncated by Road
Building in Kermānshāh,
Iran (B.D. Clark)

Development and Change Within Traditional Urban Quarters: One of the Major Roads Driven Through Kermānshāh, Iran (B.D. Clark)

Development and Change Within Traditional Urban Quarters: Bringing Piped Water to San'a, Yemen AR, Without Major Destruction of Buildings (S. Richmond)

commuter journeys of at least two hours each day.

Ankara clearly contains two very different types of *gecekondu* settlement, a feature recognised by the residents themselves. At least one-quarter of the households in Dikmen and Etlik formerly lived in the central areas and had moved out in order to obtain better accommodation. The socio-economic contrasts between the inner and outer *gecekondu* areas are such as to pose many problems for a government attempting to deal positively with such settlements. If the disorderly sprawl of Ankara is to cease, it is evident that the benign indifference which has existed to date in lieu of effective policies must change. On the other hand, the *laissez-faire* attitude has enabled diligent families to create for themselves a reasonably satisfactory living and working environment, although even in these districts the problems of confused tenure and deficient infrastructure remain to challenge government planning programmes.

But it is the older central *gecekondu* communities which pose the most complicated problems since any improvement must involve some property demolition and hence resettlement. Whilst the affected residents of these areas might favour improved credit facilities as a means of obtaining better housing, it is evident that some form of direct government contribution is necessary to help the poorer families. What form this contribution should take is difficult to determine at present because so little information is available on the character of the squatter populations concerned or the capacity of the various sectors of the building industry.

There is little point in discussing some of the more detailed aspects of *gecekondu* improvement in Ankara when the more positive elements of existing legislation have yet to be executed with any great enthusiasm. The current *ad hoc* response by both the government and the squatters has produced a not unsatisfactory situation which both sides seem content to accept. But the urban poor in Ankara, and indeed in Turkey as a whole, have not yet become aware of the political power which they hold in the existing evenly-balanced parliamentary system. The minimal pre-election improvement manoeuvres which are now used to win votes will soon be recognised for their true worth by a new generation of *gecekondu* residents who are beginning to realise how little the city has given their families over the last two decades. The very names of some of the *gecekondu* districts reflect this new determination — Yiğitler (the courageous), Caliskanlar (the hardworking) and Yılmazlar (the undaunted). The present situation thus represents a short breathing space during which new realistic policies must be formulated for the future.

Conclusion

It is apparent, even from this brief overview of low-cost housing in Ankara, that the provision of shelter for the urban poor is a complex problem and cannot be divorced from other aspects of the development process. Each city in the Middle East may differ in the specific details of its housing or employment situation but the conditioning factors are basically the same, relating to the attitudes of the individuals involved and the politico-economic setting in which development is taking place. As yet there is minimal information on the nature of the development process in the Middle East — how it compares with the situation in other parts of the Third World, how it varies within the region itself. Until this information is obtained there will be few effective responses to the difficulties currently being experienced by the cities in the region.

The goal of this chapter is not, therefore, to offer any 'solutions', but to question the isolationism of recent research in the region and encourage a wider appreciation of the origin, nature and dynamics of urban problems. In much of the Third World the current debate is on the merits of praxis rather than process — practice rather than theory. In urban studies in the Middle East we have yet to progress to theory.

References

1. F. Stambouli, quoted in P. Bairoch, *Urban Employment in Developing Countries* (International Labour Office, Geneva, 1973), p. 47.

2. See P.J. Rimmer, D.W. Drakakis-Smith and T.G. McGee (eds.), *Food, Shelter and Transport in Southeast Asia and the Pacific: Challenging Unconventional Wisdom*, Dept of Human Geography, Research School of Pacific Studies (Australian National University, Canberra, 1978).

3. For example, see W. van Rijckeghem (ed.), *Employment Problems and Policies in Developing Countries: the Case of Morocco* (Rotterdam University Press, Rotterdam, 1976).

4. F. Fanon, *The Damned* (Prescence Africaine, Paris, 1963).

5. Perhaps epitomised by W.W. Rostow, *Stages of Economic Growth: A Non-Communist Manifesto* (Cambridge University Press, Cambridge, 1966).

6. T.G. McGee, 'The persistence of the proto-proletariat: occupational structures and planning of the future of Third World cities', *Progress in Geography*, vol. 9 (1976) 1-38.

7. McGee, ibid., has termed them the proto-proletariat.

8. S. Amin, *The Maghreb in the Modern World* (Penguin, Harmondsworth, 1975).

9. M. Bennoune, 'The origin of the Algerian proletariat', *Dialectical Anthropology*, vol. 1 (1975-6) 201-24.

10. E.F. Schumacher, *Small is Beautiful: A Study of Economics as if People Mattered* (Blond and Briggs, London, 1974); S.A.N. Andersen, 'Slums of hope', *Ekistics*, vol. 34, no. 201 (1972) 114-15.

11. J. Abu-Lughod, 'Problems and policy implications of Middle Eastern urbanization', *Studies in Development Problems in Selected Countries of the Middle East, 1972* (UNESOB, Beirut, 1973), pp. 42-62.

12. See the following for summaries of this work: G. Sjoberg, *The Pre-industrial City: Past and Present* (Free Press, Glencoe, 1960); A.D. King, *Colonial Urban Development* (Routledge and Kegan Paul, London, 1976); T.G. McGee, *Southeast Asia City* (Bell, London, 1967).

13. C. Geertz, *Peddlers and Princes: Social Development and Change in Two Indonesian Towns* (University of Chicago Press, Chicago, 1963).

14. J.C. Jackson, 'Trader hierarchies in Third World distribution systems: the case of fresh food supplies in Kuala Lumpur', in P.J. Rimmer *et al., Food, Shelter and Transport*, pp. 33-61.

15. The three most comprehensive descriptions are K. Hart, 'Informal income opportunities and urban employment in Ghana', *Journal of Modern African Studies*, vol. 11 (1973) 61-89; M. Santos, 'Economic development and urbaniza-tion in underdeveloped countries', mimeograph (University of Toronto, 1972); S.V. Sethuraman, 'The urban informal sector: concept, measurement and policy', *International Labour Review*, vol. 114, no. 1 (1976) 69-81.

16. International Labour Office, *Employment, Incomes and Equality: A Strategy for Increasing Productive Employment in Kenya* (ILO, Geneva, 1972).

17. Y.M. Yeung and T.G. McGee, *Hawkers in Southeast Asian Cities: Planning for the Bazaar Economy* (IDRC, Ottawa, 1977); L. Lomnitz, 'Mechanisms of articulation between shantytown dwellers and the urban system', mimeograph, Burg Wortenstein Symposium No. 73, *Shantytowns in Developing Nations* (Wenner-Gren Foundation, New York, 1977); A. Stretton, 'Independent foremen and the construction of formal sector housing in the Greater Manila Area', in P.J. Rimmer *et al., Food, Shelter and Transport*, pp. 155-69.

18. J.C. Jackson, 'Trader hierarchies'; M.A. Johnstone, 'Squatters in Malaysian cities: some preliminary comments', in P.J. Rimmer *et al., Food, Shelter and Transport*, pp. 11-134.

19. H.W. Dick, 'Indonesian prahus and Chinese junks: some issues of definition and policy in informal sector studies', in P.J. Rimmer *et al.*, ibid.

20. H.W. Dick and P.J. Rimmer, 'An integrated alternative to economic dualism', unpublished manuscript, n.d.

21. F. Fanon, *The Damned*; P. Worsley, *The Third World* (Weidenfeld and Nicolson, London, 1964); P.W. Gutkind, 'The socio-political and economic foundations of social problems in African urban areas', *Civilisations*, vol. 22 (1972) 18-33.

22. M. Weiner, 'Urbanization and political protest', *Civilisations*, vol. 17 (1967) 44-50; J. Nelson, *Migrants, Urban Poverty and Instability in Developing Countries*, Occasional Paper No. 22, Centre for International Affairs (Harvard University, 1969); R. Cohen and D. Michael, 'The revolutionary potential of the African lumpenproletariat: a sceptical view', *Institute of Development Studies Bulletin* (University of Sussex), vol. 5, no. 2 to 3 (October 1973) 31-42.

23. O. Lewis, 'Culture of poverty', *Scientific American*, vol. 215, no. 4 (1966) 19-25.

24. J. Waterbury, *Cairo: Third World Metropolis* (Part 3: Housing and Shelter), American Universities Fieldstaff Reports, vol. 18, no. 8 (1973).

25. D.W. Drakakis-Smith and W.B. Fisher, *Housing Problems in Ankara*, Occasional Publications (New Series) no. 7, Department of Geography (University of Durham, 1975).

26. Waterbury, *Cairo*, p. 9.

27. J.F.C. Turner, 'Housing priorities, settlement patterns and urban develop-ment in modernising countries', *Journal of the American Institute of Planners*,

vol. 34 (1968) 354-63; also 'Housing issues and the standards problem', *Ekistics*, vol. 32, no. 196 (1972) 152-8.

28. For some other discussions of the model see D.W. Drakakis-Smith, 'Perspectives on urban housing problems in developing countries', mimeograph, Department of Human Geography, Research School of Pacific Studies (Australian National University, Canberra, 1975); D.W. Drakakis-Smith, 'Shelter: Overview', in P.J. Rimmer *et al., Food, Shelter and Transport*, pp. 101-10; and D.W. Drakakis-Smith, *Housing Provision and the Development Process* (Bell, London, forthcoming).

29. R. Burgess, 'Informal sector housing: a critique of the Turner school', mimeograph, Institute of British Geographers Conference on *The Urban Informal Sector in the Third World* (SOAS, London University, 1977).

30. The best collation is contained in the UNDESA Report entitled *Improvement of Slums and Uncontrolled Settlements*, E.71.IV.6 (New York, 1971).

31. D.W. Drakakis-Smith and W.B. Fisher, *Housing Problems in Ankara*.

32. UNESOB, 'Population distribution and urbanization in selected countries of the Middle East', *Studies on Selected Development Problems in Various Countries in the Middle East, 1971*, E.71.II.C.2 (New York, 1971), pp. 59-78.

33. UNESOB, 'Uncontrolled urban settlements: a case study of Amman, Jordan', *Studies on Development Problems in Selected Countries in the Middle East, 1973*, E.73.II.C.2 (New York, 1974), pp. 60-88.

34. J. Gulick, 'Baghdad: portrait of a city in physical and cultural change', *Journal of the American Institute of Planners*, vol. 33, no. 5 (1967) 246-55.

35. J. Abu-Lughod, 'The multi-form cities of North Africa: reading the urban form for social form', mimeograph, Department of Sociology, Northwestern University, n.d.

36. W. Ben Mahmoud and S. Santilli, 'What to do with Medina?', *Ekistics*, vol. 35, no. 227 (1974) 259-63.

37. For some discussion of tourism and redevelopment of *Medinas* see ibid.; and G.H. Blake and R.I. Lawless, 'Tlemcen – continuity or change', *Architectural Association Quarterly*, vol. 6, no. 1 (1974) 38-46.

38. UNDESA, *Improvement of Slums*, p. 81.

39. For some discussion see D.W. Drakakis-Smith, 'The role of the private sector in housing the urban poor', in R.D. Hill and J.M. Bray (eds.), *Geography and Environment in Southeast Asia* (Hong Kong University Press, Hong Kong, 1977).

40. M. Mozayeni, 'City planning in Iran: evolution and problems', *Ekistics*, vol. 227 (1974) 264-7.

41. K.M. Johnson, *Urbanization in Morocco*, International Urban Survey (Ford Foundation, New York, n.d.) 66-7.

42. J. Gulick, 'Baghdad'; UNDESA, *Improvement of Slums*.

43. K.M. Johnson, *Urbanization in Morocco*.

44. This is usually attributed to the work of John Turner and William Mangin in Latin America but general theoretical discussion on the nature of the informal sector has played an equally important role.

45. World Bank, *Housing*, Sector Working Paper (New York, 1975).

46. K.M. Johnson, *Urbanization in Morocco*.

47. UNESOB, 'Uncontrolled urban settlements', p. 82.

48. For some discussion of urbanisation in Turkey see R. Keleş, *Urbanization in Turkey* (Ford Foundation, New York, 1974); K.H. Karpat, *The Gecekondu: Rural Migration and Urbanization in Turkey* (Cambridge University Press, Cambridge, 1976).

49. The following sections on slums and squatters in Ankara are based on

fieldwork undertaken during 1974. A more compehensive report can be found in
D.W. Drakakis-Smith and W.B. Fisher, *Housing Problems in Ankara*.

50. R. Keleş, *Eski Ankara'da bir Sehir Tipolojisi* (Ankara Üniversitesi,
Siyasal Bilgiler Fakültesi Yayınları 314, Ankara, 1971).

51. R. Keleş, ibid.

52. X. de Planhol, 'Ankara: aspects de la croissance d'une métropole', *Révue
Géographie de l'Est*, vols. 1-2 (1973) 155-88.

6 'QUARTERS' AND ETHNICITY

T.H. Greenshields

Introduction

The purpose of this chapter is to investigate the processes involved in the formation and development of ethnic clusters in Middle Eastern cities. It is written in response to the absence of any introductory text on the subject, despite the fact that ethnic 'quarters' have long been recognised as characteristic features of Middle Eastern cities. Generalisations on ethnic 'quarters' are limited to those contained in more general studies of Middle Eastern cities and society. Nevertheless these generalisations do provide a basis for discussion. Accordingly the chapter begins with a brief review of these statements before passing on to a fresh and extensive re-examination of the processes involved, based on an investigation of available case studies. Finally, the chapter considers the relevance of ethnic clusters in the present day in the light of both the conclusions reached regarding the processes of cluster formation and development, and of comments in the general literature suggesting a tendency towards their eventual disappearance.

First, however, it is necessary to define terms. 'Ethnic' groups are here considered as population groups maintaining a particular identity based on racial, religious, linguistic or cultural status, on tribe, subtribe or family, or on region, town or village of origin. 'Ethnicity' is therefore used as a broad concept, embracing differences in identity based on several different criteria, although in many cases more than one of these criteria contribute to the sense of ethnic identity. This definition may be broader than that accepted by other writers, but its statement at the outset should avoid misinterpretation. The term 'quarter' may give rise to rather more confusion. This term has been used rather loosely by academics and others as though a quarter is a readily identifiable unit, representative of a certain pattern of social organisation, and possessing a certain structure and set of distinguishing characteristics which it shares with other quarters. In practice, not only has the term been applied to different social situations and to units of different scales, but also, even where quarters have been identified, there is often doubt about their limits, or even about the number of quarters in a given situation.[1] Given such imprecision in the meaning of the term and in the identification of quarters, it would appear necessary, in

120

discussing the spatial distribution of ethnic groups within cities, either to apply a strict socially-based definition of the term 'quarter', which would be restrictive, or to abandon the social implications of the term altogether, and focus instead on the purely spatial aspects of population grouping. It is the latter approach which is adopted in this study. In considering ethnic 'quarters', this paper is concerned with spatial clusters of members of particular ethnic groups within a city greater than 'those expected from a random distribution of all people within the city. No *a priori* assumptions are made about the nature of the social links between the individuals in the clusters, about the barriers of separation (social or physical) between the members of the clusters and the surrounding population, about the degree of segregation of members of the clusters, or about the distinctness of the cluster limits. Ethnic 'quarters' are understood simply as spatial clusters of members of ethnic groups. It follows that in discussing such clusters this chapter will exceed the limits of quarter studies based on social criteria. It is hoped that the excursion will prove refreshing.

In the general literature, the existence of ethnic 'quarters' in Middle Eastern cities has been viewed as a characteristic feature of 'Islamic' urban organisation.[2] This view has been attacked by Hourani,[3] who argues that a city cannot be merely a physical representation of a system of social ethics or social institutions. He prefers to draw attention to immigration as a generative force behind quarter formation. This relationship, between immigration and quarter formation, has been recognised by Le Tourneau and Lapidus, who also both recognise the diversity of processes involved in quarter formation, without examining them in detail.[4] Both Lapidus and Aubin, however, draw attention to the need for such a detailed investigation,[5] and it is the recognition of this need which forms the starting point for this chapter. The study in fact consists of a re-examination of the processes of ethnic cluster formation and development based on a comparative investigation of the large number of case studies now available on particular cities, particular ethnic groups, and more rarely, particular quarters.[6] If reference is made most frequently to the evolution of Jewish quarters, this merely reflects the bias of the available documentation. The framework for the discussion is provided by the realisation that ethnic clusters within cities must originate and grow through population redistribution, that is either through migration to a town or redistribution within it. Explanation of cluster formation must therefore lie in the relationship between these population movements and the socio-economic environment in which they take place. Further, such population movements may be made either at one time, *en masse*, or by individual persons or families over a period of time. Not surprisingly, the mass movements, often dramatic in nature, and sometimes the result of official decree, leave most evidence in the written record. Individual movements are less easy to identify, at least in the past. The following paragraphs consider in turn the evidence available concerning the processes involved in cluster formation through mass and individual population movements.

Processes of Cluster Formation

The successive immigration *en masse* of homogeneous migrant groups has been an important generator of ethnic 'quarters'.[7] A variety of groups has been involved. Thus ethnic 'quarters' have been created for military units (for example, in Marinid Fès Jdid, for the Christian militia and Syrian archers,[8] and in Rabat for the Abid and Oudaïa tribesmen),[9] for members of the ruling class (for example at San'ā' for the Ottomans),[10] for transferred populations (for example, the settlement of Nor Jolfā at Esfahān for Armenians transferred from Jolfā by Shah Abbās I),[11] and for refugees. Examples of refugee 'quarters' include the settlement of Moriscos within and next to the casbah of Rabat in the early seventeenth century,[12] and the creation of quarters by the Ottoman government in the nineteenth century for Circassian refugees (Mohâjrîn Osmaniyé at Antakya) and for Muslim refugees from Crete (el-Mohâjrîn at Damascus).[13] New, and still surviving 'quarters' were constructed at Aleppo (Meidan) and Beirūt (Bourj-Hammoud) for the Armenian refugees who moved into Syria and Lebanon after 1920.[14] Mansur has described in some detail the creation and survival of a quarter for Cretan refugees at Bodrum, a town on the Aegean.[15] The first group of Cretans to settle there arrived in 1912, after a temporary stay at Kos. They settled all over the town, wherever they were able to rent accommodation. In 1923, however, more Cretan Turks arrived, under the exchange of population provision of the Treaty of Lausanne, while under the same exchange, Bodrum's Greek quarter (Kumbahçe) was emptied of its inhabitants. The government then installed the new arrivals in the houses which had belonged to the Greeks. Cretans who had earlier been living in the other quarters of the town then moved to Kumbahçe to be nearer relatives and friends, and to this day Bodrum still contains two separate communities, calling themselves 'Cretan' and 'local'. For even more recent examples one need look no further than the refugee camps established for the Palestinians outside 'Amman and Beirūt.[16]

Mass regrouping into separate quarters within cities of ethnic groups, previously sometimes living intermixed with the rest of the population, is exemplified by the creation of the Jewish *mellahs*. These quarters (known as *mellah* in Morocco, *hara* in Tunisia, and simply *Jewish quarter* in Algeria) were, however, characteristic only of certain towns in North Africa and Yemen AR and appeared only in the fifteenth century. While segregation certainly operated in North Africa to some extent before that date, it was not imposed by the authorities.[17] The first *mellah* was created in Fès in the early fifteenth century.[18] Prior to that time the Jews of Fès lived in the old city. It is impossible to assert that they inhabited a special quarter there, though this seems probable. Following incidents which the chroniclers do not record clearly, in the early fifteenth century the Marinid ruler ordered the Jews to settle in Fès Jdid, next to his palace, in the quarter of Homs, which had previously contained the Syrian archers of the royal army. The motive was apparently to eliminate tension between Muslims and Jews. The name of Homs was gradually replaced in popular usage by that of Mellah, after the site of the quarter, and this name was subsequently applied to other Jewish quarters constructed in Morocco in similar fashion.[19] Several writers have pointed out the principal characteristics of these *mellahs*; that they were created to give protection to the Jews and were therefore most often situated near to the citadel.[20] In a number of instances both of these features were true. However, apart from protection there were other (possibly related) issues involved.[21] At Salé and Demnate, for example, there was a desire to segregate the Jewish population in order to avoid the ritual uncleanliness to mosques resulting from their location in clusters of Jewish inhabitants. At Marrakech and Constantine, the Jews were transferred to new quarters in order to clear land for building projects. At Tlemcen the quarter seems to have been due to Jewish initiative, while the Jews were certainly able to influence the extent or location of their *mellahs* at Marrakech and Rabat. Population growth may have been a significant causative factor. Moreover, location of the new quarter was not invariably next to the citadel; at Mogador, for example, it was at the opposite side of the town. In this respect one should note the physical structure of the towns at the time of the creation of their *mellahs*. Since the *mellahs* were all established after the initial creation of the towns in which they were located, sometimes quite late in the history of these towns, it is obvious that the choice of their location was heavily constrained by the limited availability of vacant land within the towns. In this respect, the establishment of the Jewish quarters of

Tlemcen and Oran on marshy land seems particularly instructive, for was this not the land of least quality, until then neglected for building purposes?

The formation of ethnic clusters through movements made on an individual or family basis is naturally much less well documented than the formation of clusters by more dramatic and often officially inspired mass movements. Recent work has in fact shown that where there was no mass migration or regrouping by official decree there was often intermixing of the various ethnic groups and imprecise limits to ethnic clusters.[22] Since such clusters did and do exist, however, how are they formed? In answering this question, writers have unfortunately tended to ignore population movements, preferring instead an explanation in terms of a system of social relations. Sauvaget, for example, attributes the quarter-structure of Damascus and Aleppo in large part to insecurity in medieval times.[23] It is obvious that the Jewish *mellahs* and other quarters like the strongly protected Jewish quarter at Kirman owed much to the desire for security.[24] But, as Elisséeff has pointed out,[25] without a consideration of population movements and the decisions lying behind them, insecurity is simply inadequate as an explanation of quarter structure. At Damascus, for example, it is evident from Thoumin's description of the Christian quarter of Bâb Muşallâ that the enclosure of the quarter by walls postdated the concentration of its population.[26] It is impossible to infer process from structure. Fortunately a few studies do throw some light on the processes involved, and these are summarised in the following paragraphs.

To begin with, a few writers have recognised the creation of ethnic clusters in the past by the individual immigration of members of particular ethnic groups.[27] Le Tourneau considers that such clusters were characteristic of migrant groups not completely assimilated into the city.[28] Marty has considered them in most detail, though she does not devote much attention to the processes of settlement.[29] She notes that at Tunis migrants tended to cluster in the suburbs bordering the road which led from their region. Some were rapidly absorbed into the city, others remained concentrated by ethnic group. Even when ethnic cohesion was strong, however, members of some groups were not clustered, but dispersed through the city as their occupation demanded. Families tended to rent a room in a house, but bachelors would live together in hostels which might or might not be ethnically exclusive. Marty's work is valuable because it suggests a link between past processes of ethnic cluster formation and current processes of rural-urban migration.

Mansur has illustrated another mechanism behind ethnic clustering in considering the relationship between kinship and residence at Bodrum.[30] Here the custom is that when a son marries, a house is built for him, even if it is only a one-room structure called a 'dam' (a roof). The *dam* is often built on the land surrounding the main house, for families like to be near each other, and it is very usual to find a street in which many families have the same surname. However, in recent years, people from other parts of the country have begun to acquire land along the seafront at ever rising prices. This prevents the local inhabitants who live near the sea from buying land for their children, who have to move further away. Thus there are signs of disintegration in the system. At Salé, by contrast, in the nineteenth century there was no such rigid system.[31] Relatives or friends might wish to live nearby one another, but they rarely managed to do so. These examples demonstrate considerable variation in the practices of kinship groups with respect to the setting up of new homes. Thus, while Delaval interprets the physical structure of the Algerian Saharan town simply as an image of its social organisation into a hierarchy of kinship groups,[32] it is obvious that his conclusions are locationally highly specific.

In other cases, differences in customs or mutual distrust were responsible for some voluntary segregation and clustering.[33] Goitein, for example, shows from his study of the Cairo Geniza, how cultural differences could upset the relatively widespread intermixing between the Jews and other elements of the population which prevailed in Old Cairo in the twelfth century AD.[34] In houses in which the various apartments were not entirely separated from one another it was difficult for Jews to live together with Muslims, as they did not accept the Muslim custom of secluding the female members of the family in a separate section. The inconvenience to Jewish women, together with apprehension of Muslim overbearing and the possible desecration of the Sabbath, led the Jewish authorities to promulgate a statute forbidding the sale or rent of parts of houses to Muslims. Private persons too tried to protect their womenfolk from such inconvenience. When a notable had given a house as a gift to two brothers on condition that a certain women should be permitted to live there, he stipulated a fine of 50 dinars on the recipients if they sold the house to a Muslim during her lifetime. Similarly, a woman who had donated part of a house to the poor and a small house adjacent to it to her housekeeper, stipulated that the small house should never be sold to Muslims, as this would be a nuisance for the poor. Nevertheless, the economic need to sell or let houses to Gentiles might overcome such restrictions and maintain intermixing. Thus while in one provincial town, probably El-Maḥalla, it was forbidden under penalty of excommunication to sell houses situated in the Jewish quarter to a Muslim, the prohibition was not observed. Furthermore, the charitable foundations belonging to the Jewish community found themselves forced from time to time to let rooms and apartments to Muslims and Christians.

Related to the question of cultural differences is the observed tendency of religious groups to cluster around holy sites.[35] This is very much a 'chicken and egg' problem, however, and furthermore, once such a hypothetical node has been created, it is not clear whether migrants move to it in order to be near the site, or in order to be amongst their compatriots − or at least, which is the dominant consideration. Ben-Arieh regards the tendency to cluster around holy sites as the main principle of the spatial organisation of Jerusalem's population before the nineteenth century.[36] Thus the Muslims tended to cluster around the Temple Mount area, the Christians around the Church of the Holy Sepulchre, while the Jews, forbidden residence next to the Wailing Wall, settled in relative proximity, near to existing secondary sites. Hopkins, however, while acknowledging the significance of the holy sites, gives more consideration to other influences.[37] He observes that the Christians had not always been concentrated in the Holy Sepulchre area, for in the eleventh century AD the Muslim rulers cleared out the Christians from the present Muslim quarter in order to secure for Muslims access to the Temple Mount. Thus the location of the Christians in the Holy Sepulchre area was not entirely voluntary. Nor was it necessarily because of the proximity of holy sites, for apart from the Holy Sepulchre there were few Christian holy sites within the quarter. Hopkins cites as additional contributory factors, security, and the comparative wealth of the Christian groups and their merchant interests which attracted them to the higher and hence healthier western ridge of the town and to the main gates of entry to the west. The Jews meanwhile would derive their location partly from relative proximity to the Wailing Wall, and partly from their weak position which left them the least desirable land in the city, that is the relatively low land inside the Dung Gate which received much of the drainage and effluent from above. These differences of interpretation emphasise the dangers of assuming process from observed structure without any detailed consideration of the decision-making process.

An additional point which emerges from the work of Hopkins on Jerusalem is the possible significance of socio-economic status in influencing the distribution of ethnic groups. In Cairo, Abu-Lughod explains the localisation of the Coptic population in the late eighteenth century, in port and former port areas, in terms of their preferred occupations as scribes, account-keepers and customs officials.[38] That occupation rather than ethnicity itself may at least sometimes have been the determining factor behind ethnic clustering is suggested also by the settlement patterns of the immigrant groups already discussed. Where the occupations of the immigrants were not strictly localised this could be accompanied by spatial fragmentation of an immigrant group despite its ethnic cohesion. This was also true in the past of the black slaves in North African towns who were naturally scattered all round the towns, although at Algiers in the early nineteenth century, the freed slaves and their descendants were lodged in seven houses according to origin.[39] Unfortunately, little or no work has been done examining in detail the relationship between socio-economic status and ethnic clustering in the Middle East, and we are ignorant of the processes involved.

Evolution of Ethnic Clusters

However established, ethnic clusters, far from being static features, as might be expected if they were merely the physical expression of a social system, could expand or contract, or shift their location within the city, at least when they were not rigidly delimited. This important aspect of quarter development emerges quite clearly even from some of the pioneer studies of Middle Eastern urban geography. In Antakya, for example, the population in about 1930 was divided into three groups, Turkish, Alawi and Christian, distributed between 45 'quarters'. But between the different ethnic sectors of the town there had been infiltration into neighbouring quarters, such that quarters originally united had been split into two or three. This process of fragmentation was recorded by the existence of twin quarters. Thus there existed side by side Qastal Islam and Qastal Khristiân, Moqbel Islam and Moqbel Khristiân, etc.[40] At Aleppo, the Jewish quarter migrated westward towards the periphery of the town in the face of Muslim expansion.[41] In Damascus, there was a redistribution within the city of Christians from the quarter of Bâb Musallâ from the nineteenth century onwards.[42] At Tunis, the Jewish population was already expanding outside the limits of its 'hara' by the seventeenth century[43] (Figure 6.1). Finally at Jerusalem, within the Old City there was in the nineteenth century an invasion of Muslim and mixed-population areas by expansion from the Jewish and Christian quarters[44] (Figure 6.2). There

Figure 6.1: The 'Hara' of Tunis: Quarter Expansion and Intermixing of Population (after Sebag, 1959)

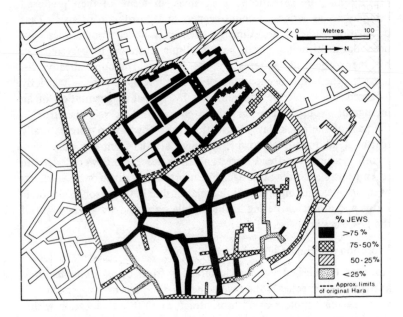

is unfortunately not the space here to reproduce these examples in detail. Collectively they demonstrate the 'dynamism' of ethnic clusters, and their explanations reveal the importance of both demographic forces, and social and economic power in explaining this dynamism. These forces have not always been responsible for such movements, however. Some have been prompted by natural disasters. Outbreaks of plague, for example, at İstanbul, caused some flight of Jewish population from the affected areas to safer zones in 1618 and 1812, while the city would appear to have been particularly susceptible to fire. There are many examples of the movement of Jews from quarters destroyed by fire to new areas of clustering, and in the seventeenth century these movements caused significant changes in the internal structure of the Jewish community.[45]

Hopkins has developed a model of quarter structure and expansion based on his study of the Jewish quarter of Jerusalem.[46] He regards the Jewish quarter as a whole as the sum of interlinked sub-quarters, each consisting of a node, containing a religious building,

Figure 6.2: Quarter Expansion in the Old City of Jerusalem in the Nineteenth Century (after Ben-Arieh, 1975)

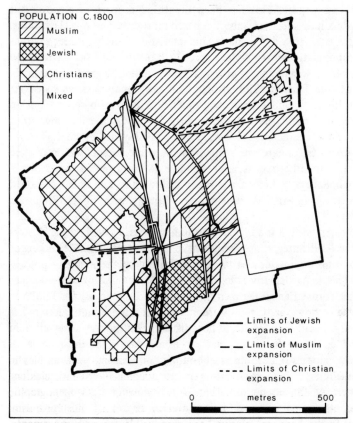

public building or bazaar, serving its surrounding houses. He observes how streets and houses were gradually taken over by Jewish settlers and a synagogue established when a local quorum was reached. Thus a new node was created, and in this way the quarter expanded by the creation of interlinked nodal points. The most interesting idea to emerge from his model is that of the importance of threshold values in determining the establishment of new nodes. Otherwise the model tells us little of the reasons for choosing new locations, or of the generative force behind the expansion. In this respect, the findings of Mansur concerning the relationship between kinship and residence may have some application.

Ethnic Clustering in Contemporary Middle Eastern Cities

A tendency to the disintegration of ethnic clusters has been suggested by several writers. This has been identified as part of a movement towards a new social organisation based on socio-economic class status, and has been regarded as more characteristic of the wealthier sections of the population than of the poorer.[47] Prothro and Diab have indeed identified a weakening of the link between kinship and residence in four Middle Eastern cities, strongest in the upper class, and weakest in the lower.[48] Gulick too found only weak clusters based on kinship or sect in Tripoli, Lebanon, although distinctive clusters did occur where these characteristics were accompanied either by homogeneous class interests, or interests related to the same area of origin outside Tripoli.[49] In other towns, however, like Bodrum or the towns of the Algerian Sahara, ethnic clustering remains vital, and there is indeed evidence to suggest that contemporary disintegration of ethnic clusters may be illusory.

To begin with, it is apparent that in many cases where ethnic clusters seem to be disintegrating, this is not so much due to the intermixing of pre-existing populations as to the emigration of the minority population. This is particularly true of the Jews,[50] but also of other peoples like the Zoroastrians of Kirman, who are deserting the city for Tehrān.[51] Elsewhere, however, the outward movement from ethnic quarters has certainly been directed to other districts within the same city, in general either to 'modern' quarters, established since the nineteenth century,[52] or into districts neighbouring the existing quarters.[53] The movement into 'modern' quarters has generally involved the wealthier members of the community. Far from involving a disappearance of ethnic clustering, however, a considerable degree of clustering may survive in the 'modern' quarters. Thus in Cairo, the Copts have shown a marked preference for the northern suburb of Shubra, an area just north of the old Coptic quarter.[54] In Baghdād, there was differential movement between the Sunnis, who tended to move northwards out of Rusafah into the district of Waziriyah, and on the other hand, the Christians and Jews (now reduced) who moved southwards into Battawiyin, Sadun and Alwiyah.[55] At Jerusalem, when from the nineteenth century the population expanded outside the walls, the religious communities tended to settle in separate homogeneous groups.[56]

The expansion from existing quarters into neighbouring districts is sometimes difficult to distinguish from the movement to 'modern' quarters, as in the movement of Cairo's Copts northwards into Shubra. Such expansion has already been identified in discussing quarter dynamics, and it seems that the principal generative mechanism is, in the present as it was in the past, demographic.[57] However, since for demographic forces to receive expression in quarter expansion, a sufficiently permissive social milieu is required, the recent expansion from the overcrowded Jewish *mellahs* in particular has been regarded as a new phenomenon, a response to the establishment of such a milieu in the nineteenth and twentieth centuries.[58] Where enclosure had formerly been rigorously enforced, this interpretation is undoubtedly valid. But in Tunis, as has been seen, this was not the case and the beginnings of expansion from the *hara* predated the nineteenth century. In other words, expansion from the *mellahs* in the nineteenth and twentieth centuries is not a process unique to modern times, but merely a contemporary example of a process which has been observed at earlier dates, and not uniquely amongst Jewish populations. Furthermore while such expansion may involve a considerable degree of intermixing with the neighbouring population, the expanding population nevertheless remains both clustered and localised. At Marrakech, for example, the direction of expansion from the *mellah* was channelled by both buying power and business considerations.[59] At Casablanca, the expansion of the *mellah* differs from that at Marrakech in that it is related not to outward movement of population (for the wealthier Jews have moved elsewhere) but to massive Jewish immigration which, originally directed to the *mellah*, has subsequently embraced the whole medina where Jews and Muslims live intermixed.[60] Such intermixing should not disguise the clustering of Jewish immigrants by preference in the medina, rather than in the bidonvilles populated by Muslim immigrants.

The partial or complete departure of an ethnic group from its original quarter, by the processes described above, leaves a vacuum which in many cities is filled by the invasion of new population elements, often of a different group, and results in an intermixing of populations similar to that which may be engendered by quarter-expansion.[61] Thus the Zoroastrian quarter of Kirman has been invaded by Muslims[62] (Figure 6.3). At Salé, Muslim and Jewish families live in the same houses in the old *mellah*.[63] In Beirūt, the departure of the Jews has been followed by a movement of Kurds into the former Jewish quarter, an interesting example of replacement of one minority group by another.[64] Such contemporary processes of invasion and succession, like the related process of quarter expansion, are only modern examples of long-established processes. The intermixing resulting should not obscure the fact that in the context of the city as a whole, the surviving remnants

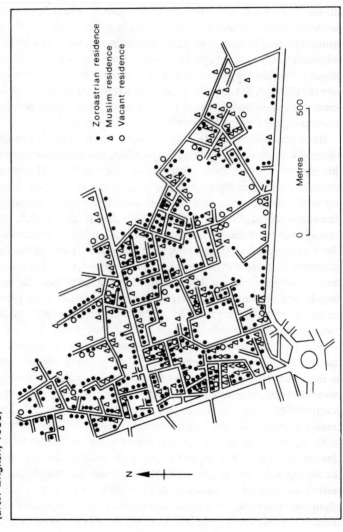

Figure 6.3: Invasion of a Quarter in Process of Desertion: The Zoroastrian Quarter of Kirman (after English, 1966)

- Zoroastrian residence
▲ Muslim residence
○ Vacant residence

0   500
Metres

of the departing group continue to be clustered.

Thus far the discussion of ethnic clustering in the present day has focused not on the formulation of new urban ethnic groupings, but on the fortunes of existing groups. It remains to consider whether or not new urban ethnic clusters are currently being formed. In fact, one example, the formation of refugee quarters in the present day, has already been described in discussing quarter formation. Another is provided by the delimitation of separate living areas in Kuwait for citizens and non-Kuwaiti migrants, a modern example of the official delimitation of ethnic quarters.[65] However, the most important feature of population movement in the Middle East today is undoubtedly the process of rural-urban migration which has reached unprecedented levels. It is therefore essential to consider to what extent this process is accompanied by the creation of urban ethnic clusters.

Rural-urban migration has already been identified as a generator of ethnic clusters in the past. Despite the change in intensity of migration this century, many studies of contemporary migrant settlement have identified a greater or lesser degree of ethnic clustering amongst the migrants, especially, but not exclusively, when they have settled in shanty-towns.[66] The basis of such clustering varies. It may be sect, tribe, family or village of origin, or a combination of these identities. The precise identification of the basis of clustering has attracted the attention of a number of writers.[67] Others have indicated the significant variations which exist between different ethnic groups in their degree of clustering.[68] Likewise, the explanation of such clustering varies. Some clusters have appeared, for example, as the result of a coincidence between socio-economic status and ethnic identity of the migrants, as in Tehrān, where Azerbaijani migrants have clustered in the low-status areas of the south and west.[69] Others have appeared as the result of a particularly sharp distinction in ethnic identity between the inhabitants of the receiving town and the surrounding countryside, as at Famagusta, where Greek migrants had by 1956 created a separate suburb, Varosha.[70] However, two processes in particular have been identified as generating and sustaining such clusters. One is the help given by established migrants in finding homes for immigrant relatives and friends near their own dwellings.[71] The second is the maintenance of ethnic solidarity as a form of migrant adjustment to urban life.[72] Some writers see the clusters generated by these processes not as permanent but as transitory features, which disappear with increasing urbanisation, and there is some evidence to support this view.[73] Nevertheless, this view does depend largely on assumptions made about the nature of urbanisation and migrant adjustment, in which migrants are seen as progressively shedding their rural ethnic identities in adjusting to a new 'urban' way of life. If, by contrast, the retention of ethnic identity and related ethnic clustering is regarded as a new form of 'urban' association, created in the process of migrant adjustment, and contributing to a new 'urban' way of life, then there seems no reason to assume that such an 'urban' association will disappear until it ceases to be useful to its members. One might assume that the usefulness of such forms of association would vary in practice according to ethnic groups, to time and to place. While there might therefore be some local tendency to disintegration, this could not be assumed to be universally operative.

Conclusion

This chapter has investigated the processes involved in the formation and development of ethnic clusters in Middle Eastern cities by means of a comparative examination of the large number of studies now available on particular towns, ethnic groups or quarters. It has been written in response to the lack of theoretical work on these processes. The focus has been specifically on quarters as spatial ethnic clusters, rather than on quarters as social entities. The framework for discussion was provided by the realisation that ethnic clusters must originate and grow through population redistribution, that is either through migration to a town or redistribution within it; that explanation of cluster formation must therefore lie in the relationship between these population movements and the socio-economic environment in which they take place; and that such population movements may be made either *en masse*, or by individual persons or families over a period of time. The investigation has revealed first of all the diversity of processes involved in cluster formation and development; the immigration of homogeneous migrant groups (military units, members of the ruling class, transferred populations, refugees), mass regrouping within cities (e.g. the Jewish *mellahs*), and population movements on an individual basis, where clustering may be related to immigration patterns, family establishment patterns, differences in customs or mutual distrust, the presence of holy sites, or socio-economic status. The discussion has revealed secondly the 'dynamism' of ethnic clusters. Far from being static features, as might be expected if they are merely the physical expression of a social system, ethnic clusters can expand or contract, or shift their location within cities, at least when they are not rigidly delimited. Finally, the investigation has revealed that ethnic clustering remains vital in a number of situations today, and that there is evidence to suggest that contemporary disintegration of ethnic clusters may be illusory. The processes operating in the present seem in many cases to be similar to those operating in the past, and it appears that the distinction between the 'traditional' and 'modern' structure of the Middle Eastern city may have been overdrawn.

This chapter is only a tentative overview of the problem and it reveals the necessity for a more detailed investigation of the processes involved in the formation and development of ethnic clusters both in the past and in the present. Investigation of past processes should be based not on inferences from physical structure, but on careful examination of archival sources, such as the Cairo Geniza and the Ottoman administrative records, whose usefulness has been demonstrated by Goitein and Lewis.[74] Investigation of contemporary processes should concentrate in particular on identifying the specific ethnic basis of clustering in each instance. Studies should be systematic and comparable. There is a splendid opportunity here to combine the linguistic skills of the Orientalist with the technical skills of the urban geographer and urban sociologist in fruitful interdisciplinary co-operation. The field for research is enormous. Only when it is undertaken may we begin to understand more than the bare outlines of the processes of cluster formation discussed here. Until it is undertaken we should be prepared to acknowledge our ignorance. Ethnic 'quarters' are by no means a dead subject. On the contrary, the work has hardly begun.

References

1. K.L. Brown, *People of Salé: Tradition and Change in a Moroccan City, 1830-1930* (Harvard University Press, Cambridge, 1976), p. 37; M. Clerget, *Le Caire étude de géographie urbaine et d'histoire économique* (E. & R. Schindler, Cairo, 1934), vol. 1, p. 263; D.F. Eickelmann, 'Is there an Islamic city? The making of a quarter in a Moroccan town', *International Journal of Middle Eastern Studies*, vol. 5, no. 3 (1974) 283-4; A. Joly, 'Tétouan', *Archives Marocaines*, vol. 4 (1905) 291; E.W. Lane, *Cairo Fifty Years Ago*, ed. S. Lane-Poole (John Murray, London, 1896), p. 59; L. Mercier, 'Rabat, description topographique', *Archives Marocaines*, vol. 7 (1906) 309.

2. X. de Planhol, *The World of Islam* (Cornell University Press, Ithaca, New York, 1959) 13-14; G. Marcais, 'La conception des villes dans l'Islam', *Revue d'Alger*, vol. 2, no. 10 (1945) 532; G.E. von Grunebaum, 'The Structure of the Muslim Town' in *Islam: Essays on the Nature and Growth of a Cultural Tradition* (Routledge and Kegan Paul, London, 1961) 147-8.

3. A.H. Hourani, 'The Islamic city in the light of recent research', in A.H. Hourani and S.M. Stern (eds.), *The Islamic City* (Bruno Cassirer, Oxford, 1970), pp. 21-2.

4. R. Le Tourneau, *Les villes musulmanes de l'Afrique du Nord* (La Maison des Livres, Algiers, 1957), pp. 18-19; I.M. Lapidus, 'Muslim cities and Islamic societies', in I.M. Lapidus (ed.), *Middle Eastern Cities* (University of California

Press, Berkeley, 1969), pp. 51, 64; I.M. Lapidus, 'The early evolution of Muslim urban society', *Comparative Studies in Society and History*, vol. 15 (1973) 40.

5. J. Aubin, 'Eléments pour l'étude des agglomérations urbaines dans l'Iran mediéval', in Hourani and Stern (eds.), *Islamic City*, pp. 72-3; I.M. Lapidus, *Muslim Cities in the Later Middle Ages* (Harvard University Press, Cambridge, Mass., 1967), p. 91.

6. Because of language difficulties, only studies in English and French have been examined. German work has sadly been ignored. This is not to deny its relevance or usefulness.

7. This emerges particularly clearly from J. Sauvaget, *Alep* (Librarie Orientaliste Paul Geuthner, Paris, 1941).

8. Le Tourneau, *Les villes musulmanes*, pp. 18-19; R. Le Tourneau, *Fez in the Age of the Marinides* (University of Oklahoma Press, Norman, Oklahoma, 1961), pp. 15-16; R. Le Tourneau, *La vie quotidienne à Fes en 1900* (Hachette, Paris, 1965), pp. 25-6, 72.

9. J. Caille, *La ville de Rabat jusqu'au protectorat français* (Publications de l'Institut des Hautes Etudes Marocaines, no. 44, 3 vols., Paris, 1949), pp. 312-13, 331-4, 347, 356; on Cairo, see Clerget, *Le Cairo étude*, pp. 213-15, and J. Abu-Lughod, *Cairo, 1001 Years of the City Victorious* (Princeton University Press, Princeton, New Jersey, 1971), p. 18; on Aleppo, see Sauvaget, *Alep*, pp. 106, 118; on the Janissaries at Algiers and Tlemcen, see P. Boyer, *La vie quotidienne à Alger à la veille de l'intervention française* (Hachette, Paris, 1963), pp. 127, 132-4, 147, and G.H. Blake and R.I. Lawless, *Tlemcen: Continuity and Change in an Algerian and Islamic Town* (Bowker, London, 1976), pp. 62-3.

10. J.M. Prost-Tournier, 'San'a; Presentation de la capitale du Yémen', *Révue de Géographie de Lyon*, vol. 50, no. 4 (1975), 366, 371-2, 376.

11. W. Blunt, *Isfahan: Pearl of Persia* (Elek Books, London, 1966), p. 103; G. Bournatian, 'The Armenian community of Isfahan in the seventeenth century', *The Armenian Review*, vol. 24, no. 96 (1971) 27-45, and vol. 25, no. 97 (1972) 33-50; V. Gregorian, 'Minorities of Isfahan: the Armenian community of Isfahan 1587-1722', *Iranian Studies*, vol. 7, nos. 3-4 (1974) 652-80. For transfers to Istanbul, see: A. Galante, *Histoire des Juifs d'Istanbul*, vol. 1 (Imp. Hüsnütabiat, Istanbul, 1941), pp. 50, 53; U. Heyd, 'The Jewish communities of Istanbul in the XVIIth century', *Oriens*, vol. 6 (1953) 305; B. Lewis, *Istanbul and the Civilisation of the Ottoman Empire* (University of Oklahoma Press, Norman, Oklahoma, 1963), pp. 100-1; R. Mantran, *Istanbul dans le seconde moitié du XVIIe siècle* (Librarie Adrien Maisonneuve, Paris, 1962), pp. 49, 53.

12. Caille, *La ville de Rabat*, pp. 213-15, 249-50. On the Andalusian resettlement see Le Tourneau, *Les villes musulmanes*, pp. 29-30.

13. J. Sauvaget, 'Esquisse d'une histoire de la ville de Damas', *Révue des Etudes Islamiques*, vol. 8 (1934) 473-4; J. Weulersse, 'Antioche, essai de géographie urbaine', *Bulletin d'Etudes Orientales*, vol. 4 (1934) 49.

14. Armenian refugee settlement in Syria and Lebanon was the subject of the author's doctoral thesis, 'The settlement of Armenian refugees in Syria and Lebanon, 1915-1939' (unpublished, University of Durham, 1979).

15. F. Mansur, *Bodrum: A Town in the Aegean* (E.J. Brill, Leiden, 1972), pp. 6-10, 21.

16. A. Bourgey and J. Phares, 'Les bidonvilles de l'agglomération de Beyrouth', *Révue de Géographie de Lyon*, vol. 48, no. 2 (1973) 107-39; J. Hacker, *Modern 'Amman: a Social Study*, Research Papers Series No. 3, Dept. of Geography (Durham Colleges in the University of Durham, 1960).

17. A. Chouraqui, *La saga des juifs en Afrique du Nord* (Hachette, Paris, 1972), pp. 92-3; S.D. Goitein, *A Mediterranean Society: The Jewish Communities of the Arab World as Portrayed in the Documents of the Cairo Geniza* (University of California Press, Berkeley, vol. 2, 1971), p. 293; H.Z. (J.W.) Hirschberg, 'The

Oriental Jewish communities', in A.J. Arberry (ed.), *Religion in the Middle East*, vol. I (Cambridge University Press, Cambridge, 1969), p. 151. Whatever were the liberties or restrictions of Islamic law with respect to the residential location of minority groups, it is apparent that they were applied unevenly in time and place. See A. Fattal, *Le statut legal des Non-Musulmans en pays d'Islam* (Imp. Catholique, Beirut, 1958), pp. 93, 144-5.

18. Chouraqui, *La saga des juifs*, p. 368, n. 43; H.Z. (J.W.) Hirschberg, *A History of the Jews in North Africa, Vol. 1, From Antiquity to the Sixteenth Century* (E.J. Brill, Leiden, 1974), pp. 370-1, 389-91; Le Tourneau, *Fez in the Age of the Marinides*, pp. 16, 30-1.

19. For Marrakech, see: G. Deverdun, *Marrakech des origines à 1912*, vol. I (Texte, Editions Techniques Nord-Africaines, Rabat, 1959), pp. 338-9, 363-7; J. Bénéch, *Essai d'explication d'un mellah* (Buckdruckerei und Verlag Heinz Rohr, Kaiserlautern, n.d.), pp. 15-16, 27; P. Flamand, *Les Communautés israélites du Sud-Marocain* (Imp. réunies, Casablanca, n.d.), pp. 120-2. For Rabat-Salé, see: K. Brown, 'An urban view of Moroccan history – Salé 1000-1800', *Hésperis-Tamuda*, vol. 12 (1971) 13, 55-7, 73-5; Caille, *La ville de Rabat*, pp. 314-15, 320, 323-4; J. Goulven, 'Esquisse historique des mellahs de Rabat-Salé', *Bulletin de la Société de Géographie du Maroc*, vol. 3 (1922) 28-31; M. Naciri, 'Salé: Etude de Géographie urbaine', *Révue de Géographie du Maroc*, vol. 3-4 (1963) 39. For Tlemcen, see: Blake and Lawless, *Tlemcen*, pp. 49-50, 56; Darmon, 'Origine et constitution de la communauté israélite à Tlemcen', *Révue Africaine*, vol. 14 (1870) 376-83. For Constantine, see M. Eisenbeth, 'Les Juifs en Algérie et en Tunisie à l'époque turque (1516-1830)', *Révue Africaine*, vol. 96 (1952) 154. For Demnate, see P. Flamand, 'Un mellah en pays berbère; Demnate', *IHEM, Notes et Documents*, vol. 10 (1952) 17, 19-20, 159-63. For Mogador, see Flamand, *Les Communautés israélites*, pp. 122-3. For Ṣanʻā', see Prost-Tournier, 'Sanʻa' ', 371-2, 376-8.

20. Chouraqui, *La saga des juifs*, pp. 93, 213, 216; G.S. Colin, 'Mellah', *Encyclopédie de l'Islam*, vol. 3 (E.J. Brill, Leiden, 1936), pp. 523-4; Flamand, *Les Communautés israélites*, pp. 126, 129.

21. For precise references, see note 19.

22. A. Adam, *Casablanca, essai sur la transformation de la société marocaine au contact de l'Occident*, vol. 1 (CNRS, Paris, 1972), pp. 35-6; Chouraqui, *La saga des juifs*, pp. 92-3; Flamand, *Les Communautés israélites*, p. 119; Goitein, *A Mediterranean Society*, pp. 289-93; Hirschberg, *A History of the Jews*, pp. 197-8; Le Tourneau, *Les villes musulmanes*, p. 18; B. Lewis, *Notes and Documents from the Turkish Archives; a Contribution to the History of the Jews in the Ottoman Empire* (Central Press, Jerusalem, 1952), pp. 7-8.

23. Sauvaget, 'Esquisse d'une histoire', 450-3 and *Alep*, pp. 105-6.

24. P.W. English, *City and Village in Iran* (University of Wisconsin Press, Madison, 1966), p. 42.

25. N. Elisséeff, 'Damas à la Lumière des théories de Jean Sauvaget', in Hourani and Stern, *Islamic City*, pp. 173-4.

26. R. Thoumin, 'Deux quartiers de Damas', *Bulletin d'Etudes Orientales*, vol. 1 (1931) 101-2, 112-14.

27. Boyer, *La vie quotidienne*, p. 164; Brown, *People of Salé*, pp. 34-5; Le Tourneau, *Les villes musulmanes*, pp. 19, 29-30; G. Marty, 'A Tunis: éléments allogènes et activités professionelles', *IBLA*, vol. 11 (1948) 159-88; G. Marty, 'Les Algériens à Tunis', *IBLA*, vol. 11 (1948) 301-34; G. Marty, 'Les Marocains à Tunis', *IBLA*, vol. 12 (1949) 25-32.

28. See note 26.

29. See note 27.

30. Mansur, *Bodrum*, pp. 22-4.

31. Brown, *People of Salē*, pp. 37, 39.

32. B. Delaval, 'Urban communities of the Algerian Sahara', *Ekistics*, vol. 38, no. 227 (1974) 252-8.

33. Boyer, *La vie quotidienne*, p. 173; Galante, *Histoire des Juifs*, p. 56; Goitein, *A Mediterranean Society*, pp. 292-3; Hirschberg, 'The Oriental Jewish Communities', p. 150 and *A History of the Jews*, pp. 197-8; P. Sebag, *L'évolution d'un ghetto nord-africain. La hara de Tunis* (PUF, Paris, 1959), pp. 14-17.

34. See note 33.

35. Y. Ben-Arieh, 'The growth of Jerusalem in the nineteenth century', *Annals of the Association of American Geographers*, vol. 65, no. 2 (1975) 252-7; J. Gulick, 'Baghdad, portrait of a city in physical and cultural change', *Journal of the American Institute of Planners*, vol. 34 (1967) 249; I.W.J. Hopkins, 'The four quarters of Jerusalem', *Palestine Exploration Quarterly*, vol. 103 (1971) 68-85.

36. See note 35.

37. See note 35.

38. Abu-Lughod, *Cairo*, p. 59.

39. Boyer, *La vie quotidienne*, pp. 165-7; Le Tourneau, *La vie quotidienne à Fes*, p. 33.

40. Weulersse, 'Antioche, essai de géographie urbaine', passim.

41. Sauvaget, *Alep*, pp. 61-2, 174, 226-9.

42. Thoumin, 'Deux quartiers', 115-16.

43. Sebag, *L'évolution d'un ghetto nord-africain*, pp. 11-17.

44. Ben-Arieh, 'The growth of Jerusalem in the nineteenth century', 257-62.

45. Galante, *Historie des Juifs*, 49-69; Heyd, 'The Jewish communities of Istanbul', 312-13.

46. Hopkins, 'The four quarters of Jerusalem', 78-81.

47. A. Adam, 'Urbanisation et changement culturel au Maghreb', in R. Duchac et al., *Villes et sociétés au Maghreb – études sur l'urbanisation* (Centre de Recherches et d'Etudes sur les Sociétés Méditerranéenes, Aix-en-Provence, 1974), pp. 219-20; G. Baer, *Population and Society in the Arab East* (RKP, London, 1964), p. 192; G. Baer, *Studies in the Social History of Modern Egypt* (University of Chicago Press, 1969), pp. 216-18; C.W. Churchill, 'An American sociologist's view of seven Arab cities', *Middle East Economic Papers*, vol. 14 (1967) 35; B.D. Clark and V. Costello, 'The urban system and social patterns in Iranian cities', *Transactions of the Institute of British Geographers*, vol. 59 (1973) 108; de Planhol, *The world of Islam*, pp. 39-40, 99-100.

48. E.T. Prothro and L.N. Diab, *Changing Family Patterns in the Arab East* (AUB, Beirut, 1974), pp. 68-9.

49. J. Gulick, *Tripoli: A Modern Arab City* (Harvard University Press, Cambridge, Mass., 1967), pp. 66-7, 137-9.

50. Abu-Lughod, *Cairo*, pp. 190, 200-1; Adam, *Casablanca*, pp. 202-4; Blake and Lawless, *Tlemcen*, p. 104; Clark and Costello, 'The urban system', 108; J.I. Clarke, *The Iranian City of Shiraz*, Research Papers Series No. 7 (Dept. of Geography, University of Durham, 1963), pp. 48-51; V. Costello, *Kashan, A City and Region of Iran* (Bowker, London, 1976), p. 90; Gulick, 'Baghdad, portrait of a city', 252; Naciri, 'Salé', 39; Sebag, *L'évolution d'un ghetto nord-africain*, pp. 27-8.

51. English, *City and Village in Iran*, pp. 47-9.

52. Adam, *Casablanca*, pp. 44-6; Blake and Lawless, *Tlemcen*, p. 90; Clarke, *The Iranian City of Shiraz*, pp. 48-51; H. de Mauroy, 'Mouvements de population dans la communauté Assyro-Chaldéene en Iran', *Révue de Géographie de Lyon*, vol. 43 (1968) 349-50; H. de Mauroy, 'Les minorités non-Musulmanes dans la population Iranienne', *Révue de Géographie de Lyon*, vol. 48, no. 2 (1973) 173;

X. de Planhol, 'Recherches sur la géographie humaine de l'Iran septentrional CNRS', *Mémoires et documents*, vol. 9 (1964) 65; X. de Planhol, 'Geography of settlement' in W.B. Fisher (ed.), *Cambridge History of Iran, Vol. 1, The Land of Iran* (Cambridge University Press, Cambridge, 1968), p. 458; M. Eisenbeth, *Les Juifs de l'Afrique du Nord* (Imp. du Lycée, Alger, 1936), p. 39; Galante, *Histoire des Juifs*, p. 58; J.M. Landau, *Jews in Nineteenth-century Egypt* (University of London Press, London, 1969), pp. 30-1; Sauvaget, 'Esquisse d'une histoire', 474; Sebag, *L'évolution d'un ghetto nord-africain*, pp. 17, 19, 21.

53. Adam, *Casablanca*, pp. 43-4, 47-8; Bénéch, *Essai d'explication*, pp. 271, 274-5; Eisenbeth, *Les Juifs de l'Afrique du Nord*, pp. 27-39; Flamand, *Les Communautés israélites*, pp. 137-50; R. Lespes, *Iran, Etude de Geographie et d'Histoire Urbaine* (Collection du centenaire de l'Algérie, Paris, 1938), pp. 129-30.

54. Abu-Lughod, *Cairo*, pp. 61-2, 176-7, 210-12.

55. Gulick, 'Baghdad, portrait of a city', 251-2; P. Marthelot, 'Baghdad, notes de géographie urbain', *Annales de Géographie*, vol. 74 (1965) 34-5.

56. D.H.K. Amiran, 'The development of Jerusalem, 1860-1970', in *Urban Geography of Jerusalem: A Companion Volume to the Atlas of Jerusalem* (Massada Press, Jerusalem, 1973), pp. 20-52; Ben-Arieh, 'The growth of Jerusalem in the nineteenth century', 262-9; J. Parkes, *The Story of Jerusalem* (Cresset Press, London, 1949), pp. 18 ff; U.O. Schmelz, 'The evolution of Jerusalem's population', in *Urban Geography of Jerusalem*, pp. 53-75.

57. Chouraqui, *La saga des juifs en Afrique du Nord*, pp. 211-23.

58. E.g., Chouraqui, ibid., Chap. 12 and Flamand, *Les Communautés israélites*, p. 140.

59. Flamand, ibid., pp. 137, 140-3, and Bénéch, *Essai d'explication*, pp. 271, 274-5.

60. Adam, *Casablanca*, pp. 43-4, 47-8.

61. Abu-Lughod, *Cairo*, pp. 190, 200-1; Blake and Lawless, *Tlemcen*, p. 162; Bourgey and Phares, 'Les bidonvilles de l'agglomération', p. 109; Clarke, *The Iranian City of Shiraz*, pp. 48-51; de Planhol, *The World of Islam*, pp. 39-40; English, *City and Village in Iran*, pp. 47-9; Flamand, *Les Communautés israélites*, pp. 142-3; Gulick, 'Baghdad, portrait of a city', 252; Lespes, *Oran*, pp. 124-5; Naciri, 'Sale', 39; Sebag, *L'evolution d'un ghetto nord-africain*, p. 21.

62. English, *City and Village in Iran*, pp. 47-9.

63. Naciri, 'Salé', 39.

64. Bourgey and Phares, 'Les bidonvilles de l'agglomération', p. 109.

65. A.G. Hill, 'The population of Kuwait', *Geography*, vol. 54 (1969) 88; A.G. Hill, 'Segregation in Kuwait', in B.D. Clark and M.B. Gleave (eds.), *Social Patterns in Cities* (IBG Special Publication, London, 1972), pp. 127-31.

66. A. Adam, 'Le bidonville de Ben Msik à Casablanca', *Annales de l'Institut d'Etudes Orientales d'Alger*, vol. 8 (1949-50) 104-5; R. Baron, Ltnt. Huot and L. Paye, 'Conditions d'habitations des émigrants indigènes à Rabat', *Révue Africaine*, vol. 79 (1936) 889-91; Bourgey and Phares, 'Les bidonvilles de l'agglomération', 115-16, 119-22; S. Delisle, 'Le Proletariat Marocain de Port Lyautey', in *Cahiers de l'Afrique et l'Asie*, vol. 1 (n.d.) 148-9; de Planhol, 'Recherches sur la géographie humaine', 75 and 'Geography of settlement', 460-1; R. Descloitres, J.-C. Reverdy and C. Descloitres, *L'Algérie des Bidonvilles* (Mouton & Co., Paris, 1961), pp. 233-4; J. Gulick, 'Village and city: cultural continuities in twentieth century Middle Eastern cities', in I.M. Lapidus (ed.), *Middle Eastern Cities* (University of California Press, Berkeley, 1969), pp. 148-9; R.S. Harrison, 'Migrants in the city of Tripoli', *Geographical Review*, vol. 57 (1967) 407-14; K. Karpat, *Rural Migration and Urbanisation in Turkey: The Gecekondu* (Cambridge University Press, Cambridge, 1976), pp. 66-70, 78, 83,

117-30; F.I. Khuri, *From Village to Suburb: Order and Change in Greater Beirut* (University of Chicago Press, Chicago and London, 1975), Chapter 2, passim; A. Melamid, 'The geographical distribution of communities in Cyprus', *Geographical Review*, vol. 45 (1956) 360; R. Paskoff, 'Oujda: esquisse géographique urbaine', *Bulletin économique et social du Maroc*, vol. 21 (1957) 78; A. Prenant, 'Facteurs du peuplement d'une ville d'Algérie: Sétif', *Annales de Géographie*, vol. 62 (1963) 450; P. Sebag, 'Le bidonville de Bourgel', *Cahiers de Tunisie*, vol. 6 (1958) 277n; P. Suisse, 'Physionomie du douar "Doum" ', *Bulletin Economique et Social du Maroc*, vol. 20 (1956) 102; P. Suzuki, 'Encounters with Istanbul: urban peasants and rural peasants', *International Journal of Comparative Sociology*, vol. 5 (1964) 210; R. Montage, *Naissance du proletariat marocain* (Cahiers de l'Afrique et l'Asie, no. 3, n.d.), p. 170.

67. Adam, 'Le bidonville de Ben Msik', 104-5; R. Descloitres, J.-C. Reverdy and C. Descloitres, 'Organisation urbaine et structures sociales en Algérie', *Civilisations*, vol. 12 (1962) 233-4; Karpat, *Rural Migration*, pp. 117-30; Khuri, *From Village to Suburb*, Chap. 2; K.K. Petersen, 'Villagers in Cairo: hypothesis versus data', *American Journal of Sociology*, vol. 77 (1971) 567-78, 571-2.

68. Adam, 'Le bidonville de Ben Msik', 106-7; R. Baron, Ltnt. Huot and L. Paye, 'Logements et logers des travailleurs indigènes à Rabat-Salé', *Révue Africaine*, vol. 81 (1937) 737-8; Delisle, 'Le Proletariat Marocain', 149; Montagne, *Naissance du proletariat marocain*, p. 170.

69. De Planhol, 'Recherches sur la géographie humaine', 75 and 'Geography of settlement', 460-1.

70. Melamid, 'The geographical distribution of communities in Cyprus', p. 360.

71. M.M. Azeez, 'Geographical aspects of rural migration from Amara Province Iraq, 1955-1964', PhD thesis (University of Durham, 1968), 263; Delisle, 'Le proletariat Marocain', 148; Gulick, 'Village and City', 148-9.

72. V. Costello, *Urbanisation in the Middle East* (Cambridge University Press, Cambridge, 1977), pp. 48-51, 56-9; Delisle, 'Le proletariat Marocain', 149; Karpat, *Rural Migration*, pp. 34-8, 41-7; Khuri, *From Village to Suburb*, pp. 56-7; R.A. Lobban, 'Alienation, urbanisation and social networks in the urban Sudan', *Journal of Modern African Studies*, vol. 13, no. 3 (1975) 491-500.

73. Adam, 'Urbanisation', 220; Naciri, 'Salé', 46-9; A. Prenant, 'Rapports villes – campagnes dans le Maghreb: l'exemple d l'Algérie', *Revue Tunisienne des Sciences Sociales*, vol. 5, no. 15 (1968) 199; Sebag, 'Le bidonville de Bourgel', 277n; see also the example of the Quarantine quarter at Beirut, described by Bourgey and Phares, 'Les bidonvilles de l'agglomeration', 125-7.

74. S.D. Goitein, 'Cairo: An Islamic city in the light of the Geniza documents', in Lapidus, *Middle Eastern Cities*, pp. 80-96; Goitein, *A Mediterranean Society*; Lewis, *Notes and Documents from the Turkish Archives*.

7 THE EVOLUTION OF RETAILING PATTERNS

V.F. Costello

Introduction

To many in the West the Middle Eastern town has been seen as, above all, an emporium; perhaps because so much of the West's borrowings from Middle Eastern culture between about AD 800 and 1800 have lain essentially in the domain of trade — imported foods, cloths, implements, weapons, ornaments and luxuries of all kinds.[1] The region's position at the cross-roads of three continents has helped the development of external city-based contacts; and it is the great caravan cities of the Middle East and North Africa that have been best known outside the region. Historically cities such as Fès, Cairo, Damascus and Mashhad fluctuated with commercial and political changes, the presence of political power contributing significantly to long-distance trade. The demand for luxury items created by a court could in itself enable a city to develop higher order functions than the numbers and wealth of the local inhabitants would normally warrant, as in the case of Tlemcen in Algeria under the Abd al-Wadids.[2] Equally the removal of political power could lead to a decline in the city's commercial role, as many of the towns of western Turkey experienced,[3] after a reorganisation of the Ottoman administrative hierarchy early in the twentieth century. Although these functions may have stimulated commercial life, the cities of the Middle East and North Africa in the past were not, of course, supplied with the immediate necessities of life, food and drink, by caravans or overseas trade. They relied on their local regions for these. Two partly contradictory views of the nature of the relationship between city and hinterland are taken in the current literature on the subject. On one side the traditional role of the city in urban-rural relations is seen as parasitic: rural surpluses were removed from the countryside by taxation or absentee landlords and dissipated in nonproductive urban consumption, thus, incidentally, stimulating commerce within the city. The process was carried out by political means before the last century, through taxation,[4] while in the nineteenth and twentieth centuries the spread of rent capitalism has concentrated economic power in the hands of private individuals.[5] The overconcentration of wealth in cities has led in the present century to even further concentration in a few cities. On the other side some of the literature, particularly by geographers, emphasises the mutually reciprocal relations of city and rural hinterland, in which goods, mostly agricultural produce, are sold by the rural population in return for merchandise, manufactured goods and services which are provided in the city.[6]

This chapter will look first at the traditional pattern of retailing in the Middle Eastern city, then at the transition which has taken place in that pattern to the present day. A major problem here is how far one can use 'fossilised' examples of retailing patterns found in the present day to demonstrate points to be made about the past. Increasingly also the distribution of urban populations may bear little spatial relation to traditions of urban life. Our fine example however shows that even in one of the largest and most modern metropolises patterns of retail and service provision are strongly influenced by traditional social life.

The Traditional City

It was only in the larger settlements that retail provision apart from the level of the general store was continuous, for only here was aggregate demand for goods and services large enough to support permanent shops, which could be reached in a short space of time on foot. Outside the larger settlements low per capita demand and the limitations imposed by primitive transport technology kept, and still do keep in many areas, the level of demand below that necessary to support a permanent market. Traders visited several markets on a regular basis, and by so travelling extended their market area to the point where they were able to survive. The commodities traded at periodic markets varied, and vary, according to their level. Mikesell has recognised two types of market in north Morocco:[7] a local market where emphasis is on the distribution of local products and the exchange of rural surplus for urban goods, with a market radius of 16 to 20 km and containing a few hundred people, most engaged in sedentary subsistence agriculture; and a regional market drawing on a larger population, perhaps with a radius of 30 km, often located at the junction of complementary zones of production or on the convergence of important routeways. In the larger markets there is greater emphasis on the sale of higher value articles such as pottery or millstones, and the sale of foreign imports.

These markets are temporary and periodic, their function to sell or exchange goods and services. In Charpentier's terminology they are 'selling bazaars'[8] as opposed to permanent bazaars which are more complex in their structure, and many contain manufacturing, usually

by producer retailers; though in those crafts which have a more extensive division of labour, such as textiles, manufacturing premises and
design premises may be quite separate from retailing outlets. The links
between rural populations and these markets varied a great deal in
frequency and intensity, and the commercial transactions which take
place are only one of a number of types of movement and communication between city and village — economic, social or political.[9] Reflecting this, the term 'bazaar' or *sūq* has a number of related but distinct
meanings: as an element in the social life of cities the bazaar could be
identified as the more powerful merchants and entrepreneurs and the
people who worked for them; institutionally the urban bazaar could
be a collection of craft guilds; it could act as a credit information
system, as a central business district, as a religious and recreation
centre, while it was set apart from the rest of the city by its distinctive
morphology.

Bazaars in the cities of central Iran have been the subject of much
attention in recent years; the writings of English, Costello, Bonine and
Bazan,[10] as well as the work in German by Ehlers and Wirth[11] now
provide a coherent picture of the nature of urban-rural relations and
of the patterns of retailing within urban areas in cities with important
traditional bazaars which have not yet been swamped by recent rapid
urban growth. Most bazaars in the Middle East and North Africa tend
to be grouped around some central point, a principal mosque or a
citadel, around which was a concentric zonation of product types.
Iranian bazaars, however, such as that in Kashan,[12] tend to be linear
and the types of product sold are grouped in sections, each known by
that product, so that there is a bazaar of the copper scourers, a bazaar
of the goldsmiths, a tailors' bazaar and so on (Figure 7.1). The main
thoroughfare was a continuously vaulted passageway that ran for about
1,000 m with a number of side branches which become increasingly
subdivided towards the bazaar centre. At the centre is a complex of
mosques and caravanserais. These caravanserais, or serais called *khāns*
in much of the Arabic and Turkish speaking worlds, are two- or three-
storey structures built around a central courtyard, often with a pool
in the middle. Serais dealing in perishable or more expensive goods
might be roofed over, and the carpet serais were the most expensively
decorated. Serais tended to specialise in a limited range of goods; the
upper floors were used for wholesale transactions, while the ground
floors and basement were used for storage.

The social functions of such a bazaar are described by the
ethnographer Centlivres:[13] 'Centre commercial, artisanal, religieux,

administraf, on peut définir le bazar comme un lieu public où s'excercent, dans un espace restreint, des activités masculines par l'opposition d'habitat, réservé à la vie privée, et aux zones de culture et d'élevage où activité est uniforme et dispersée.' A significant feature of life in the larger urban bazaars was the craft guilds, which regulated the quantity and quality of a particular manufactured good sold in the city. In Iran and the Ottoman Empire the guilds were developed under the protection of the government as an instrument for the effective control of the state's population and economy.[14] The number of shops, movement from one grade to another in the guilds' hierarchy, and the prices of goods were carefully regulated. The guilds were taxed as a unit and in Iran they chose their own chief and officers. They were also associated with a number of religious and social functions, but it was their fiscal and administrative roles which were of most importance and these were assigned to them by the state. One advantage which accrued to the bazaar merchants through membership of the guilds was security,

Figure 7.1: Sketch Map of the Kashan Bazaar (1973) showing the Covered Arcade, Serais and Specialist Bazaars

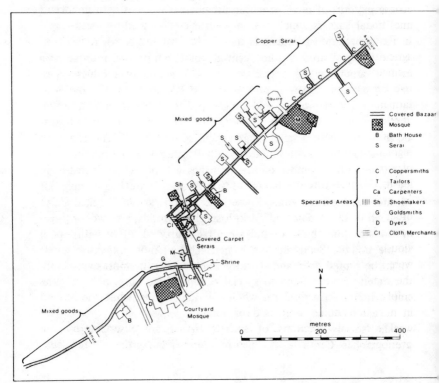

particularly necessary when so many were producer-retailers. Apart from specialised or highly expensive imported luxury items, manufactured goods were produced in the bazaar, in small workshops which also served as retail establishments. There was little division of labour, and from raw material to finished product the process was often in the hands of one man. Industrial linkages were simple: the potter, for example, acquired his clay and fuel from the local countryside, copper oxide from the coppersmith, and what few tools he might use from the carpenter. From the eighteenth century onwards, however, as European merchants set up in business in the Middle East and North Africa and began to import European factory goods in bulk, this mode of production became increasingly uneconomic. The effect was disastrous for many of the producer-retailers and the craft guilds.

Changes in Traditional Patterns

In the transition from the traditional patterns of hinterland and central place relations, and the organisation of retailing within the city, it was urban-rural relations which began to change first. The relations changed radically in the nineteenth century as the largely self-sufficient rural economies of the region were transformed into export-oriented economies tied to the industrial economies of Europe and North America.[15] In Egypt and many of the lands eastward the growth of a domestic agricultural market bound to foreign exports encouraged the development of some provincial towns as wholesale markets and as administrative centres for central government. Commercialisation enabled rural farmers to market in larger, more distant centres, aided by the gradual development of better roads. The hinterlands of the higher-level centres expanded, to include many areas which had formerly been outside any regular urban sphere of influence. In the Maghreb, likewise, the creation of a modern communications network following the French conquests led to the emergence of more integrated city systems, with interlocking or overlapping spheres of influence, and the acquisition of higher-order services by some centres as a result of increased nodality.[16] A new hierarchical structure began to emerge, slowly replacing the previously relatively isolated collection of urban centres. These hierarchies were compounds of traditional urban centres with colonial cities, but the overall pattern of interaction was shifted in favour of the major colonial urban areas on the coast. In the present day Smitz has shown in north Morocco how the local periodic central place network of weekly markets, which are all about equally ranked and have non-overlapping hinterlands, has become articulated into the hierarchically ordered system of the urban economy.[17] Smitz maintains however that the persistence of oriental rent capitalism differentiates this hierarchy from superficially similar central European systems.

In many instances, as in central Iran, the arrival of wheeled traffic expanded and intensified the existing pattern of routeways rather than creating a new one. The effect of an improvement in the road network was not always however beneficial to particular settlements. In the Ula region of Turkey better roads and the availability of credit together with the opportunities for cash cropping has in recent decades greatly increased the wealth of the agricultural hinterland; increased market knowledge has enabled rural inhabitants to acquire local services in villages and higher order goods and services from more distant cities.[18] The effect has been to bypass the small town of Ula. The response of Ula's merchants has been to shift to itineracy, travelling out to the villages in an attempt to capture lost trade, and offering improved credit facilities. This erosion of the importance of intermediate centres in a trading hierarchy following an improvement in transport and communications is well documented for other central place systems: the process of differential growth cause the very smallest centres to vanish, intermediate size centres to suffer a relative decline and larger centres to grow. Environmental conditions in the Middle East and North Africa have some influence here. Beguin and others have found that in general richer agricultural regions, with more dense populations, have an urban trading hierarchy not dominated by a single centre; poorer regions with lower population densities tend to have fewer intermediate centres anyway and are frequently dominated by a single urban centre.[19]

The progressively greater linking of the urban systems of the Middle East and North Africa with the capitalist West had further consequences for the organisation of retailing within the city. The number and importance of producer-retailers has everywhere declined as the cities have become the outlet for mass-produced, often imported, manufactured goods. The distinction in function between manufacture, wholesale and retail has led to increased land-use differentiation and specialisation within cities. Morphological changes in the structure of traditional cities have been manifold: new suburbs were grafted onto the old quarters and in some cases completely surrounded it, leaving it as an enclave, frequently divided by modern highways, and sometimes demolished altogether. Baghdād serves as a good example of one of the largest cities.[20] The pre-industrial commercial centre of Baghdād was near the eastern bridgehead of the river Tigris; some of the buildings, on the eve of the First World War, dated back to the thirteenth century, and the bazaar area as a whole remained relatively untouched. During that war the Turkish army was advised by German military engineers to cut a highway through the old city to facilitate the movement of artillery. This was done, demolishing houses and sūqs. The British forces who occupied Baghdād after the war regraded and paved this New Street, later called Rashid Street, and equipped it with a water supply, drainage and street lighting. Shops were established along the street, which sported arcades and shaded sidewalks and was linked to the traditional sūqs by covered side alleys. Another new street, Kifah Street, opened in 1936, laid out parallel to Rashid Street and connected to it, has developed as a secondary business centre. Specialised automobile repair facilities then began to cluster on the highways in the eastern part of the old city, but little retail concentration has occurred away from the old city. Baghdād's suburbs have expanded steadily in the years following the First World War, but they contain only a minimim of commercial establishments, providing low-order goods and services, such as bread, meat, groceries, barber shops and a coffee shop. Occasionally there is a supermarket. The expansion of commercial and government establishments in the old core of the city has resulted in a progressive loss of its residential nature. Although most of Baghdād's centrally located shops are on modern avenues, the greatest concentration is still in the old city around the site of the traditional sūqs, or bazaars. This is in contrast to other large cities such as Damascus and Mashhad, where suburban expansion has led to the development of new, separate town centres. Until the 1960s suburban expansion in Mashhad was almost all to the west of the old city and by then commercial activity was centred around two areas, the core of the old city, the golden-domed shrine of the Imam Reza, with its attendant bazaars, and the new extramural administrative centre to the west. At that time Mashhad had two distinct peaks in land values, reflecting this bipolarity.

The physical reorganisation of retailing was but one aspect of a series of changes resulting from a shift in individual producing and retailing to corporate organisations; and an increasing influence of the state in Middle Eastern society. Guild organisations, where they existed, lost much of their former influence. Other changes took place in many countries as the Islamic framework of society was loosened and there was a shift to secular values; thus, for example, the codes of conduct laid down for commercial transactions in Iran and Turkey before the twentieth century regulated business deals according to a religiously-based code of ethics, to which merchants could refer. A religious judge gave advice and rulings in doubtful cases. In modern times the codes have been superseded by government regulations, which are claimed to embody the original religious principles, but which are enforced by the secular authorities. The bazaar retains some influence as an institution in some countries, being a powerful force for conservatism in Iran. A study of the Qasvīn bazaar by Rotblat has, however, shown that the lack of expansion and reorganisation in dealings with goods such as agricultural produce are the result, not of the absence of entrepreneurial talent or values, but of structural impediments, such as the widespread use of commission agents, which frustrate enterprise.[21]

Changes in the values of commercial life accompany to some extent the division of the urban economy into, broadly, three sectors — the bazaar sector, the corporate sector and the individual enterprise sector — each of which has its characteristic retail outlets. The traditional bazaar-type outlets, sometimes still producer-retailers, are run by family enterprises, producing and selling commodities to the poor mass-market, using locally-produced raw materials. Such enterprises have survived in many instances by substituting high labour inputs in place of capital. They are under pressure from the modern corporate sector in two ways: it is difficult to produce goods matching in quantity, quality or range those made in mechanised factories; and the sites they occupy in the bazaars are frequently coveted by higher-order retail outlets selling modern goods. Such modern retail outlets represent the second sector, the corporate sector of the economy, which is capital-intensive, uses high levels of technology and productivity, with a division in function and geographical location between production, wholesaling and retailing. The third sector, the unemployed workers of the street economy, are the least documented, yet the visual impression they make in the city is vivid. In those countries not experiencing a major economic boom this sector may account for 10 to 40 per cent of the total urban labour force. One survey of Cairo migrants showed that 22 to 26 per cent were self-employed as hawkers.[22] Among the retail and service activities available are those from the numerous street hawkers, sellers of lottery tickets, boot-blacks, panders and prostitutes. A brief survey by Clarke in Shīrāz revealed no less than 51 types of pavement trader.[23]

The distribution of retailing activities within the city has increasingly been controlled by conscious planning on the part of central government or local authorities. It has taken a number of forms, and reflects in some measure the changes in Western planning thought during recent decades, in particular away from just crude highway construction towards a more subtle and detailed land-use planning. In Damascus, for instance, municipal decrees since 1949 have designated streets or portions of streets where shops can be constructed. The wholesale planning of new towns has usually involved provision for retailing; in the case of Sidi Ammar in Algeria, having a projected population of 75,000, a two-tier hierarchy of shopping centres is planned, with a town centre and neighbourhood units, each with no more than ten shops which are to serve approximately 6,500 people.[24] By contrast the new town of Umm Said in Qatar will have a three-tier system of community facilities at town centre and neighbourhood levels. The scale of planned development in Middle Eastern cities has increased from the single-street planning of Baghdād in the 1920s to the grandiose scheme of the Kuwait government at Subbīyya, where a wholly new city is being constructed, or the Iranian government's development of 'Shahestan Pahlavi', a projected new centre for Tehran, covering 554 ha, 25 ha of which is intended for retail and hotel development. Some 14,000 people will be employed in retailing and hotels. However, the amount of retail provision for a particular population at a particular demand level in most planned schemes seems still to be a matter of guess-work. One further planned element to be noted is the tourist bazaar. Bazaars like that of İstanbul and many of the larger cities of the Maghreb have been tourist attractions for decades, though the great majority of their customers were indigenous; the bazaars of a number of towns have recently been remodelled with the tourist in mind. Eşfahān has acquired such a new section to its bazaar; it is brighter, cleaner and, one may add, notably more expensive than the old.

Tehrān — A Case Study

The distribution of retailing and other services within urban areas is determined not only by the market forces operating in the central place system or legislation founded on the ideas of a planning profession which has been educated in Western techniques of land-use planning; it is determined also by the city's socio-cultural milieu. The social gradient which exists in Tehrān, from the poor traditional south of the city to the wealthy north has been documented by a number of authors, but Vielle and Mohseni[25] have given a most detailed study of the influence of the city's social geography on the distribution of service establishments providing leisure and similar facilities. They analyse the location of a number of facilities, including traditional style tea houses, where people can drink tea, gossip, discuss business, relax, or even in some cases use it as a market place for casual labour; Westernised cafeterias and bars, where alcoholic drinks may be consumed; kebab restaurants, serving Iranian food, and sandwich bars; guest houses and hotels; Iranian 'houses of strength' for traditional athletics, and modern sports clubs; cinemas, libraries and the provision of prostitution. The greatest density of nearly all these activities, whether customary Iranian or more foreign in character, is found in a zone running north of the central bazaar, but outside this zone there are secondary nuclei with mixes of leisure facilities peculiar to themselves. The north-west of Tehrān comprises residential zones where the life-style is for the most part Westernised and cosmopolitan. Mosques are almost absent, and there are the main hotels, social clubs, bars, cabarets and restaurants serving foreign cuisine. The cinemas have high admission prices and a higher than average proportion of the films are dramas, westerns, romances and detective stories. The population is both Iranian and foreign. The area is one of cultural and economic contrast between Iran and abroad. The rest of Tehrān is in contrast to this zone and may be divided into a mixed zone in the west, containing intermediate social categories, and the whole of the rest of Tehrān. The major concentration of retail and service establishments serving the rest of the city is in and around the bazaar, at the centre of the old town. There are numerous mosques, tea houses, kebab restaurants and religious libraries. In the residential quarters on the avenues, tea houses and kerbside barbecue salesmen provide the passer-by with refreshments. In general, 'houses of strength' are preferred to sports clubs, and the cinemas tend to show more comedies, heroic adventures and musicals. There are however sections of the city set aside for prostitution – an activity disapproved of by Islamic morality, but implicitly tolerated in the big city. One such area is around Avenue Lalehzar, which was the principal zone of contact between Iranians and foreigners in Tehrān until the 1950s; another is in the south-west around the Gomruk and Qasvīn gates, where travellers from the provinces first arrived in Tehrān. It is here that the 'reserved quarter' was established by the municipality. Veille and Mohseni point out that the reserved quarter is not an innovation in the Islamic city, nor are areas where alcoholic liquor can be bought. Such districts in the traditional parts of Tehrān cannot therefore be regarded as zones where a transition from customary Iranian Islamic life-styles to Westernised life-styles is taking place.

The division of Tehrān into various zones, reflected in the types of goods and services provided in each, stems from the wide social and cultural divisions in Iranian society, divisions which the events following autumn 1978 have shown to be profound and long-lasting. Iran is not unique in this respect: Cairo can show similar features. The resurgence in traditional values is likely to occur in many of the countries of the Middle East and North Africa, but there are differences in emphasis from one country to another, and from one city to another. In the traditional quarters, cafes, tea houses, icecream parlours — where women can go — are often divided into two parts, with a mezzanine floor or an inner secluded section for families. Males who are not accompanying their family are politely kept out, and the women themselves will not enter unless accompanied by at least one male member of their immediate family. Only in Westernised hotels, bars and restaurants does this not apply. Again, differences between cities are illustrated by Kuwait and Tripoli[26] in Lebanon: in the latter women may go unaccompanied to the cinema in pairs, if lightly veiled, and once inside they may smoke, whereas in Kuwait City the cinemas are divided completely into a family half and a half reserved for men.

Conclusion

The provision of retailing in Middle Eastern and North African towns may be related to the structural changes and tendencies to be found in the city as a whole, as outlined by Wirth.[27] Most of the cities appear to be a mixture of ancient, traditional elements, of modern elements of a purely Western pattern, of Western acculturation taking place in some respects, a 're-Orientalising' process taking place in others. The larger cities show a number of characteristic features. First, the traditional trading centre, the bazaar and its neighbouring caravanserais where these have survived, has lost some of its importance, but in most cases still retains a large part of its retailing if not manufacturing functions. Physically, socially and functionally the traditional commercial district is no longer the centre of urban life. The residential quarters of the old city have declined also, and there is only small-scale retail provision at the local level. Although in the smaller towns differentiation between old and new is not so marked, modern commercial districts have developed in the newer suburbs of most towns, not so much competing with the bazaar but supplementing it and providing services for the more Westernised sectors of society. The residential districts where these are housed have a highly mobile population living at low densities. Retail provision is small scale as a result. Increasingly the demands of the motor vehicle prescribe the layout of many districts, even to the extent in Kuwait City of dictating the entire structure of the city. Shopping for the wealthier, more mobile sections of the urban community is increasingly likely to follow North American patterns of out of town shopping centres. For the mass of the poorer population, living in newly built suburbs, the patterns of retailing are largely unknown. It is in these areas, where the overwhelming majority of the inhabitants of Middle Eastern towns live, that least research has been done. The bazaar has always attracted Western scholars, perhaps because of its exoticism; and the processes giving rise to modern commercial centres are reasonably well understood by analogies with Western experience, but what is happening in most of the city is still largely a closed book.

References

1. G.M. Wickens, 'What the West borrowed from the Middle East', in R.M. Savory (ed.), *Introduction to Islamic Civilisation* (Cambridge University Press, London, 1976), pp. 120-5.

2. R.I. Lawless and G.H. Blake, *Tlemcen: Continuity and Change in an Islamic Town* (Bowker, London, 1976).

3. P. Benedict, *Ula, An Anatolian Town* (E.J. Brill, Leiden, 1974).

4. I.H. Harik, 'The impact of the domestic market on rural-urban relations in the Middle East', R. Antoun and I. Harik (eds.), *Rural Politics and Social Change in the Middle East* (Indiana University Press, Bloomington, Indiana, 1972).

5. H. Bobek, 'Zum konzept des Rentenkapitalismus', *Tidjschrift Voor Economische en Sociale Geographie*, vol. 65 (1974) 73-8.

6. P.W. English, *City and Village in Iran: Settlement and Economy in the Kirman Basin* (University of Wisconsin, London, 1966).

7. M.W. Mikesell, 'The role of tribal markets in Morocco', *Geographical Review*, vol. 48 (October 1958) 494-511.

8. C.-J. Charpentier, *Bazaar – e – Tashqurghan* (Uppsala, 1972), p. 11.

9. L. Nader, 'Communication between city and village in the modern Middle East', *Human Organisation*, vol. 24 (1965) 18-24.

10. P.W. English, *City and Village in Iran*; V.F. Costello, *Kashan, A City and Region of Iran* (Bowker, London, 1976); M. Bonine, 'Yazd and its hinterland: a central place system of dominance in the central Iranian plateau', unpublished PhD thesis (University of Texas at Austin, 1975); Bazan, M. 'Qom, ville de pèlerinage et centre régional', *Revue Géographique de l'Est*, vol. 13 (1973) 77-136.

11. E. Ehlers, 'Die Stadt Bam und ihr Oasen – Umland/Zentraliran: Ein Beitrag zu Theorie und Praxis der Beziehungen ländlicher Räume zu ihren kleinstadtischen Zentren in Orient', *Erkunde*, vol. 29, part 1 (1975) 28-52; E. Wirth, 'Zum problem des bazars (sūq, çarşi)', *Der Islam*, vol. 51, part 2, 203-60, vol. 52, part 1, 6-46 (1974-5).

12. V.F. Costello, *Kashan*.

13. P. Centlivres, *Un Bazar d'Asie Centrale* (Dr. Ludwig Reichert, Wiesbaden, 1972).

14. W.M. Floor, 'The guilds in Iran – an overview from the earliest beginnings until 1972', *Zeitschrift der Deutschen Morgenländischen Gessellschaft*, vol. 125 (1975) 99-116.

15. I. Harik, 'The impact of the domestic market on rural-urban relations'.

16. R.I. Lawless and G.H. Blake, *Tlemcen*

17. H. Smitz, 'Bildung und Wandel Zentralörtlicher systeme in Nord-Marokko', *Erdkunde*, vol. 27, part 2 (1973) 120-31.

18. P. Benedict, *Ula, An Anatolian Town*.

19. H. Beguin, *L'organisation de l'Espace au Maroc* (Academie royal des sciences d'outre-mer, Brussels, 1974).

20. W.C. Fox, 'Baghdad: a city in transition', *East Lakes Geographer*, vol. 5 (1969) 5-23.

21. H. Rotblat, 'Stability and change in an Iranian provincial bazaar', unpublished PhD thesis (University of Chicago, 1972).

22. K.K. Petersen, 'Villagers in Cairo, hypotheses versus data', *American Journal of Sociology*, vol. 77 (1971) 560-73.

23. J.I. Clarke, *The Iranian City of Shiraz*, Department of Geography Research Papers No. 7 (University of Durham, 1963), p. 34.

24. H. Roberts, *An Urban Profile of the Middle East* (Croom Helm, London, 1979).

25. P. Vielle and K. Mohseni, 'Ecologie Culturelle d'une ville islamique: Tehran', *Revue Géographique de l'Est*, vol. 9, 3-4 (1969) 315-59.

26. J. Gulick, *Tripoli: a Modern Arab City* (Harvard University Press, Cambridge, Mass., 1967), p. 5.

27. E. Wirth, 'Strukturwandlungen und Entwicklungstendenzen der orientalischen stadt', *Erdkunde*, vol. 22, part 2 (1968) 101-28.

8 URBAN PLANNING: PERSPECTIVES AND PROBLEMS

B.D. Clark

Introduction

In view of the wide range of subjects which are covered by the term urban planning, this chapter must of necessity be highly selective. Whilst certain broad generalisations will be made about the nature of urban planning, it must be borne in mind that this presents difficulties not only because of the great contrasts in resources and economic opportunities in Middle Eastern countries but also because of the historical, political and cultural diversity. Despite these practical and indeed conceptual difficulties, it is suggested that generalisations about contemporary urban planning problems do have validity.

The chapter will consider various themes. First, a review will be made of the scope of urban planning in the Middle East. This will be followed by an evaluation of the processes, which, as a result of recent rapid urban growth in most Middle Eastern countries, are increasingly necessitating the introduction of a range of interventionist policies; policies which have had to be related to the scale and spatial forms of growth in an attempt to try to solve what can be described as a malfunctioning of individual cities, or parts of towns and cities, and in some countries the whole of the urban system.

An analysis of the development and nature of urban planning in selected countries to show the form that planned intervention has taken then follows. By way of conclusion and in order to obtain a broad overview of contemporary urban planning problems in the Middle East, certain key planning themes will be selected to evaluate the strength and weaknesses of current planning policies and to suggest what form future strategies may take.

The Scope of Urban Planning

When applied to countries of the Middle East, the term urban planning is a concept which not only covers a wide range of topics but which is also open to a number of interpretations.[1] It can refer to interventionist policies at a variety of scales including the relationship of urban land-use planning to regional and national planning strategies. In many countries this scale of planning is weakly developed and is more a pious hope than a practical reality.[2]

Often, however, urban planning is a concept which specifically relates to physical land-use planning at the city or town scale. This concept of planning is usually concerned with the production of city 'master plans' with emphasis being placed on zonation of land in order to achieve a more rational pattern of future development including policies for redevelopment or conservation of existing structures. It is perhaps unfortunate that this form of urban planning is often believed to be the most practical means of controlling or initiating change in land-use patterns. As an exercise it is often superficial and highly idealised. Many of the city master plans which have been produced are design-orientated and bear the imprint of the engineer with many failing to take into account social and economic considerations, or the needs and aspirations of those being planned for. Public participation is usually minimal or non-existent.[3] Even when master plans are approved, powers may not exist to enforce them. Indeed in some instances, Baghdād, Kuwait and Tehrān, for example, consultants have been requested to propose legislative procedures to facilitate plan implementation. Not only is lack of legislation and enforcement procedures a major weakness of planning in many Middle Eastern countries but also there is often no real desire to implement. This situation arises because the decision-makers are often the landowners and as land speculation is now so rife within cities, many stand to lose out if rigid planning is enforced.[4]

Whilst a move towards integrated urban planning is now apparent in most Middle Eastern countries other scales of intervention exist. Particularly important are the range of small-scale actions which are designed to improve the physical, social and economic fabric of towns and cities. These types of action such as road building, provision of low-cost housing, sewerage systems and piped water, etc., are perhaps the dominant theme of urban planning in the Middle East at the present time and are likely to remain so until a more integrated overall planning strategy can be implemented. Piecemeal often unco-ordinated interventionist policies help to account for the often haphazard admixture of land-use types and inefficiency in the functioning of the city which ostensibly the developments are attempting to resolve.[5] It could be described as a policy of incrementalism whereby it is hoped that the sum of the actions will lead to a better planned city. But it also helps to emphasise that not only is there a lack of administrative power at the city level to enforce co-ordination of policies but also that many of the actions are planned and financed by central government ministries or agencies as part of their narrowly defined sectoral objectives. Inefficiency therefore often results and can be seen in the lack of co-ordination between what should be complementary policies.[6]

All of the above types of actions, together with many others such as policies for conservation of historic centres (see Chapter 9), are part of the complex and constantly evolving urban planning process. Any attempt to generalise about problems of planning in the Middle East must therefore take account of the wide range of topics which are encompassed by the concept. Two further dimensions of the concept must, however, also be considered and these relate to scale and time. The scale dimension refers to the size of the unit at which planning operates. This ranges from metropolitan areas, usually with capital cities such as Cairo, Baghdād and Tehrān with a total population of several millions and seemingly insatiable growth, to medium sized towns and cities where stagnation is often discernible, to small towns which have had contrasting patterns of growth in recent years.[7] Many are now declining as a result of changing transport technology or a dwindling resource base whilst others are acting as the pre-industrial nucleus for rapid urban growth. A good example of this latter category are towns in the eastern province of Saudi Arabia and on the Gulf littoral where exploitation of oil has seen the transformation of traditional oasis communities together with the creation of new oil company towns such as Dhahran.[8] In the case of Iran many small fishing ports on the Gulf have been developed by the government as part of their national spatial planning strategy.[9]

Urban planning policies therefore tend to vary markedly depending on the size of the city or town being planned. Policies range from bold, imaginative, often politically prestigious schemes in capital cities to small-scale developments in provincial towns. Overall it could be described as expediency planning which in the poorer countries of the region is severely constrained by lack of adequate finance. It makes an interesting contrast to planning in European countries. For in Europe it is possible to generalise about mandatory planning systems, both of development control and forward planning, which would apply and be enforced throughout the whole of a country. In the Middle East, however, any planning framework that exists is usually fragmentary in scope and has been established in an attempt to solve specific problems or help resolve a particular crisis. Because these problems are usually associated with the largest cities, planning tends to be concerned with the country's capital and a few other major cities but plan-making and development control policies are often not co-ordinated.[10]

The remaining dimension that must be briefly mentioned is that of time. For in the Middle East urban planning, at least in certain countries and in some form, has had a long and respectable history.[11] It is fashionable to assume in some quarters and particularly amongst foreign planning consultants that because the old cores of many Middle Eastern cities appear to be haphazard, radical planning and restructuring is normally required to bring order out of chaos. Nothing could be further from the truth and much harm has been done as such policies have been imposed.

There are many examples over the years which indicate that positive planning has existed in some form. It ranges from small-scale planning of residential units which were inward-looking but planned for people rather than as part of some grandiose design scheme, to sympathetic design and landscape planning of buildings and squares seen nowhere to more effect than in the Maydān-i-Shah, Eṣfahān.[12]

There is now an increasing awareness that a great architectural and design heritage has been lost as a result of the ruthless drive towards modernisation and commercial gain whether this be self-inflicted as in Kuwait or externally imposed as in Morocco. Beirūt bears testimony to this perhaps better than anywhere else in the Middle East and prior to the current political troubles and the physical destruction of parts of the city all that remained of the old city was the area of the emaciated central bazaar. As George Shiber has so eloquently argued there is a vast heritage in the traditional city which can act as a more satisfactory basis for contemporary design than many of the alien concepts now being imported. Let it not be forgotten that one of the earliest planned working-class housing schemes was located in the Middle East at Kahun in Egypt (*c.* 2600 BC) and attempts at vehicle/pedestrian segregation were adopted in some Middle East cities at the time of the Roman Empire![13]

Urban Growth and Urban Planning

Certain key themes can be identified when considering the impact of the rapid urban growth that has occurred in the Middle East and the way that urban planning has attempted to respond through a series of control mechanisms. First there is the question of the nature of urban growth, the processes generating it and the methods that have been introduced to control and manipulate the spatial form that it takes. Next there is the question of urban primacy and overconcentration of population and productive capacity in a limited number of cities, usually the country's capital, and whether policies of spatial redistribution, including decentralisation, are desirable or attainable. Thirdly, there is the problem of the provision of a range of facilities in urban areas, such as housing, public utilities and health and welfare facilities. This clearly raises the question of social equity for different groups in society and whether urban planning is reducing inequality or, as some studies suggest, increasing it.[14] Although each of these themes will be considered in turn it should be stressed that each one is closely related and dependent on the others.[15]

As has been shown in Chapter 2, the rapid urban growth that is occurring results from high rates of natural increase and net immigration. In many countries of the Middle East, particularly where net immigration is a major component of the high urban growth rates as in Iraq, it can be argued that perhaps the most important urban planning policy that has been introduced is the indirect attempt that has been made to restrict and control the migration component that is directed towards the largest cities. Unfortunately the development of the agricultural sector, and linked rural settlement strategies and counter magnets of growth have not had a particularly successful history in most Middle Eastern countries. Often they have been difficult to link to specific urban policies again reflecting the lack of overall national spatial planning strategies. Likewise control of the natural increase component of urban growth by population policies has not had the success that proponents would have wished.[16]

Because of their inability to control the processes which are generating urban growth, urban planners are increasingly being forced to react to the visible evidence of this failure. This includes intense overcrowding in the core of cities with their associated social problems and an increase in the population of shanty settlements which have been built, usually on the city periphery. This theme will be considered in more detail later in the chapter but the problems facing a planner in a city of say two million people with a growth rate of 5 per cent per annum, means that an additional 100,000 residents have to be catered for each year. This is presenting almost insurmountable problems particularly when it has to be combined with attempts to control or demolish shanty settlements, restrict densities in the core residential areas by policies of renewal, rehabilitation or redevelopment or provide adequate minimum standard housing for immigrants, those displaced from development zones and others who are in the housing market.

Not only is the amount of urban growth now one of the major urban planning problems in the Middle East but also the spatial form that it is taking is increasingly significant. For the new spatial patterns that are evolving, whether they be planned or spontaneous, are leading to the concept of the dispersed city in many Middle Eastern countries. This is particularly apparent in the capital cities and the rapidly growing towns in certain of the Gulf Emirates. To appreciate the significance of these new spatial forms, and how planning is attempting to control and manipulate them, one must be aware of the traditional urban forms onto which these new developments are being appended. As the urban form of Middle Eastern cities is described in Chapter 9, only certain features which impinge on urban planning need be highlighted.

Many Middle Eastern cities consist of an older often walled city, the *medina*, surrounded by recent developments extending, in the case of the larger cities like Kuwait and Beirūt, up to 15 km from the city centre. Land uses within the city are poorly differentiated with relatively little segregation of function although there are some exceptions to this general rule. New arrivals to the city lived as close as possible to their place of work, which in many cases meant lodging with friends or relations from the same area of origin already established in the city.

Two new developments are modifying this basic pattern. First it seems that in the Middle East as in Europe, a middle class is emerging with aspirations to own and live in detached villas or houses at some distance from the noise and crowding of the central city. Secondly, as a result of greater involvement by national governments in economic development, in particular with reference to the establishment of large-scale industry, an urban industrial working class is emerging.[17]

These new developments are imposing a considerable strain on the already overworked urban administrators and planners in the Middle East. The concept of a corporate body or *baladīya* responsible for the well-being of all the inhabitants of a city is itself a novel concept in parts of the region while the complexity of urban land ownership and of the national legal systems which must be employed to expedite the transfer of property is making heavy demands. Corruption and nepotism in government and administration are part of the reason why few cities of the region have implemented a comprehensive development plan, for from Bahrain to Beirūt the key issue of compensation for compulsory purchase of land or property in urban areas often thwarts the developer's purpose.

At present, therefore, Middle Eastern cities are expanding rapidly but in a piecemeal and unco-ordinated fashion, with growing car ownership amongst the new middle classes. Beirūt's suburbs now extend high into the Lebanon mountains putting increasing pressure for expenditure on suburban roads which could more usefully be spent elsewhere. An increasing proportion of the GNP is being spent on transport systems to allow the elite groups living outside the city centres to travel to work and to use the service facilities which remain in the central city.

The second major component of the urban population, the new industrial proletariat, are also moving out of the central city as houses are replaced by higher-order functions such as retailing and offices. Many are moving into houses vacated by higher-status groups who themselves are moving further out of the city. It is here also that immigrants are acquiring accommodation, usually rented, helping to inflate the value of land and increase the density. In view of the fact that there is a weakly developed public housing sector, the pressures on the city periphery have tended to see an admixture of spontaneous housing such as shanty dwellings which exacerbates the piecemeal and unco-ordinated patterns of development of middle-class housing.

The second major theme that will be discussed under the broad heading of urban growth and planning is the question of primacy (Figure 8.1). It can be argued that the major planning problem of rapid urban growth is not the growth *per se*, but that it has been concentrated in a limited number of cities. This is linked to a belief held by many planners that a balanced hierarchy of settlements is desirable and that urban primacy reflects a malfunctioning of a country's urban system. Many policies therefore have attempted to reduce the pattern of allometric growth in order to create a balanced hierarchy of settlements. This concept is now being questioned and Janet Abu-Lughod suggests that many Middle Eastern countries, when compared with developed countries in the nineteenth century, are

> developing under very different circumstances of transportation and communication. They appear to be moving into the new larger scale of urban hierarchy, by-passing that intermediate stage that gave rise to what we have mistakenly called 'normal' or 'balanced' urban hierarchies . . . it would be foolhardy to aim at the creation of a hierarchy scaled to a now defunct technological situation simply because it conforms to norm.[18]

Whether or not the creation of a balanced hierarchy of settlements is in fact sound planning policy is debatable, but there can be no doubt that certain primate cities such as Cairo, Baghdād and Tehrān are attracting too high a percentage of the urbanising population.[19] The basic problem is whether control of growth can be achieved and what form of decentralisation should be attempted?

Figure 8.1: Primacy as Shown in Iran, is also a Major Planning
Problem in Many Other Middle Eastern Countries

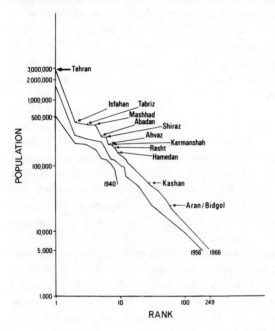

An overall assessment of decentralisation policies in the Middle East
suggests that, as part of an overall regional planning policy, measures
are not well developed. Attempts, therefore, to stimulate growth in
subregional centres by a policy of creating growth poles or growth
zones linked to decentralisation of industry from the primate cities
and giving them preferential tax treatment and heavy subsidies has not
met with much success. An alternative type of decentralisation policy
has been the attempt to build satellite settlements away from the
primate cities but usually within the metropolitan labour market.
Laudable though this concept may be, it still remains an ideal which has
rarely been achieved other than as a plan. All of this means that the real
pressures are being placed on the existing primate and other large cities,
for in practice the rapid growth is having to be absorbed by the cities
themselves.

Nowhere is the problem more severe than in the central area of the
traditional city, where

Ancient commercial cores designed for smaller populations producing goods under pre-industrial techniques and distributing them by
animate means of transportation have suddenly been called upon to
adapt to the commercial needs of mass production and distribution
and the transportation requirements of speed and bulk. The results
have often been devastating. Traffic congests commercial centres . . .
land use alterations have not taken place at the rate required or
according to any rational plan.[20]

The entrepreneurial and 'market' response to this problem was relatively straightforward and saw the establishment of an alternative, more
efficient location. It is this process, when combined with the creation
of new residential areas aided by the building of new roads, with a
population that has greater purchasing power, that has now led to the
dual nature of many cities in the Middle East.[21] In general, the duality,
which can be measured in physical, economic and social terms, is not,
with certain notable exceptions such as in the cities of Morocco, a
planned policy. Rather it has been market mechanisms giving a lead
that planning has belatedly been attempting to control and manipulate.

Overall, therefore, the real planning problems of the rapidly growing
primate cities are related to their size, complexity and increasing social
polarisation. Decentralisation as a concept which would see the establishment of free-standing settlements is advocated by many but in
reality it turns out to be synonymous with peripheral development. It is
now on the sprawling, often unplanned periphery that increasingly both
the rich and poorer elements of society fight for supremacy through the
legal or illegal acquisition of land.

The final theme to be considered in this section, which is using the
nature of rapid urban growth to try to understand some of the key
urban planning problems of Middle Eastern cities, relates to the provision of urban facilities. Throughout much of the region there appears
to be both inadequate planning and provision of a wide range of facilities. This particularly applies to housing although severe difficulties are
being experienced as a result of inadequate sewerage and piped water
systems and the lack of health and welfare facilities. Many recent
studies have shown that the distribution of existing facilities strengthens
the divide between different social groups.[22]

The crux of the problem, however, relates to housing. Not only is
there an absolute deficit of housing units but also much of the existing stock, whether it be in old inner-city locations or in peripheral
areas such as shanty-towns, lack minimum standards and need to be

redeveloped, rehabilitated or provided with basic amenities. Inadequate housing is not a new phenomenon but what is of growing concern to the planner is the scale of the problem. Attention is increasingly being focused on the health and environmental aspects of substandard housing by agencies such as WHO and UNDP who are encouraging governments throughout the Middle East to intervene more positively.

Two aspects of the housing problem which are closely related will be considered. First, the planning problem of traditional housing in the core of the city and secondly the planning implications of shanty settlements.

In theory, planners have a number of options when attempting to intervene in the housing market in the old residential areas of cities. In practice the opportunities are severely restricted and an example illustrates the dilemmas being faced. In many of the older quarters, the housing stock is declining in quality at a time when additional demands are being placed upon it. Densities are increasing as a result of a number of factors, including improved child survival ratios (itself a reflection of improved social and health planning), and immigration. If these housing units are destroyed there is usually no obligation to provide alternative accommodation and so the number of homeless is increased. At the same time there is a need for land in these residential areas to provide more adequate schools and health and welfare facilities. This is proving almost impossible to achieve. Unless the land is required for specific purposes, such as conservation policies which isolate key buildings by creating a cultural *cordon sanitaire* (which may see buildings destroyed), for road-building, or for commercial gain, the main policy appears to be one of patch and mend or ignoring it.

Many would argue that the shanty-towns, and the growing number of refugee camps, are now one of the most pressing urban planning problems in the Middle East. These shanty settlements, usually peripheral but sometimes within the city on land of a low quality ignored by earlier development such as marsh land and unstable terrain, have been developed with or without the tacit agreement of the government. They are not a new phenomenon and in some countries were an important feature of cities in the 1920s. Shanty dwellings do, however, represent a form of minimum shelter which have been provided at low or nil cost to the community. In many cases they represent an improvement on the rural houses from which the occupants may have come. On the other hand they present serious health hazards, lack facilities and utilities and can be considered as a physical and psychological blight on the country at large. They also restrict the options open to a planning authority in that their location is often fortuitous, new developments are unpredictable and their development often conflicts with a more optimum land use planned for the area such as low-cost housing. Once established it is very difficult to provide any facilities except in a piecemeal and unco-ordinated manner.

Various solutions have been attempted. In some countries shanty settlements have been bulldozed away and the occupants forcibly moved. This tends to shift the problem to a new location rather than resolve it. In other instances low-cost housing has been provided but rents are often so high that those displaced cannot afford them.[23] Some countries have tried to control the location and form that shanty development takes by allocating land and providing minimum facilities. As a form of self-help this policy would appear to have much to commend it.

Housing, therefore, in a wide variety of guises, illustrates the inadequacy of facilities in many Middle Eastern cities. New policies are being tried including the building of low-cost 'popular' housing, the creation of special housing banks and housing corporations and the development of self-help housing associations. Free or subsidised land allocation is also being introduced but overall the gap between supply and demand is still very great and whilst urban planning has had some impact there is still a long way to go to meet existing shortages, improve the present housing stock and develop more satisfactory facilities and amenities.

Urban Planning in Selected Middle Eastern Countries

Three countries, Iran, Morocco and Kuwait, have been selected to illustrate the contrasting urban planning policies that are found in the Middle East. It is believed that they represent a range of approaches to urban problem-solving. Iran helps to emphasise many of the general points relating to city planning made in earlier sections of the chapter; rapid urban growth and the planning response, a weak administrative planning structure, duality in cities but signs of increasing attempts to try to introduce more optimum spatial patterns at a range of scales. Morocco reflects the impact of imposed colonial planning concepts and how with independence the country has tried to integrate different levels of planning. Kuwait is symbolically representative of several of the Gulf Emirates where a radical transformation has occured as a result of the availability of almost unlimited resources and where foreign expertise has been utilised to propose solutions.

Iran

The first administrative attempt to improve conditions in cities was the Municipal Act of 1913. City Councils were established but they achieved very little apart from the introduction of street cleaning. They were abolished in 1917 when the Ministry of the Interior became responsible for urban affairs. This position lasted until 1949 when the Law of Independence of Municipalities was passed. The Ministry however retained responsibility for certain urban functions in small towns until the 1970s. This included the preparation of guide plans for land-use development.[24]

With the exception of certain planned squares and parade grounds the single most important physical planning action up to the post Second World War period was the decision of Reza Shah (1925-41) to attempt to modernise the major cities of the country. His solution was simple, brutal and extremely effective, for he decided to drive a major network of long straight roads (*Khiabans*) through the heart of the traditional cities. Whilst many cities were inefficient in terms of their ability to cope with the increasing number of motor cars, the new roads created a monotonous townscape, truncated existing residential areas and commercial activities and bear testimony to the fact that this was essentially single-element planning, predominantly an engineering solution, with little regard being paid to the social and economic disruption which ensued. It was this road-building programme which encouraged many commercial activities to move out of the old city and which eventually led to the development of new commercial centres in many cities of Iran.[25] At the same time many city walls were demolished and in Tehrān most of the fine Qajar architectural heritage was destroyed as part of what many would argue to be ill-conceived redevelopment planning.[26]

In the post 1945 period urban planning was incorporated as a component, albeit a small one in financial terms, of the national development plans. In the first two plans, urban development was given a low priority with emphasis being placed on the provision of potable water, electricity production and street improvements. Lacking resources the municipalities were dependent on allocation of funds from central govenment. There was no overall planning strategy and the nature of development was a reflection of the capabilities of individual municipal officials.

It was not until the third national plan (1962-6) that steps were taken to allow the preparation of city master plans. In practice most were commissioned and developed during the late 1960s and early

1970s under the fourth national plan.[27] In 1965 a High Council for City Planning was created. It had power to guide and advise on the preparation of master plans, set planning standards and approve plans once they were submitted. Seventeen cities were initially selected for the preparation of master plans and this was extended to a further nine in the fourth plan. Several of these plans have now been produced and are acting as the basis for the broad planning policy of the city. But the lack of effective planning laws, difficulties of interpretation and limited qualified personnel means that there are great problems in detailed implementation of the proposals. In the case of the Tehrān master plan, the consultants were requested to write their own legislative proposals as to how the plan should be implemented.[28]

During the period of the fifth development plan (1973-8) a new trend can be seen. Master plans are now being produced for the majority of the largest cities of Iran, but there is a realisation that many of the earliest ones were too concerned with physical planning. Now

Within the framework of the Master Plan for each urban centre, development programmes will be based on more comprehensive objectives stressing the quality of urban life and as far as possible the establishing of diverse objectives for social and economic development programmes will be avoided.[29]

As well as intimating that broader social and economic factors will be taken into account a second major trend is the desire that urban planning should be integrated into a broader regional and national planning strategy. To this end a Centre for National Spatial Planning has been established with wide powers of research, training of planning personnel and formulation of planning policy. A National Spatial Strategy Plan has been produced and in comparison with many earlier reports on planning it is a critical and realistic document about alternative options for planned development. It notes that inequalities are increasing and that a high target rate of economic growth will lead to a deterioration in the quality of life.

Another major trend is the desire to decentralise not only decision-making, but also decision-makers, to the provincial cities. To this end a far more positive policy of movement of civil servants to the provincial capitals has been set in motion. Finally, there is now a recognition of the need for greater intervention in the housing market. With a short-fall of between two and three million houses in urban areas this decision is certainly to be welcomed. Because rents in the cities are now so high, the major drive will be to provide cheaper housing.[30] To encourage this a new Construction Bank was established in 1974 and money is being invested in factory-built housing units. Many of the major industrial developments have associated housing programmes and it is clear that a far higher standard of social facilities have been provided than in both the traditional core and new housing areas within the cities.

Two major problems need to be resolved. First it has been estimated that in Tehrān in 1976 over 100,000 houses were standing empty because of new tax laws which made owners reluctant to rent property. This indicates how significant the speculative element is in the housing market giving rise to great resentment amongst those without accommodation. Second, a lack of effective planning is still seeing too many resources being diverted to housing developments for middle- and upper-income groups. Recent events in Iran bear devastating testimony to the fact that one of the causes of current unrest is that there has been little attempt to improve facilities in poorer quarters of the cities. Despite the fact that planning is now playing a greater role there is a great need for further action to reduce the increasing social polarisation.

Morocco

Modern town planning in Morocco can be said to date from 1912 when France established a Protectorate over the country.[31] Marshal Lyautey who was nominated 'Résident Général' had been a town planner prior to his appointment and his post gave him a new opportunity to develop his interests. Three initial decisions that he made were of great significance in the development of planning. First, he transferred the capital from Fès to Rabat. Secondly, he created a modern harbour at Casablanca and, thirdly, he created a new port, now called Kénitra. Following on from these decisions, which directed future growth to the coast, he appointed foreign planners insisting that three broad principles of planning would have to be followed. First, European quarters would have to be separated from Moroccan residential quarters, the medinas. It has never been clear whether this was a policy of enforced segregation or a desire to maintain the cultural identity of the Moroccans based on respect. Secondly, he stipulated that the cultural heritage should be maintained. In effect this was a policy of preserving and enhancing urban sites and features such as city walls and also ancient monuments. Thirdly, he insisted that the most up-to-date methods of town planning should be applied in the development of the segregated European quarters of cities. This was made law in 1914 and the Act was a far-sighted statement of good planning practice.

Unfortunately, most of the work of Lyautey's planners was directed towards the European population and the local population were largely ignored in the increasingly overcrowded medinas. The 1920s and 1930s saw a lack of investment in the cities because of the economic depression at a time when their population was increasing. The consequences of this were severe because the flow of migrants could not all be accommodated in the medinas.[32] As well as an increase in the density of the medinas two other developments occurred. Bidonvilles were erected at random sites and the authorities attempted to regroup them into larger controlled units. Whilst this policy seems to have worked, the scale of the problem has not diminished and the population in the bidonvilles of Casablanca alone has increased from 50,000 in 1940 to an estimated 270,000 in 1975. The second development was the growth of what have been called clandestine settlements. These were housing areas developed on small plots of land sold by unscrupulous landowners without the knowledge of the municipal authorities. They developed into poor quality housing areas lacking facilities and amenities which constituted a great health hazard.

In the post Second World War period the development of urban planning became enmeshed in various national economic plans that were prepared. Attempts to stimulate the rural economy were given a massive boost as also were plans to improve the European quarters of the city. One man, however, stamped his imprint on the form that urban planning took in the period 1946 to 1953 and his actions are still visible today. Michel Ecochard, when appointed to develop planning in the country, adopted a dynamic line of approach. He set in motion policies of decentralisation from Casablanca, provided low-cost housing, now heavily criticised because of its monotony of design, built up a massive land bank of municipal-owned land for future urban developments and developed a range of plans at a variety of scales. As Jean Dethier has rightly said

> His successors were left with a clear cut situation: possibilities of decentralization; an active policy toward low-cost housing; considerable land reserves; up-to-date and broadened legislation; new ideas in urban planning; and an impressive series of plans, both general and detailed, for a multitude of built-up areas and in particular for Casablanca.[33]

After independence in 1956, the Moroccan government continued to follow the urban policy established by the French administration.

However, an increase in the total urban population and a reduction in finance meant that urban planning and housing policies were accorded a lower priority. A neglect of planning, particularly in the medinas — which were allowed to deteriorate — has proved very costly and has compounded the problems that\face planners today. In one sense this situation is a direct result of economic planning policies in the mid-1960s which have tried to divert investment towards rural projects. By so doing it was hoped to slow the exodus of rural migrants to urban centres. Concurrent with the government's policy for rural development was a deliberate decision not to invest money in urban development projects, the logic being that it would repel potential migrants from the city.

In the 1968-72 National Development Plan, emphasis was again given to urban planning policies. In general it was a negative attitude towards cities, the policy being to slow down their growth and dilute their influence. Policies were also formulated to eliminate bidonvilles. Some were in fact demolished but they soon sprang up again on the same site or nearby. In the period 1973 to 1977 urban development has again been accorded a higher priority. A significant advance has been the proposed introduction of a new law to govern regional and urban planning in Morocco. It is the first serious attempt to reorganise and reform the system of physical planning in the country since the law passed during Ecochard's period of control in the 1950s.

The law established a three-tier planning structure:

(1) Regional plans — which are intended as a general plan for the overall development of large regions. These plans will include guidelines for economic and social development, for industrial location, and for the development of the transportation network and other major public installations.

(2) A second tier consisting of master plans for cities and rural centres. Theoretically speaking the regional plans should be able to point to areas that require a more detailed plan. The law stresses that the plans should be programme- and investment-orientated.

(3) The third level of planning proposed in the law involves the preparation of land-use plans for specific, clearly defined districts of a city, town or village.

The reawakening of interest in urban development has stimulated the Moroccan government to call upon international assistance. The aid requested has been for technical assistance, but more importantly, large amounts of credit for private housing construction.

Kuwait

The final example to be briefly considered is the city state of Kuwait. With one of the highest per capita incomes in the world, the nature of urban development that has occurred raises many points of interest to urban planners. One of the most interesting features related to the rapid growth in the last 30 years has been the development of a resi- dential segregation policy which discriminates in favour of Kuwaitis at the expense of other nationals.[34] Central to the issue of residential segregation is the government's programme of property acquisition, started in 1952 as a means of expediting urban redevelopment in the old city. The government agreed to pay owners of land or property generous sums to sell up and move out of the old city into newer suburban areas. As George Shiber has stated: 'The impact of revenue on urban landscapes has been meteoric, radical, ruthless. It has all but obliterated in one hectic decade nearly all physical and social land- marks of the past.'[35] The old city has been virtually destroyed or changed out of all recognition. Sprawling low-density suburbs have been established with the car and the road system dominating the landscape (Figure 8.2). It is in this environment that planning policies have evolved.

Detailed planning for the inevitable growth and change did not take place until the 1950s when a foreign planning consultant was appointed to produce a town plan.[36] The proposals, which were formulated in London and not in Kuwait, suggested a road system which was almost a duplicate of the dense pattern of streets found in the old city. The plan necessitated the destruction of much property and led to the break-up of the old city by the introduction of wide streets, new commercial activities and government buildings, and the imposition of a restructuring totally lacking an awareness of the Arab urban heritage. This plan has remained the basic scheme for the expansion of the city to the present day. It proposed a scheme of radial and circumferential roads that were to be imposed on the desert, incorporating the concept of a series of neighbourhood units between the major arterial routes.

Despite the existence of a physical plan with laws for its imple- mentation, problems arose. Traffic planning got out of hand and unco- ordinated development was occurring on the city periphery. After much discussion it was decided in 1968 to appoint Colin Buchanan and Partners to prepare a National Physical Plan for the State of Kuwait, a Master Plan for Greater Kuwait and Action Area Plans.[37] This is not the place to go into details as to what the various plans proposed but what is of interest is the reaction to the plans in Kuwait.[38] For quite

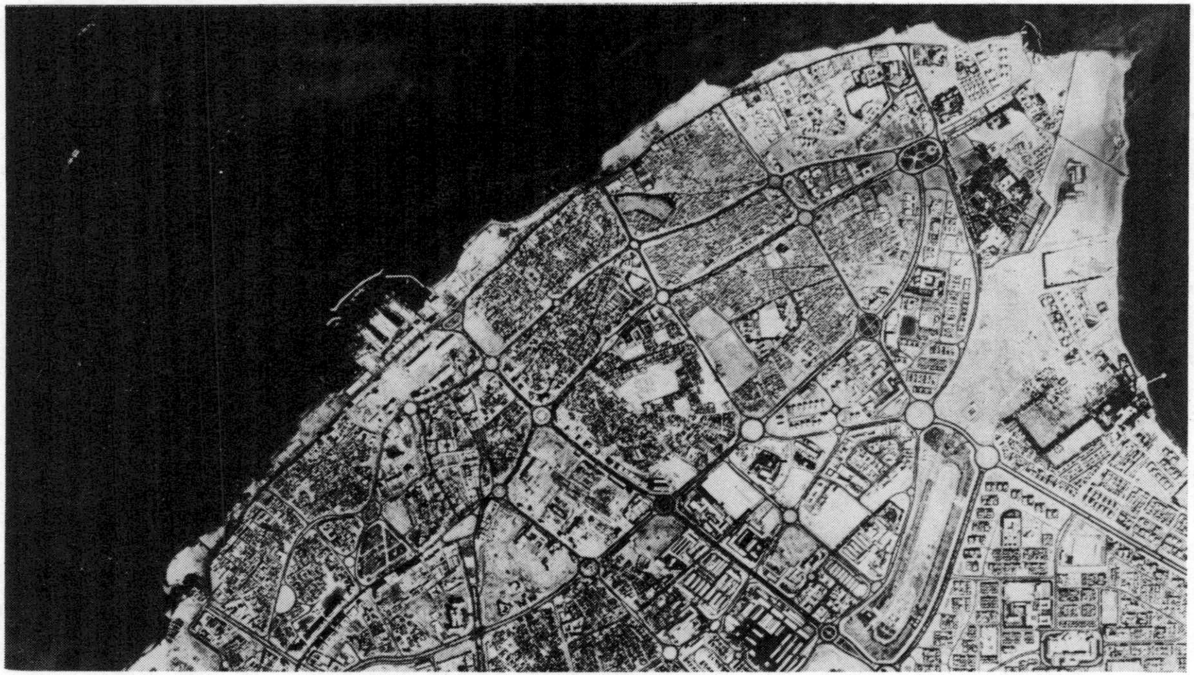

Figure 8.2: The Car and Massive Road-building Programmes in Kuwait not only Dominate the Urban Landscape but also Influence Attitudes towards Planned Solutions

clearly it is illustrative of a growing feeling in many Middle Eastern countries that there are dangers in 'importing' planning expertise to try to resolve local problems. Criticisms have been that the local counterpart team were not fully involved in policy formulation, instead they were used largely for data collection; no serious training programme to implement the plan was established; participation was minimal; and concepts formulated to develop the plans were based on external experience rather than on local knowledge. Again it is not important whether these criticisms are correct. What is important is that within the planning literature these kind of views are increasingly being expressed.

In many respects Kuwait can afford to make mistakes in the development of its urban planning because it has the resources to correct them. In a positive sense it has spent heavily but wisely on a wide range of infrastructure projects and also in the field of social planning. But it has destroyed its historic core and has failed as a result of its policy towards non-Kuwaitis to provide adequate housing for immigrant workers including the Bedouin on whom the Kuwaiti population and their economy are dependent.[39]

Conclusions

Given the complexity of urban planning it is difficult to draw anything but the most tentative conclusions about its current status in the countries of the Middle East. In the three countries considered it has been shown that a range of different policies have been adopted and that they have all met with different degrees of success. At the heart of nearly all the urban problems, however, has been the rapidity of growth. If other Middle Eastern countries are included further distinctive policies can be identified. Israel, for example, has adopted an urban planning policy that has given particular emphasis to the creation of new settlements but even more important it has the legal powers and a willingness to implement planning policies which are approved. In this sense it is somewhat exceptional, for throughout the rest of the Middle East there would appear to be an ambivalent attitude to the whole concept of planning. On the one hand there is a great desire to integrate urban planning with other scales of planning (national, regional, economic, etc.) and also a desire to produce plans to improve the quality of life in the city. On the other hand there is an unwillingness to enforce planning policies (and most countries have a great deal of planning legislation) in a way that makes the interpretation unequivocally clear to all actors in the process such as central government officers, municipal officials, the developers and the public at large.

Much of this problem stems from the general attitudes of the population in the Middle East to the role of state intervention in matters which are held by some to be matters of personal choice. Limited intervention may be acceptable to those who have power and influence, who own their property and who can afford to defend their own personal interests. It is, however, no comfort to those living in abject poverty in the bidonvilles in Morocco, Lebanon and Iran where jobs are few and prospects for the future bleak. For these people, there may be a need for stronger powers of intervention, on the grounds of social equity. Overall, however, there is now perhaps a greater willingness to accept that planning has to be developed but it is inevitable that for a variety of reasons people will attempt to by-pass or thwart its objectives.

Perhaps the most general policy that has been adopted throughout the Middle East has been the production of city master plans (Figure 8.3). Designed to modify existing land uses and develop optimum patterns for new growth, they vary in content, sophistication and degree of relevance to the real urban issues of the day. Generalising about their utility, the following points could be made

(1) Although many plans are approved very few have been implemented. Reasons for this include lack of planning legislation, lack of resources or lack of manpower.

(2) Many plans have been prepared with a lack of understanding and sympathy for the requirements of the city. Often there has been hostility and lack of co-operation between the planners and the planned-for. The wishes of the public are very rarely taken into account and participation and involvement is virtually nil.

(3) Many plans produced cannot operate because there is no framework of planning into which they can fit.

(4) Many of the concepts included in the plans are too complex to be understood by those who have to implement the proposals.

In sum, much has been achieved as a result of the development of different scales of urban planning and some of the successes have been considered in this chapter. Certain of the small-scale design elements found in cities throughout the Middle East, for example, are superb by any standard. However, planning has largely failed to achieve the oft-stated objectives of restricting the growth of the large expanding cities and still has a long way to go to improve the quality of life in cities

Figure 8.3: Proposed Land Uses Contained in the Master Plan for Beer Sheva, Israel (after E. Spiegel, *Neue Städte in Israel*, Karl Krämer Verlag, Stuttgart, 1966, p. 141)

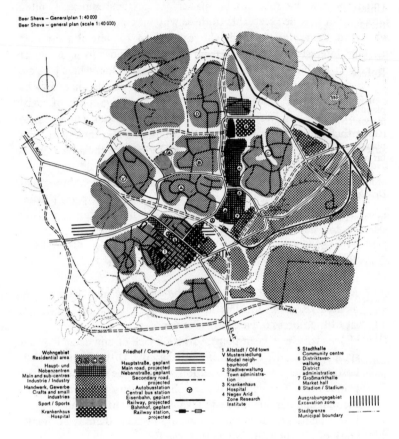

Beer Sheva – Generalplan 1 : 40 000
Beer Sheva – general plan (scale 1 : 40 000)

Wohngebiet / Residential area	
Haupt- und Nebenzentren / Main and sub-centres	
Handwerk, Gewerbe / Crafts and small industries	
Industrie / Industry	
Sport / Sports	
Krankenhaus / Hospital	

Friedhof / Cemetery
Hauptstraße, geplant / Main road, projected
Nebenstraße, geplant / Secondary road, projected
Autobusstation / Central bus station
Eisenbahn, geplant / Railway, projected
Bahnhof, geplant / Railway station, projected

1 Altstadt / Old town
V Mustersiedlung / Model neighbourhood
2 Stadtverwaltung / Town administration
3 Krankenhaus / Hospital
4 Negev Arid Zone Research Institute

5 Stadthalle / Community centre
6 Distriktsverwaltung / District administration
7 Großmarkthalle / Market hall
8 Stadion / Stadium

Ausgrabungsgebiet / Excavation zone
Stadtgrenze / Municipal boundary

and provide adequate minimum urban facilities.

In the future it is likely that there will be changes in the field of urban planning. There are signs that legislation is being strengthened and that the will to enforce policies and plans is growing. Planning will increasingly have a more significant social and economic input, creating in cities something that is more than just a respectable form of architecture or engineering. Whilst planning is at present elitist and imposed it is likely that it will become more involved with the wishes and aspirations of the population. This will only be possible if more resources are put into education, training and the development of planning and city management programmes. At the present time a great deal of lip-service is paid to the concept of urban planning in Middle Eastern countries. Unless greater effort is made to convert ideas and ideals into positive measures the future of cities looks bleak.

References

1. Two of the most important works on definitions, scope and nature of urban planning in the Middle East are by the late George Shiber: *The Kuwait Urbanization* (Government Printing Press, Kuwait, 1964) and *Recent Arab City Growth* (Government Printing Press, Kuwait, 1967). These are seminal works on urban planning in the Middle East. The title of the first volume is misleading as it covers far more than urban planning in Kuwait.

2. See, for example, Secretariat of the High Council for Urban Planning, Ministry of Development and Housing, Government of Iran, *Urban and Regional Development Planning in Iran*, vol. 1 (Tehran, 1971).

3. An informative study on lack of participation is given by H. Ghaffarzadeh in 'Hamadan. An evaluation of the urban planning process', unpublished PhD thesis (Department of Geography, University of Aberdeen, 1979).

4. An excellent study of the complex relationship between urban land policies, urban planning and speculation in Iraq, Jordan, Lebanon and Syria, is contained in *Urban Land Policies and Land Use Control Measures*, vol. V, Middle East, (Department of Economic and Social Affairs, United Nations, New York, 1973).

5. A good example of this can be seen in the chapters on Cairo and Beirut, in *From Madina to Metropolis*, ed. L. Carl Brown (The Darwin Press, Princeton, 1973). A detailed example is seen in *Kermanshah: An Iranian Provincial City*, J.I. Clarke and B.D. Clark, Centre for Middle Eastern and Islamic Studies (University of Durham, Publication no. 1, 1969).

6. In many major cities in the Middle East, this lack of co-ordination is particularly noticeable with regard to transport programmes and land-use proposals (central areas and peripheral industrial and housing developments), the provision of utilities and building land and the non-separation of polluting industry and housing. See for example Chapter 6, 'Land use and land values' in *Tehran, An Urban Analysis*, H. Bahrambeygui (Tehran, 1977).

7. Major demographic trends can be seen for cities in *Populations of the Middle East and North Africa*, ed. J.I. Clarke and W.B. Fisher (University of London Press, London, 1971).

8. G. Schweizer, *Saudi-Arabian* (Horst Erdmann Verlag, Tubingen, 1976), pp. 247-9.

9. Centre for Research and Training in Regional Planning, *National Spatial Strategy Plan* (Tehran, 1976), pp. 17-21.

10. *Urban Land Policies and Land Use Control Measures*, pp. 13-19.

11. The most important sources on the early planning history of the Middle East are: A.E.J. Morris, *History of Urban Form* (G. Goodwin, London, 1974); F. Hiorns, *Town Building in History* (G.G. Harrap, London, 1956); A.M. Hourani and S.M. Stern (eds.), *The Islamic City. A Colloquium* (Bruno Cassirer, Oxford, 1970); L. Cari Brown (ed.), *From Madina to Metropolis*, pp. 290-333. A useful summary of early city planning is included in: P. Beaumont, G.H. Blake and J.M. Wagstaff, *The Middle East: A Geographical Study*, Chapter 6, 'Towns and Cities' (J. Wiley & Sons, London, 1976), pp. 189-221.

12. E.E. Beaudouin and A.U. Pope in *A Summary of Persian Art*, ed. A.U. Pope (City Plans, vol. 2, London, 1938/39), pp. 1391-410.

13. A.E.J. Morris, *History of Urban Form*, p. 52.

14. See, for example, J.I. Clarke and B.D. Clark, *Kermanshah*, H. Ghaffarzadeh, *Hamadan*, and also A.A. Al-Moosa, 'Bedouin shanty settlements in Kuwait: a study in social geography', unpublished PhD thesis (University of London, 1976), 314-22.

15. For one of the best summaries on the whole question of urban growth and planning strategies see J.L. Abu-Lughod, 'Problems and policy implications of Middle Eastern urbanization', in *Studies on Development Problems in Selected Countries in the Middle East, 1972* (UN, New York, 1973), pp. 42-62.

16. A.G. Hill, 'Some political, social and economic implications of population policy and growth in the Middle East and North Africa', unpublished mimeo (Office of Population Research, Princeton, New Jersey, 1975), pp. 1-75.

17. For a discussion of these changes see C. Issawi, 'Economic change and urbanization in the Middle East', in *Middle Eastern Cities*, ed. I.M. Lapidus (University of California Press, Berkeley and Los Angeles, 1969), pp. 102-21.

18. J. Abu-Lughod, 'Problems and policy implications', p. 52.

19. For purposes of the production of the Master Plan of Tehrān it was projected in 1969 that the population of the city would be 5.5 million in 1991. It now appears that it will have reached this figure by 1980! M. Moeinzadeh, 'Urbanisation in Tehran: problems and opportunities', *International Union of Local Authorities Newsletter*, vol. 9, no. 9/10 (1975) 12. For Cairo, see J. Abu-Lughod, *Cairo: 1001 Years of the City Victorious* (Princeton University Press, Princeton, 1971).

20. J. Abu-Lughod, 'Problems and policy implications', p. 53.

21. R. Ettinghausen, 'Muslim cities: old and new' in L. Carl Brown (ed.), *From Madina to Metrpolis*, pp. 290-318.

22. G. Payne in *Urban Housing in the Third World* (Leonard Hill, London, 1977) considers some of the wider issues of housing provision and polarisation. Detailed studies of this polarisation are included in A.G. Hill, 'Segregation in Kuwait', in *Social Patterns in Cities*, IBG special publication no. 5 (March 1973) 123-42. See also J.I. Clarke and B.D. Clark, *Kermanshah*, pp. 105-26.

23. A.A. Al-Moosa, 'Bedouin shanty settlements in Kuwait', 267-310.

24. These guide plans were simple statements of the possible land-use patterns that should be adopted in small towns. Many during the 1960s and 1970s were prepared by Americans working for the Peace Corps. Some guide plans were based on detailed study, others more on speculation!

25. J.I. Clarke, *The Iranian City of Shiraz*, Department of Geography Research Papers Series no. 7 (University of Durham, 1963), and J.I. Clarke and B.D. Clark, *Kermanshah*, pp. 18-22.

26. H. Bahrambeygui, *Tehran: An Urban Analysis*, pp. 34-48.

27. A. Mozayeni, 'City planning in Iran: evolution and problems', *Ekistics*, vol. 38, no. 227 (October 1974) 266.

28. This included the establishment of a five-year 'service' line beyond which no development would be allowed without special permission. This line would move outward every five years until it reached the outer boundary of the plan in 25 years time. Needless to say this policy has not been fully enforced and much peripheral development has occurred.

29. Plan and Budget Organization, *Iran's 5th Development Plan 1973-1978 Revised. A Summary* (Tehran, 1974), p. 372.

30. Bank Rahni Iran, *Summary of the Twenty Five Year Plan for Housing in Urban Areas from 1345-1370 (1966-1991)* (Tehran, 1970), pp. 1-36.

31. Much of the material that follows is based on the excellent summary of

urban planning contained in *From Madina to Metropolis* in the chapter entitled J. Dethier, 'Evolution of concepts of housing, urbanism and country planning in a developing country: Morocco, 1900-1972', pp. 197-243. This chapter also contains a comprehensive bibliography.

32. G.H. Blake, 'Morocco: urbanization and concentration of population', in J.I. Clarke and W.B. Fisher (eds.), *Populations of the Middle East and North Africa* (University of London Press, 1972) pp. 419-22.

33. J. Dethier, 'Evolution of concepts of housing', 221.

34. A.G. Hill, 'Political, social and economic implications of population policy', 127-31.

35. G. Shiber, in *From Madina to Metropolis*, p. 170.

36. Miniprio, Spencely and Macfarlane, *Plan for the Town of Kuwait* (London, 1951).

37. Colin Buchanan and Partners, *Kuwait Master Plan and Action Area Studies: First Report, the long-term strategy; second report, the short term plan* (Reports on Action Area 1 and Action Area 2, 1971/72).

38. K. Jamil, 'Kuwait: a salutary tale', *The Architects Journal* (December 1973) 1452-7.

39. A.A. Al-Moosa, 'Bedouin shanty settlements in Kuwait', 314-22.

9 THE FUTURE OF HISTORIC CENTRES: CONSERVATION OR REDEVELOPMENT?

R.I. Lawless

The Historic City Under Threat

Beginning in the nineteenth century, the introduction of Western culture and the industrial revolution resulting from advances in technology, interrupted the evolutionary processes of urban development in the Middle East. There was a sharp break in the continuum, and a rejection of the architectural heritage of the past as modernisation became synonymous with Westernisation.

The impact of modernisation on the historic city has been profound, but has varied in both time and space. The process began as early as the mid-nineteenth century in some major coastal cities, for example Algiers, in Algeria, which soon began to dominate the new urban hierarchy. Other centres, however, particularly those in the interior, and the smaller provincial towns outside the modern economic enclaves created by the intrusion of capitalist modes of production, remained scarcely touched by the modern world until recently. Towns such as San'a in the Yemen AR, and Mecca and Medina in Saudi Arabia for example retained their integrity but at the price of relative and sometimes absolute decline. Today, although most historic cities have survived at least in part, they are often encircled and dwarfed by modern extensions resulting in a striking juxtaposition of urban styles. The most extreme examples of this phenomenon are the 'dual cities' of Morocco which experienced the more openly intrusive form of colonialism, European settler colonisation. It was the policy of the French Resident-General Lyautey 'to avoid the unhealthy mixture of races'. Existing cities such as Fès and Marrakech were preserved intact. New cities built by Europeans for European occupation and laid out with straight and wide streets to accommodate motorised traffic were established some distance away, leaving a *cordon sanitaire* between old and new in order to separate as completely as possible the life of the colonial population from that of the Moroccans. As part of the same policy the walls surrounding the old cities of Salé and Rabat were not only left intact but were actually strengthened and repaired by the French after 1912 in order to maintain what Janet Abu-Lughod has described as 'the self-sufficiency of the apartheid quarters'.[1] Elsewhere the boundary between the *medina* and the modern, Western-style appendages was less strictly defined, as in Tunis and Cairo, and in a number of cases the modern city has made deep inroads into the adjacent historical core. The eastern section of the old city or *Casbah* of Algiers for example was demolished by the French in order to build new port facilities, military installations and residential accommodation for the early European settlers.[2] In Iran, Reza Shah's policy from 1926 onwards of cutting a network of strategic routes straight through the tight-packed fabric of all major towns has produced a grid of broad, direct avenues, articulated at their crossing points by large ornamental roundabouts, and interrupting the earlier street network at haphazard angles.[3] This arbitrary, superimposed pattern has been repeated elsewhere in the region with varying degrees of sympathy for the old town's structure – for example at Aleppo in Syria[4] (Figure 9.1), Baghdād[5] in Iraq and Göynük in Turkey.[6] In only a few cases, notably Beirūt[7] and Kuwait,[8] and some of the smaller pre-colonial towns in Algeria, has the process of modernisation swept away virtually all traces of earlier urban patterns. In Beirūt a relatively insignificant, although extremely old, historic centre was ruthlessly converted and modernised. In the case of Kuwait, the fact that the historical heritage was unimpressive and the financial resources at hand relatively unlimited, resulted in a decision virtually to raze the old city and rebuild a capital better suited to the requirements of modern transport and commerce. Most cities in the Middle East, however, have neither had the financial capacity to trade old for new, nor have they inherited historic centres of so little intrinsic interest that they can afford to destroy them.[9]

If much of the traditional urban fabric has survived, dramatic changes in economic and social organisation have occurred within the historic centres. A swing of emphasis away from the old town to the modern quarters is probably the most striking development. The economic, professional and cultural focus of urban life has moved to the modern city, and in varying degrees the old centres have become peripheral to modern administrative functions and economic activities. Until the early twentieth century, public services in the towns were rudimentary and government land use limited to the traditional citadel area. However, the government's role, once confined almost exclusively to that of tax collecting, conscription and keeping of an often precarious peace, has now changed to that of major investor in health and welfare services, educational facilities, infrastructure and industrial and agricultural development programmes. As a consequence of this growing complexity of government at both national and local levels, the need

Figure 9.1: The Historic Centre of Aleppo showing the Completed
North Relief Road (20 m wide) and the Proposed South Relief Road.
The western half of the old Jewish quarter, now isolated by new
roads is to be redeveloped as a new commercial centre (after
Cantacuzino, 1975)

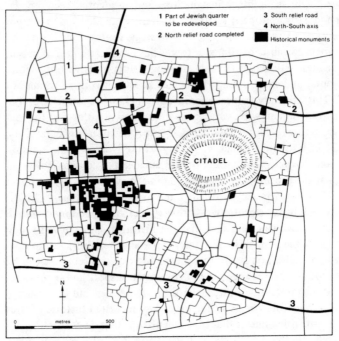

for building space has increased rapidly. In some cases areas conti-
guous to the citadel have been adapted to administrative functions, but
many government buildings have been accommodated on cheaper or
government-owned vacant land beyond the old town.

In many cities separate commercial centres have appeared outside
the historic core, and these new central business districts have begun to
absorb most of the evolving modern retailing facilities and banking
functions. Nevertheless the old town remains the most powerful low-
income commercial centre of the city, serving an increasingly dense,
poor residential population as well as traditional provincial customers.
However, intrusion of foreign manufactured goods, changing demands

and aspirations of the people, and in some cases the influence of international tourism, have greatly modified the *sūqs*. Production patterns have also altered. Many of the small workshops located in and around the bazaar complex have disappeared and declined through competition from both imported and local mass-produced factory goods. The large, modern factories established in recent years are located outside the old city where cheap land is available for building.[10]

Economic changes in the old city have been accompanied by a breakdown in social organisation and the emergence of new social patterns. Wealthy upper- and middle-class families were among the first to desert the old city for houses in the modern suburbs. Gradually these early defectors were joined by upwardly-mobile elements who hoped to join the ruling elite. In those countries which experienced direct European rule, minority groups such as the Copts in Egypt and the Maghreb Jews quickly made alliances with the new colonial power, and also left the older parts of town to live as near the foreign community as possible.[11] This exodus has resulted in an almost total proletarianisation of the traditional quarters. With few exceptions the historic cores have become reception areas for large numbers of poor migrants from the countryside. Most of the rural migrants found their first urban occupation in the old city, occupying first the *funduqs* and *wakālas* (dormitories for itinerant merchants and travellers in earlier days) and then the palaces and large town houses vacated by the departing upper and middle bourgeoisie.[12] These buildings have been rapidly subdivided to absorb the growing demand for housing. As densities increased not only the wealthy families but ordinary citizens declassed through a decline in traditional industries and trades began to look to areas of peripheral spontaneous settlement and public housing schemes in order to escape the overcrowding and 'ruralisation' of the old quarters.

Under the impact of high densities and serious overcrowding, residential property has deteriorated for lack of adequate maintenance. Religious, cultural and educational buildings have lost their wealthy patrons who have moved elsewhere; maintenance is therefore minimal if it is carried out at all, and the environs of historic monuments have been swamped by other uses. At the same time traditional systems of sanitation and water supply, already inadequate and sometimes neglected even before the twentieth century, have been totally overwhelmed by the recent influx of poor people and more often than not have collapsed under the strain.

The Concept of Conservation

Until the middle of the twentieth century few countries in the world appreciated the value of their old cities. In Europe conservation of historic structures was limited to the most notable ancient and medieval remains. Attention focused on individual monuments which were considered separately from their surroundings, and areas adjacent to such major monuments as Notre Dame in Paris were thoughtlessly demolished. It was the Second World War in particular and the extent of the destruction to the historic fabric of the major European cities which heightened an awareness both of the monuments and of their urban settings. This awareness has been further accentuated during the last 30 years by the rapid pace of industrial development and social change in Europe which has gravely threatened the artistic and historical heritage. After the Second World War, Germany, Italy, Britain, France and Poland totally or partially repaired the damage to their historic cities, and governments now recognise the urgent need of extending protection from individual monuments to groups of historic buildings.

At the same time increasing criticism has been voiced about the modern quarters of Western cities where high-rise structures, stark cubical forms, the use of metals and eventually plastics in place of traditional materials dominate architectural design, and where buildings and furniture are thought of in terms of 'machines' for living. The economic advantages of high-rise structures are now being seriously challenged, and many thousands of case studies have been made to investigate the social and psychological problems that result from unsatisfactory housing and living conditions in the modern cities of Europe and the United States.

> The artificiality of new quarters humiliatingly expresses our ignorance or lack of perception of what people truly need. Hostile forms intimidate and condition us, prevent a response to the needs of body, soul and social life. They reflect an uneasy superificiality, a chronic frustration, the loneliness of the individual swallowed up in the crowd, and are one of the root causes of urban dehumanisation. The environment we are creating is an impersonal machine, soulless and unfeeling.[13]

The negative aspects of the removal of the old to make way for the new are now recognised, and dissatisfaction with the concept of urban renewal has become widespread, particularly in the United States where it has occurred at the most rapid rate. A number of leading critics have reviewed the programmes to rebuild and redesign the interior of cities, highlighting the negative effects of displacement and resettlement on the original inhabitants of areas which have been 'renewed'.

> The post-relocation experiences of a great many people have borne out their most pessimistic pre-location expectations . . . for the majority it seems quite precise to speak of their reactions as expressions of grief. These are manifest in the feelings of painful loss, the continued longing, the general depressive tone, frequent symptoms of psychological or social or semantic distress.[14]

From this debate has emerged the idea of 'urban retrieval';[15] not the wholesale removal of the old or the passive protection of the historic fabric, but the revitalisation of old quarters so that they are given a role in the modern life of both the individual and the community. Some planners and architects now argue that it is easier to restore and modernise old buildings than was at one time thought and the cost of doing so can be less than that of demolishing and putting up new buildings to give equivalent accommodation. The revitalisation of old areas, it is suggested, can therefore be the quickest and least costly way of providing an element which humanises our ever-growing built-up areas.

> By their very nature, historic centres keep the contacts with the past and with the art and history they embody; the inhabitants subconsciously identify with the social and cultural atmosphere that surrounds them. When a town loses this quality of being an *agora*, a market and meeting place, it becomes sterile, and its society becomes de-urbanised rather than over-urbanised. It is in this sense that a revitalised historic centre can make urbanisation human by facilitating contacts between people and classes.[16]

Recent years have therefore seen a growing acceptance in the industrialised countries of the concept of the protection and planning of historic environments. Conservation has become a special form of planning involving a comprehensive approach for dealing with total environments as against single buildings. However, while conservation has been extensively discussed, debated and practised in the developed world, it remains practically a new concept in the Middle East, as in most Third World areas. Throughout the Middle East the attraction of imported Western technology remains strong; modernisation is still equated with Westernisation, and the traditional heritage despised as backward and unfashionable. Indeed if anything, these processes, both economic and socio-cultural, have accelerated since the dramatic rise in the price of oil in 1973 and the massive increase in revenues accruing to the major oil producers. Almost everywhere the historic centres are under threat either by destruction through large-scale road schemes or decay from within through neglect. Most of İstanbul's historic core has already been destroyed, leaving the great Ottoman mosques isolated and surrounded by modern developments. A recent survey revealed that more than 20 per cent of Baghdād's historic fabric has been lost since the First World War,[17] and even the holy cities of Mecca[18] and Medina[19] have finally succumbed to the sudden, rapid and often ruthless imposition of Western technology.[20]

Against these pressures the concept of conservation has as yet made little effective progress in the Middle East. Legislation and administrative machinery, where it exists, is largely prohibitive in nature and contains no financial incentives or tax reliefs to the owners of private buildings of historic interest. Very few historic towns in the Middle East have documented their cultural heritage, and most vernacular architecture remains unlisted and unprotected. Because of lack of enforcement, legislation, where it exists, has proved ineffective in solving the problems which beset historic areas. Local conservationists are few in number and face a much harder task than their contemporaries in the West. Alongside the torrent of Westernisation and its powerful exponents and many adherents, there is widespread apathy towards the region's cultural heritage and almost total lack of civic action groups. Even formidable personalities such as Hassan Fathy and Saba Shiber, whose ideas and writings on the merits of the region's architectural heritage[21] have won acclaim in the West, have been unable to exert any significant influence over the planning process in the Middle East. Conservation is essentially a Western concept, imported into the region by a few Western planners and architects, and occasionally by local planners educated at Western institutions or Western-oriented national institutions.

The exponents of conservation policies emphasise that the comprehensive and integral approach to planning historic centres is especially relevant to the traditional Middle Eastern city where individual buildings cluster together in such a compact and physically interdependent way that consideration of a single structure is often impossible. The benefits, they argue, can be considerable. They include the retention and restoration of buildings of cultural interest; and overall physical as well as visual improvement in the quality of the urban environment; but also the retention and improvement of the traditional housing stock, even those of minor architectural value, which if destroyed could seriously aggravate the already serious housing shortages affecting most Middle Eastern cities. The attraction of areas of cultural interest for tourism, a major source of revenue for a number of Middle Eastern countries, is considered to be a further advantage favouring the revitalisation of the region's historic cities.[22] Nevertheless, the possible dangers of adopting conservation policies formulated in the West have not been ignored.

The introduction of Western philosophy of conservation, which is accepted largely without question because of its origin, is in itself a very positive pressure on nations whose whole economy and much of its thought process is subject to rapid change. Sheer imitation of established Western procedures will sometimes lead an emergent regime to copy — lock, stock and barrel — conservation ideas (and even legislation) based on Western models without serious analysis of their relevance.[23]

Conservation policies should be formulated to suit the particular conditions of each country, and at the same time be adaptable to the different regions within that country.

Planning the Past — Case Studies of Tunis, Jerusalem and Eşfahān

In the last few years a number of conservation studies have been prepared — largely by foreign planning firms — and various general development plans for Middle Eastern cities also include conservation programmes (see Table 9.1). It would be impossible in the space of this chapter to describe all the conservation projects which have been prepared; some have never left the drawing board, while others gather dust in planning departments, their recommendations ignored and never implemented. Three case examples have therefore been selected of major projects in progress in order to illustrate different approaches to the conservation of the region's historic environments and in particular to highlight the various problems which such programmes encounter.

Tunis

The historic centre or *medina* of Tunis covers an area of 270 ha and contains 140,000 inhabitants, almost a fifth of the population of the city as a whole. After the establishment of the French protectorate in

Table 9.1: Some Conservation Studies Prepared for Middle Eastern Cities

Location	Comments
Fès, Morocco	UNESCO and the Technical Cooperation Bureau of the UN were responsible for the preparation of a master plan for the imperial city of Fès, completed in 1977. Preservation and rehabilitation of the city's historic centre is the main aim of the new plan but proposals are put forward for the whole city, including the medina and the modern appendage. Historic buildings are to be restored and their occupants, many of whom are poor rural migrants, housed elsewhere. (Ref. M.A. Escoffier and M.S. Bianca, *Rapport de Mission* (effectué pour le compte de l'UNESCO à l'atelier du Schēma Directeur de Fès) Fès, September 1976.)
Algiers, Algeria	A study for the renovation and rehabilitation of the Casbah of Algiers was completed in 1971. It was commissioned by the Government-agency COMEDOR (Comité Permanent d'Etudes, de Developpement, d'Organisation et d'Amenagement de l'agglomeration d'Alger) and carried out with the help of Italian specialists. Socio-economic conditions in the Casbah were studied in some detail but only very general recommendations were made about rehabilitation. Little action has been taken since the report was published. (Ref. COMEDOR, *Etude pour la rēnovation et la restructuration de la Casbah d'Alger*, 6 vols., Alger, 1971.)
Tunis, Tunisia	UNESCO sponsored study of conservation and rehabilitation of the medina — Project Tunis/Carthage. Preliminary studies carried out by Association sauvegarde de la Médina (ASM), 1969-74.
Tripoli, Libya	A pilot study has been carried out by Colin Buchanan & Partners to assist the Antiquities Department in their efforts to conserve the old city. The aim is to retain the existing character of the area but provide modern living and working conditions for the inhabitants.
Jerusalem, Israel	Master plan for the old city prepared for the Ministry of the Interior and Municipality of Jerusalem after the Israeli occupation of East Jerusalem in 1967. The work of rehabilitation is now well advanced.
Nazareth, Israel	A comprehensive outline scheme has been prepared, its object being to ensure protection of the holy sites and the preservation of the old city's character.
'Akko, Israel	After preparatory studies and research the central government and the local authority undertook to reconstruct the entire old city.

Table 9.1–*cont.*

Location	Comments
Cairo, Egypt	Official and semi-official measures to reverse the decline of Cairo's medieval core and conserve the monuments there are reviewed in P. Bergne, 'Cairo — can the medieval city be saved', *Architectural Review*, vol. CLXIV, no. 978 (August 1978) 113-26.
Arbīl, Iraq	A feasibility study for the preservation, conservation and revitalisation of the Qala or citadel area was completed in July 1971 for the Directorate General of Planning and Engineering and the then Ministry of Northern Affairs. The work was carried out by the Iraqi architectural firm of Iraq Consult in association with Colin Buchanan & Partners. This study was never implemented, and the citadel has been allowed to fall into further decay. (Ref. Iraq Consult (in association with Colin Buchanan & Partners), *The Qala'a of Arbil — a Feasibility Study for the Preservation, Conservation and Revitalization of a Historic Town*, Baghdād, July 1971.)
Kirkūk, Iraq	A study to conserve and revitalise the citadel area or Qala'a of Kirkūk was prepared by Doxiadis Associates in 1973 in conjunction with a master plan for the city of Kirkūk as a whole. The object of the study was to halt the decline of this historic area by endowing it with those facilities that would enable it to prosper with minimum disruption to the historic fabric. Because of political tensions it seems unlikely that the project will be implemented in the near future. (Ref. D. Ladas, 'Revitalizing a historic citadel', *Ekistics*, vol. 43, no. 256 (March 1977) 140-3.)
Karbalā', Iraq	A master plan for this historic town was prepared in 1974 by the Directorate General of Planning & Engineering. The plan provided for the protection of the old town but did not elaborate on its detailed conservation. (Ref. Directorate of Planning and Engineering, *A Report on the Special Study to Develop the Mosques Area in Karbalā'* (in Arabic), prepared by Adil Said, Baghdād, 1974.)
Mosul, Iraq	The master plan for the city prepared by SCET International, Paris and Dar al-Imara, Baghdād in 1972 included a conservation study of a part of the old town.
Baghdād, Iraq	A conservation study of Kadhimiya, one of the city's four surviving historic cores, was prepared in 1974 by Polservice Consulting Engineers, Warsaw as part of their recommendations for the planning and development of Baghdād to the year 2000.

Table 9.1—*cont.*

Location	Comments
Eşfahān, Iran	Several reports have been prepared by the Shankland Cox Partnership, London for UNESCO since 1968/69 on the preservation of the city and its monuments.
Yazd, Iran	A conservation study forms part of the master plan for the city prepared by a team of experts for the College of Fine Arts and Architecture in 1977.
San'a, Yemen AR	A planning study to develop and preserve the cities of San'a, Al Hudaydah, Ta'izz, Ibb and Dhamar, is being undertaken by Louis Berger International of the US and Kampsax International of Denmark and will be completed in late 1978. The study aims at retaining ancient and distinctive Yemeni architecture.
İstanbul, Turkey	Following a motion for a resolution dated 7 October 1975, the Committee on Culture and Education of the Council of Europe was instructed by the Assembly to prepare a report on the protection of İstanbul's architectural heritage. The report noted that protection plans exist but seem to be having little effect on present developments. Though the major historic monuments such as Topkapi and the Blue Mosque are not at risk, the small monuments and wooden houses in the old district are threatened. They concluded that action to protect İstanbul would demand enormous financial resources, and that it was essential to associate UNESCO and other international organisations in a campaign to safeguard the city. (Ref. *Report on the Protection of the Architectural Heritage of Istanbul*, Council of Europe, Strasbourg, 10 September 1976, Doc. 3845.)

1881 and the construction of a new European-type city to the east of the medina, the historic core was subjected to profound social, economic, cultural and architectural changes. These processes accelerated after independence in 1956 transforming the medina into a low-income residential and commercial area. At the time of independence there was a massive exodus of the high and middle bourgeoisie from the medina to the modern city, and burgeoning suburbs vacated by the exodus of the French settlers. In turn their houses were occupied by a wave of migrants from the countryside; indeed, between 1956 and 1972 the medina became the main reception area for these new urbanites. Today 65 per cent of households living in the medina and 50 per cent of those

in the northern and southern extensions (known as *rbatts*) are migrants; some 38 per cent of the migrant households settled in Tunis
during the first decade of independence. Today densities in the
medina are very high (550 inhabitants per ha) compared with the
average for the city of Tunis (114 inhabitants per ha). Pressure of
numbers has resulted in the subdivision of many traditional houses,
originally single-family residences, but now occupied by several
families. There are 15,000 houses in the medina and rbatts occupied
by 28,000 families; 46 per cent of all families live in one room each.
In the process of subdivision, the nature and meaning of the houses
also changed. The courtyard, originally a private space, became transformed into a public space (in practice an extension to the street)
when the house was occupied by several families. Severe overcrowding, subdivision among poor families possessing few resources (48 per
cent of all households receive an average monthly income of only 20
Tunisian dinars*) and high rates of tenancy (over three-quarters
of households live in rented accommodation) have contributed to the
rapid physical deterioration of the historic city's traditional fabric
through lack of maintenance. Housing conditions are therefore extremely bad — 50 per cent of dwellings are in a poor state of repair,
some lie in ruins — and basic services are poor and outdated — 60
per cent of houses do not possess piped drinking water and 53 per cent
are compelled to use communal lavatories.

Transformed into a low-income popular zone, the medina has
become the most powerful low-income commercial centre in the entire
city. New commercial activities have expanded considerably (particularly textiles and foodstuffs), responding to an increasing popular
demand, and if some traditional trades and crafts have declined, others
have survived and found new markets among the growing number of
foreign tourists who visit the medina every year. Traditional commercial activity, partly adapted to tourism, remains around the Great
Mosque and new tourist shops have expanded along the Rue Djamaa
Zitouna whereas new popular commercial activities have developed
along the north-south axis. There are now some 5,800 shops and workshops in the medina enjoying an annual revenue of between 33 million
and 35 million Tunisian dinars and employing about 16,000 people.
The physical expansion of commercial activities has been achieved by
conversion of residential and public building into commercial spaces,
and productive activities have penetrated all parts of the urban fabric.

---

* 1 Tunisian dinar = £0.7800 (March 1978).

Maintenance of the premises used for commerce and small industries is minimal, aggravating the general deterioration of the traditional fabric.

Maintenance of most of the religious, cultural and educational buildings in the medina is also poor. Since the sale of *habous* properties (religious foundations to manage donated properties, part of the profit being used to maintain the foundation), many of these monuments have been neglected and the majority converted to new uses — housing, storage and workshops. Whereas in 1956 there were 219 *zāwiyas*, only 38 remain today, and only 5 of the medina's 31 *madrasas* retain their original functions.

Faced with the marked physical deterioration in the traditional urban fabric the *Association sauvegarde de la Médina* (ASM), founded in 1968, asked UNESCO for financial support, and in 1969 UNESCO agreed to sponsor a study of the conservation and rehabilitation of the Tunis medina which became known as *Projet Tunis/Carthage* (PTC). Financial support was provided by UNPS, UNESCO and the Tunisian government, and the study was carried out by ASM. The results and recommendations were presented in February 1974.[24]

After carrying out a general socio-economic survey of the medina and investigating the extent of deterioration in the urban fabric, the PTC team made a number of major proposals. They recommended that the entire medina together with the two rbatts should be declared a *secteur de sauvegarder*. Within this area they identified three zones based on the value and quality of the architectural heritage (Figure 9.2).

1. *Zones monumentales à protéger*: those quarters where important concentrations of major monuments are located — principally the western section of the medina. They propose that no modification of the external architecture of the buildings or of their internal structure be permitted in future; traditional structures should be restored and modern architectural intrusions gradually removed.
2. *Zones de protection de la morphologie traditionnelle*: those quarters containing few prestigious monuments and of only modest architectural value. They emphasise the need to preserve the traditional morphology — the courtyard house and the pedestrian street pattern — but permit limited modification and partial renovation of structures.
3. *Zones d'environnement*: areas bordering the medina where it is suggested that construction must not conflict with the architecture and morphology of the historic city.

Figure 9.2: The Tunis Medina: Proposed Planning Zones to Protect the Architectural Heritage (after Association Sauvegarde de la Medina, 1974)

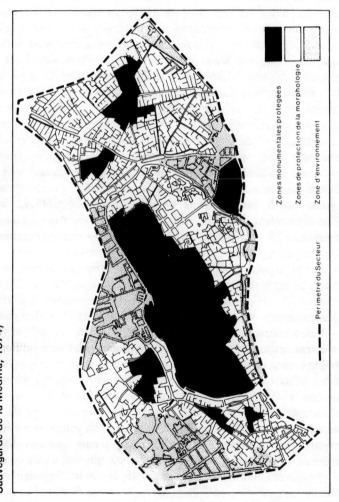

Zones monumentales protegees

Zones de protection de la morphologie

Zone d'environnement

--- Perimetre du Secteur

The PTC team proposed that any rehabilitation of historic monuments and areas should be accompanied by their re-use for appropriate activities — socio-cultural (libraries, museums and cultural centres) and for tourism. Acknowledging that the traditional specialisation of the *sūqs* has been replaced by a new segregation according to income level and socio-economic groups, they suggest that this trend be reinforced, and favour the creation of a high standard tourist and high-income axis (east-west linking the Great Mosque and the Avenue Bourguiba) and the concentration of commercial activities serving low income groups along a north-south axis. For the residential areas, the report is firmly opposed to any large-scale demolition and redevelopment. Instead it emphasises the need to keep the current number of houses — given the city's acute housing shortage and the very low incomes of the medina's inhabitants — and to improve physical conditions for the existing population. It is recognised that most of the tenants are too poor to bear even part of the costs of renovation, and the prevalence of multi-ownership (where a building is owned by more than one person) discourages landlords from investing in the maintenance and improvement of their properties. Although greater use could be made of credits from the *Fonds National pour l'Amélioration de l'Habitat* (FNAH), the report acknowledges that the Tunis Municipality must bear much of the responsibility for the rehabilitation of the medina and the provision of adequate physical and socio-cultural infrastructures.

The PTC report recommended that the ASM be given overall responsibility for co-ordinating the work of conservation and rehabilitation. Unfortunately, in practice the ASM's role has become purely advisory, the consequences of which are clearly illustrated by the Hafsia project. The Hafsia quarter was designated for redevelopment as early as 1928, but it was not until the early years of independence that the insanitary dwellings were finally demolished. The plan prepared by the ASM for the rehabilitation of the central part of this area proposed the reconstruction of the covered bazaars, new houses built in the traditional style for the low-income families who had been displaced, and the maintenance of a pedestrian street network. The actual execution of the programme, however, was carried out by a state company, *Société Nationale d'Investissement Tunisienne*. They ignored ASM's proposal for low-income housing, and, anxious to maximise financial returns from the project, built dwellings for high-income families (those with monthly incomes of over 70 Tunisian dinars).

Certain weaknesses and contradictions in the PTC's basic proposals have also been identified. Much attention is devoted in the report to the causes of poor housing standards and the deterioration in the urban fabric. Owner-occupation is seen as the best guarantee of improved maintenance of properties in the future by encouraging investment on the part of the dwellers themselves. Solutions are put forward to end multiownership of properties, but no mention is made of schemes to give tenants access to ownership or other recognised positive legal forms of tenure. Ben Mahmoud and Santelli have criticised the PTC study because they believe it proposes 'two policies which seem opposite and contradictory in a free market economy. The first one, a money-making rehabilitation: restoration of historic monuments to develop tourist activities. The second one, a non-profit-making rehabilitation: improvement of the existing housing standards of the current population'.[25] They predict that given the dynamics of the market economy, the first policy, the profit-making strategy, will become dominant, and rehabilitation of the medina will quickly become tourist-oriented, a place of speculation for the Tunisian well-to-do. Recent trends appear to confirm their predictions. The major bazaars and the leading historic buildings are being restored in order to attract tourists who will buy the most marketable products of Tunisian handicrafts. Little is being done to improve the living conditions or physical environment of the poor residents and renewal schemes such as the Hafsia project exclude low-income families. The creation of the District of Tunis in 1972 with responsibility for physical planning in the entire Tunis conurbation has further weakened the ASM's influence over planning decisions in the city's historic centre.[26]

Jerusalem

Soon after the Six Day War in 1967 when Israel occupied East Jerusalem, a team of architects were commissioned by the Ministry of the Interior and the Jerusalem Municipality to prepare a town-planning scheme for the Old City of Jerusalem and its immediate environs — notably the Valley of Hinnom to the west and south, and to the east the Valley of Kidron and the slopes of the Mount of Olives, Mount Scopus, the Mount of Offence and Government House Hill.[27] Despite its troubled history, the Old City had preserved much of its medieval character, the result in part of a number of town-planning schemes prepared during the period of British rule in Palestine 1918-48. Whilst not all these recommendations were put into effect, their action ensured that the city walls were preserved, the height of building was restricted, and only local stone was used for construction. Certain historic buildings within the Old City were also restored during this period.

Nevertheless, several urgent problems faced the Israeli planners in 1967. Basic infrastructure was inadequate, and vital public services were absent. More than half of the historic city's 24,000 inhabitants were concentrated in the Muslim Quarter where serious overcrowding had led to the deterioration of both streets and buildings. Most houses were subdivided among several families, each living in one or two rooms; population densities averaged 444 per ha, reaching 1,380 persons per ha in the overcrowded central areas. Parts of the Jewish Quarter, which had fallen into disrepair before the 1948 war, had been partially or totally destroyed during the hostilities, and the area was occupied by poor Arab refugees living in overcrowded dwellings. The central bazaars were in need of extensive repairs; skylights and airvents were broken and the interiors disfigured and poorly maintained. The belt of open spaces just inside the walls, once covered with gardens and reserved for public use, had largely disappeared, and the built-up area extended right up to the walls. All that separated the north and west walls from the densely built-up areas of new Jerusalem adjacent to the historic centre were narrow, overcrowded streets, derelict buildings, temporary shacks and rubble.

The town-planning scheme, completed in 1970, presented the general lines along which the Old City and its environs should be developed and represents part of the overall master plan for Metropolitan Jerusalem. As a preliminary, a comprehensive survey of the entire area was undertaken in order to determine and regulate land use within the zone,

> to demarcate the residential areas, both existing and projected, and prescribe the maximum density and height of their buildings; to designate special sites for religious, cultural and social institutions, public buildings, hotels and pilgrim centres; to preserve areas for archaeological excavations, public open spaces, gardens, parks and nature reserves; and to provide for a variety of public services, including a network of roads to be co-ordinated with the communications master plan for the entire city.[28]

The outline town-planning scheme goes into more detailed planning for the Old City than the rest of the zone with specific recommendations on a number of key issues. The serious encroachment on open space inside the walls is deplored, and it is strongly recommended that the open space and green belt inside the walls be preserved and where possible extended. A minimum distance of 10 m from the walls for new buildings within the historic centre and 75 m from the walls for buildings outside is established. Motorised traffic must be excluded from the historic centre as far as possible, and its character as a pedestrian city preserved. Vehicles should only be allowed in special service lanes, catering for the immediate needs of the population and for emergencies, and should be restricted to fixed hours in the early morning and evening. It is strongly recommended that all new surfacing of streets and alleyways inside the Old City should be in stone as in the past. Taking into account the proposed slum clearance programme for the Muslim Quarter and the new housing schemes for the Jewish Quarter, the planners suggest that the number of residents in the Old City should not exceed 20,000. After a special field survey of significant buildings and monuments in the Old City, many of these sites were registered and classified according to three categories — historical, religious and architectural. The outline town-planning scheme for the historic centre emphasises the importance of preserving these sites, although it is recognised that certain minor changes may be necessary. Such changes should be effected only with the approval of the Special Architectural Commission. As to the architecture of new structures inside the Old City, the scheme limits itself to two main requirements: they must be built in local stone and kept in scale with the existing environment. Any new building, building addition or renewal must be designed as an organic part of the existing ensemble. Outside the city walls the deep valleys of Hinnom and Kidron, the slopes of Siloam village, Yemin Moshe Quarter and the Mount of Olives are to be preserved as part of a National Park already approved by the government. In the rest of the special planning zone, which includes the amphitheatre of hills surrounding the Old City to the south and east, extensive open spaces are demarcated, and strict building regulations are recommended. Most new residential areas are planned as extensions to existing settlements and are intended to house people relocated from the slum quarters of the Old City and also those whose dwellings are on land required for widening roads or marked for archaeological excavation.

Work has already progressed on a number of major projects. A modern drainage and sewage system has been installed in large parts of the historic city, and the old water pipes have also been replaced in streets where the sewage system has been modernised. Work is continuing elsewhere. The labyrinth of overhead electricity cables and telephone wires are being removed and replaced by underground systems, and an intensive effort is being made to remove the forest of television antennae dotting the roofs of the Old City. The Armenian Quarter has already been cleared of private aerials. Restoration work is underway in the main bazaars to clear and repair the facades, replace shutters, vitrines and other fixtures, and install special lighting. Restoration work on the Goldsmith's Bazaar has already been completed. Plans to restore the spacious plazas inside the Yafo and Damascus Gates are well advanced, and a new pedestrian route has been completed linking the two gates. The empty and neglected land in the recessed north-west corner of the city wall has been converted into a paved garden piazza named Zahal Square, and a second piazza is planned on the elevated enclosure outside the city wall, west of the Citadel, and close to the Yafo Gate. In a later phase of the plan, two underground car parks are to be built on underdeveloped land in front of the Damascus and Yafo Gates, and the areas above them may be developed as large public squares with appropriate civic buildings. Motorised traffic will terminate here and access to the historic centre will be restricted to pedestrians.

But the most extensive rehabilitation project involves the reconstruction of the Jewish Quarter, now nearing completion (Figure 9.3). Immediately after regaining control of the Old City the Israeli government decided to reconstruct and resettle the Jewish Quarters demarcated as an area of 14 ha, about 16 per cent of the Old City's total area. Almost half the area had been partially or totally destroyed. A government authority, the Company for Reconstruction and Development in the Jewish Quarter of the Old City, was placed in charge of reconstruction with the aim of developing this quarter 'as a national, religious and historic site, which includes a residential area and public services for its inhabitants and visitors'.[29] The work includes renovation of existing buildings, the completion of partially ruined buildings and complete reconstruction of destroyed and evacuated areas. The many synagogues are either being renovated or newly planned, and some of the *yeshivot* (Jewish religious seminaries) have already been re-established. The commercial centre is being reconstructed as part of the central bazaar system, and an underground terminal close to the south wall is planned for parking and various other services and is to be linked to the commercial centre. Wherever possible the traditional pattern of building has been retained and the building material used is rectangular natural stone. Buildings are two to four storeys high, so as not to spoil the skyline, and many have inner courtyards. Special attention has been given to the replanning of alleyways and squares. The lanes, 2.5 to 4 m wide, are only for pedestrian use, and the shops

Figure 9.3: Master Plan for the Jewish Quarter, Jerusalem (after Sharon, 1973)

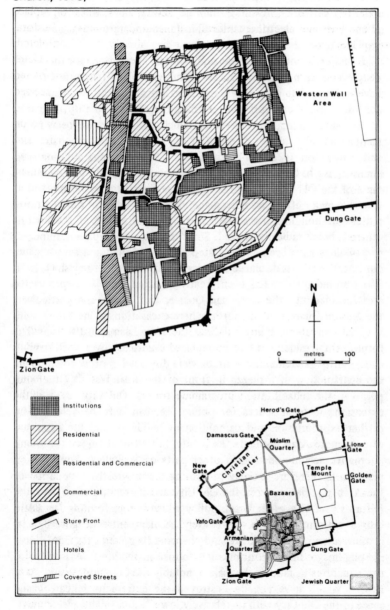

and houses will be serviced by special vehicles suited to negotiate the lanes. To supplement the present poor utility services a new infrastructure network (including drainage, sewage lines, water pipes, telephone lines and electrical cables all installed underground) is now being implemented.

Jerusalem's unique religious and political associations for the Jewish people and its present-day status as the capital of the state of Israel have ensured that abundant public and private funds are made available for the preservation and rehabilitation of the Old City. The scale of this undertaking, the speed at which the plans have been implemented, and the quality of much of the actual work of reconstruction and renovation is certainly impressive. But the rehabilitation programme also has important negative aspects, particularly for the inhabitants of the Old City, the Arab Muslim and Christian majority. For although a major effort has been made to preserve much of the traditional pattern of building, the social and religious structure of the historic centre is being radically altered. Since the Israeli occupation, hundreds of buildings have been expropriated and demolished and several thousand Arab residents displaced in order to reconstruct the Jewish Quarter. The restored quarter has been greatly enlarged, and the expropriated area intrudes into the Armenian Quarter to the west and particularly the Muslim Quarter in the north, where excavations along the western Wall have threatened many buildings, including Islamic institutions. The former Arab residents are to be replaced eventually by Jewish families and yeshivot students. More Arabs were displaced in order to complete the construction of a piazza in front of the West Wall.[30] Other proposals in the rehabilitation programme for the Old City, such as the extension of open spaces for public use, can only be achieved by further expropriation and demolition of buildings, and the expulsion of even more Arab residents. As before, not all of them will be found alternative accommodation in other parts of Jerusalem. Conservation planning is therefore actively promoting the progressive evacuation of the Arab population from the Old City and its repopulation by Jews. It forms part of a wider Israeli policy which is transforming Jerusalem into a uniformly Jewish, aggressively secular centre of government, commerce and entertainment, and changing its sacred sites from places of pilgrimage into profit-making tourist attractions. Massive highrise structures in modern Jerusalem, notably the Commodore and Plaza Hotels, which have already destroyed the extremely delicate visual space of the Old City with its relatively low site and small scale, immortalise in stone and reinforced concrete present Israeli policy.[31]

Figure 9.4: The Major Architectural Features of Eṣfahān
(inset Safavid Eṣfahān *c.* sixteenth century) (after Ardalan and
Bakhtiar, 1973)

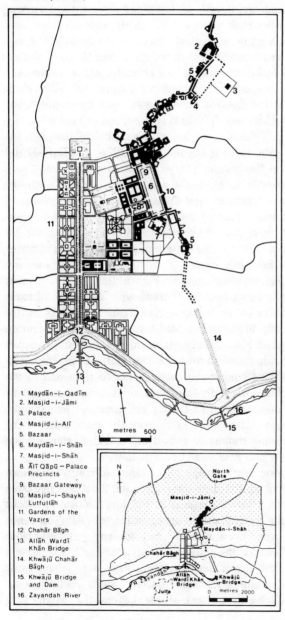

1. Maydān-i-Qadīm
2. Masjid-i-Jāmi
3. Palace
4. Masjid-i-Alī
5. Bazaar
6. Maydān-i-Shāh
7. Masjid-i-Shāh
8. Alī Qāpū – Palace Precincts
9. Bazaar Gateway
10. Masjid-i-Shaykh Lutfullāh
11. Gardens of the Vazirs
12. Chahār Bāgh
13. Allāh Wardī Khān Bridge
14. Khwājū Chahār Bāgh
15. Khwājū Bridge and Dam
16. Zayandah River

Eṣfahān

More than either Tunis or Jerusalem, Eṣfahān is a city where the past still dominates the present. The major architectural features are mainly of the sixteenth and seventeenth centuries and represent the work of the great Safavid ruler Shah Abbas I (1587-1629), who was determined to make Eṣfahān worthy of a great capital. They include the vast Maydān-i-Shah, seven times the size of the Piazza San Marco of Venice, and its associated buildings; much of the extensive bazaar system; the Chahār Bāgh or ceremonial avenue; and the magnificent Allāh Wardī Khān bridge across the Zāyandah river (Figure 9.4). By its unity, and the quality of its monuments Eṣfahān is as important as Venice.[32]

Today, although Eṣfahān is no longer the capital of Iran, it is the country's second city (with a population in 1976 of 672,000) and designated as one of the country's major industrial growth poles. Very rapid population growth, the expansion and modernisation of the urban area, and the establishment of new industries pose a major threat to the city's historic past. Much of the urban fabric of the old city survives, but the historic centre has been cut up by straight roads built for the motor car and unrelated to the pattern of growth or the integrity of the old quarters. Eṣfahān's master plan, prepared by Organic and Associates of Tehrān together with the French architect and planner Beaudouin in 1967, shows the city overlaid with a network of roads which cut the arteries of the old quarters (Figure 9.5). Only part of the plan has actually been implemented but the dramatic and often disastrous consequences are clearly visible in the townscape. Sepah Avenue, one of the first modern roads, brought traffic to the Maydān-i-Shāh and has attracted commercial development to itself and to the Chahār Bāgh which is now solidly lined with stores, offices and cinemas to the detriment of the Maydān's trading activities. A later example, Abdorrazzaq Avenue, actually breaks through the main route of the bazaar, and is drawing commerce away from it and accelerating the decline of an already poorly serviced urban quarter.

Within the historic centre, many of the large old courtyard houses are being demolished so that their owners can sell the subdivided plots or obtain even better financial returns by building multistorey blocks of flats. Indeed the government as an incentive for 'slum' clearance offers exemption from tax for three years for any proprietor who replaces his old house with a new building. This law has become a serious threat to the urban heritage. Its effects are perhaps most evident in Julfa, the former Armenian quarter, which has been radically transformed during the present decade. Beyond the old city new

Figure 9.5: Master Plan for Eşfahān by Organic and Associates and E.E. Beaudouin Showing the Proposed Road Network to be Superimposed on the Old City

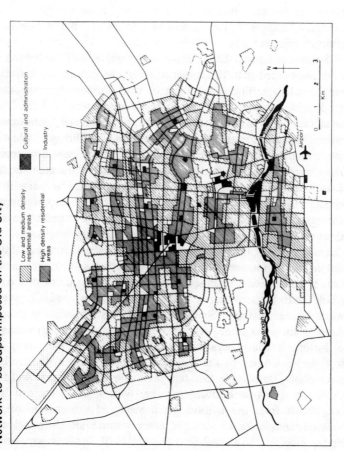

housing is everywhere expanding the limits of the city and eating into the rich agricultural land around. Whether it is private or public, piece-meal or planned, the new constructions are in the European style of flats or two-storey houses. Under the Fifth Development Plan it is the government's avowed policy to encourage apartment living in urban areas. The city is already encircled by industry and the river polluted with its effluent. Further expansion will completely destroy Eşfahān's beautiful rural surroundings leading to total industrialisation of a region stretching from the new steel complex at Aryashahr in the south, to Shahin Shah in the north and from Najafabad in the west to the new airport in the east. Increased traffic flows between these centres will inevitably impose further cross-town journeys on the existing city streets[33] (Figure 9.6).

Successive Iran/UNESCO missions to Eşfahān over the last ten years have emphasised that 'the conservation of the historic town, its monuments and its setting is an object of world importance, national and local pride, and vital for the tourist development of Iran'.[34] They conclude that it is possible to conserve the historic city with its monuments, building groups, squares, gardens and bridges, while also modernising the city and expanding it to absorb new developments. Their reports identify the main pressures which threaten the city's historic heritage and put forward concrete proposals to deal with their impact. Unfortunately, even though two of these reports appeared before publication of the city's master plan by Organic, the advice given by UNESCO over the last decade has been largely ignored.

One of UNESCO's major recommendations was that 'the quality and frequency of monuments is such that, with their setting, their preservation and maintenance cannot be separated from that of the city as a whole'.[35] In practice exactly the opposite has happened. Conservation work has concentrated almost exclusively on the major monuments. After many years of neglect, a new and positive approach to the care of historic buildings began with the appointment of the French architect André Godard to the Directorate of Antiquities in the reign of Reza Shah. During the last ten years the office of the Ministry of Culture and Art in Eşfahān, together with a skilled team of Italian consultants from the Istituto per il Medio ed Estremo Oriente have been responsible for a number of major restorations which include the Friday Mosque, the Chehel Setoon and Ālī Qāpū; plans have also been prepared for the rehabilitation of the Maydān-i-Shāh, the restoration of the Allah Wardī Khān bridge, and the recreation of the royal gardens in the area between Chehel Setoon, Hasht-Behesht and Chahār Bāgh.

Figure 9.6: The Eşfahān Region Showing Existing and Proposed Developments around the Historic City (after Cantacuzino, 1976)

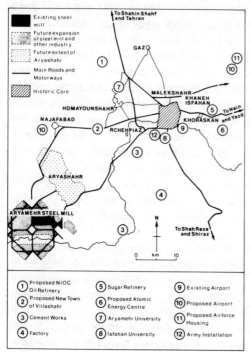

Today, one of the most striking features of Eşfahān is the remarkable condition of its famous cultural and historic monuments; but the wider objectives of conservation — the preservation not only of the monuments but their relationship to each other and the conservation of the urban fabric which make up the historic structure of the city — have been neglected.[36] 'What is required is not only the preservation of the fabric of the building but the retention of its social and urban significance through its setting.'[37]

Since the early 1970s, however, the Eşfahān Office of the Ministry of Culture and Art has at least begun to appreciate the importance of proper conservation planning. They have strongly criticised the master plan and have succeeded in obtaining some fundamental changes. It has now been accepted that further expansion of the built-up area must be prohibited, and the limits of the urban area established on the line of present building activities. Furthermore, the Ministry of Housing is being asked to transfer money which would have been devoted to new suburban housing to finance the rehabilitation of old houses within the historic city. This new emphasis on rehabilitation is encouraging, and Organic have calculated that some 400,000 extra people could live in the city if the traditional houses were repaired and converted. As a preliminary step they have set up a pilot project in Dardasht,[38] the old quarter north of the bazaar area and west of the Friday Mosque. The intention is to avoid a purely architectural solution which would result in the depopulation of the historic centre and its transformation into a dead museum-like area. Instead, the existing population are being encouraged to stay, residential buildings are to be maintained in residential use, and the local population involved in the work of restoration and rehabilitation through an education programme. The aim is to adapt the traditional fabric of the quarter to the demands of modern life, to provide access and services, to re-use existing buildings or find new uses for them by restoring, converting or even adding to them where required, and to secure the active participation of the inhabitants in the project.

Organic, under pressure from the Ministry of Culture and Art, have also agreed to abandon certain projected road schemes, although they have not yet accepted the need to stop all further road-building in the historic centre. The Eşfahān office believe that the existing structure of new roads imposed over the older pedestrian pattern must be accepted and that the old structure cannot resist the new. However, they are convinced that the influx of modern traffic must be modified and regulated in order to minimise damage to existing structures.

Another positive development has been creation of a co-ordinating committee, the first of its kind in Iran, set up by the late Empress with representatives from all the authorities concerned with the planning and future development of the city. At the moment, responsibility for the planning and development of Eşfahān and its region is shared by the municipality and several ministries with the result that decisions are often taken independently of and in some cases in conflict with each other. This inadequate and unsatisfactory administrative structure has been a major constraint on proper conservation planning. The new committee is intended to produce a more co-ordinated approach to the solution of the city's problems. It has already secured agreement that further migration to Eşfahān and industrial expansion in and around the city must be stopped, but at the moment it lacks the legal powers to enforce its decisions and has already been overruled on a number of occasions. A recent UNESCO report concluded that in reality the key to decision-making on development issues lies in the particular strength and influence of ministerial and government personalities and the degree of importance they may attach to the master plan and the conservation of Eṣfahān.[39]

Significantly, there is still no comprehensive social and economic development strategy for the city region as a whole, and yet it is only within the framework of a regional plan, in which conservation of the historic city forms an important objective, that conflicting priorities can be evaluated and the physical development of the region viewed in total. Unless there is effective co-ordination and recognition of the value and importance of conservation planning, the historic city will be destroyed.

Conclusion

The balance sheet to date is gloomy. Destruction of the historic fabric of the Middle Eastern city continues, and throughout the region both the pace and scale of redevelopment has increased dramatically during the last decade. Few conservation plans have actually been implemented, and the examples reviewed reveal not only the difficulties encountered but also draw attention to a number of important negative aspects which have appeared. Indeed, it could be argued that in most conservation schemes in the Middle East attention has focused almost exclusively on the most profitable projects, often geared to an expanding tourist market, while the poor inhabitants of the historic centres have either been totally neglected or in some cases forced out to make way for new tourist developments or rehabilitation schemes which benefit higher income groups. If this trend continues there is a real danger that in the future only fragments of the historic heritage will survive, surrounded by a sea of modern development with the monuments deprived of life and function, reduced to mere relics of the past for tourists to visit. Conservation planning must avoid simply the static preservation of a past architectural pattern and the fossilisation of lifestyles. A conservation area should not be a dead area. What are urgently required are conservation policies which not only maintain the essential quality of the historic city through urban form, height of buildings, character and scale, but which also encourage change and modernisation, providing facilities necessary to improve the lives of the inhabitants. Historic towns, like living organisms, have evolved in the past and must be allowed to evolve now and renew their cells in order to stay alive. All cities incorporate elements of architecture and planning which are as valid today as they were in the past, and which should therefore be preserved; other elements have to be altered or adapted to changes in social and economic conditions; and some have become obsolete and should be replaced.[40] New buildings, however, must be designed to fit in, in scale and style, with existing structures. The architectural heritage of the past must not be rejected but utilised selectively together with new design concepts and relevant new technology to create buildings with modern amenities which are in harmony rather than conflict with the existing urban fabric.[41] The aim of architects and planners should be modernisation without blind Westernisation. In this way we may at last begin to repair the sharp break in the evolutionary process of urban development which lies at the heart of the conservation problem.

In order to achieve a new and positive approach to conservation planning there must be a more radical dimension to research in architectural design in Middle Eastern countries; urban land reform to limit the commercial exploitation of urban land and property, curb speculation and provide tenants with access to ownership; and finally, new forms of political and administrative organisation for the city which will operate effectively at the level of the urban quarter, encouraging public participation and involvement in the rehabilitation of historic centres. At present the forces opposed to such policies are numerous and powerful. They include urban landlords, speculators, many architects and planners, the major construction companies, and especially important, their political allies. For ultimately policies are politics, and it is no revelation that they are formulated to serve the interests of the politically powerful — after all, what else are policies for? In the end, therefore, only profound political change can arrest the destructive processes which are currently transforming the historic centres of the Middle East and permit new planning policies which will secure healthy urban development in the future. It may already be too late.

References

1. J.L. Abu-Lughod, 'Developments in North African urbanism: the process of decolonization', in B.J.L. Berry (ed.), *Urbanization and Counter-urbanization*, Urban Affairs Annual Reviews, vol. 11 (Sage Publications, Beverley Hills, California, 1976), p. 205.

2. *Etude pour la rénovation et la restructuration de la Casbah d'Alger; Les transformations du tissu de la Casbah pendant la période coloniale*, Comité Permanent d'Etudes, de Developpement d'Organisation et d'Amenagement de l'agglomeration d'Alger (COMEDOR) (Alger, 1971).

3. K. Scharlau, 'Moderne Umgestaltung im grundriss Iranischer Städte', *Erdkunde*, vol. 15, no. 3 (1961) 180-91.

4. S. Cantacuzino, 'Aleppo', *Architectural Review*, no. 944 (October 1975) 241-50.

5. E. Fethi, 'Urban conservation in Iraq with special reference to Baghdad', unpublished PhD thesis, Department of Town and Regional Planning (University of Sheffield, 1977), vol. 1, 100-17, 125-82.

6. *Göynük – A Town in a Timber Region*, Department of Restoration, Faculty of Architecture (Middle East Technical University, Ankara, 1970).

7. S. Antonius, *Architecture in Lebanon* (Beirut, 1965).

8. S.G. Shiber, 'Kuwait: a case study', in L.C. Brown (ed.), *From Madina to Metropolis – Heritage and Change in the Near Eastern City* (The Darwin Press, Princeton, 1973) pp. 168-93.

9. J.L. Abu-Lughod, 'Problems and policy implications of Middle Eastern urbanization', in *Studies on Development Problems in Selected Countries of the Middle East, 1972* (United Nations, New York, 1973), p. 53.

10. V. Costello, 'The industrial structure of a traditional Iranian city', *Tijdschrift voor economische en sociale geografie*, vol. 64, no. 2 (1973) 108-20.

11. J.L. Abu-Lughod, 'Developments in North African urbanism', 207.

12. E.H. Eckert and J. El-Kefi, 'L'espace traditionnel de la ville de Tunis, La Médina et les deux Rbat: faubourg ou gourbiville', in *Les influences occidentales dans les villes Maghrébines à l'époque contemporaine*, Etudes Méditerranéennes 2 (Editions de l'Université de Provence, 1974), pp. 211-35.

13. P. Gazzola, 'Back to the agora', in *The Conservation of Cities* (Croom Helm, London and The UNESCO Press, Paris, 1975), p. 58.

14. M. Fried, 'Grieving for a lost home; psychological costs of relocation', in *Urban Renewal: The Record and the Controversy* (MIT Press, 1966), p. 359.

15. H. Daifuku, 'Urban retrieval too', in *The Conservation of Cities* (Croom Helm, London and The UNESCO Press, Paris, 1975), pp. 9-23.

16. P. Gazzola, 'Back to the agora', pp. 57-8.

17. I. Fethi, 'Urban conservation in Iraq', 428.

18. S.A.S. El-Hamdan, 'The pilgrimage to Mecca – a study of the physical planning problems with special reference to the increasing numbers of pilgrims and changing modes of travel', unpublished PhD thesis, Department of Town and Regional Planning (University of Sheffield, 1976), vol. 2, pp. 405-10.

19. A.H.M. El-Sayed, 'Conservation and development in the historic centre of Medina', unpublished MA thesis, Faculty of Architectural Studies (University of Sheffield, 1976).

20. Ironically, as the Middle Eastern countries are busily destroying their urban heritage, some planners and architects in the West are beginning to appreciate the values of the traditional Middle Eastern city or medina. Bianca, for example, conscious of the general failure of architecture and planning in the West, sees the medina as an alternative solution to contemporary urban problems. S. Bianca, 'The Islamic city: physical layout', a paper read at a Colloquium on the Islamic city held in Cambridge, England, 19-23 July 1976, 1-2.

21. H. Fathy, 'Constancy, transposition and change in the Arab city', in L.C. Brown (ed.), *From Madina to Metropolis*, pp. 319-33; S.G. Shiber, *Recent Arab City Growth* (Government Printing Press, Kuwait, 1967).

22. G. Shankland, 'Why trouble with historic towns?' in *The Conservation of Cities* (Croom Helm, London and The UNESCO Press, Paris, 1975), pp. 24-42.

23. J. Warren, 'Conservation in Islam', *The Architect* (June 1970) 20.

24. Projet Tunis/Carthage, *Sauvegarde et mise en valeur de la Médina de Tunis, Rapport de synthèse: Dossier No 1 Protection du patrimoine monumental; Dossier No 2 Mise en valeur des monuments historiques; Dossier No 3 Patrimoine*

immobilier; Dossier No 4 Descriptif et estimation sommaire des coûts —
Hypothèse de financement; Dossier No 5 Activités opérationnelles de l'A.S.M.;
Dossier No 6 Opérations de réhabilitation de l'îlot 111 E-50; Dossier No 7
Artisanat — propositions de développement; Dossier No 8 Commerce: principes
d'une politique commerciale (Tunis, 1974).

25. W. Ben Mahmoud and S. Santelli, 'What to do with medina', *Ekistics*,
vol. 38, no. 227 (October 1974) 263.

26. District of Tunis, *Schéma directeur d'aménagement et d'urbanisme:*
Rapport d'Orientation (Tunis, December 1975).

27. A. Sharon, *Planning Jerusalem: the Old City and Its Environs* (Weidenfeld
& Nicolson, Jerusalem, 1973).

28. Ibid., p. 139.

29. Ibid., p. 177.

30. A critical analysis of the outline planning scheme for the Old City,
together with a well-documented account of the expropriation and demolition
of Arab property and the expulsion of the residents can be found in A.M.
Goichon, *Jérusalem — fin de la ville universelle* (G.P. Maisonneuve et Larose,
Paris, 1976). See also N. Nazzal, 'The encirclement of Jerusalem', *Middle East*
International, no. 80 (February 1978) 18-20.

31. A. Kutcher, *The New Jerusalem, Planning and Politics* (Thames and
Hudson, London, 1973).

32. M.F. Siroux, 'Iran: the vitality of Isfahan', in *The Conservation of Cities*
pp. 146-58.

33. S. Cantacuzino, 'Can Isfahan survive?' in *Isfahan* by S. Cantacuzino and
K. Browne, a special issue of *The Architectural Review*, vol. CLIX, no. 951
(1976) 293-330.

34. G. Shankland, *The Planning of Isfahan; a Report to UNESCO* (Shankland
Cox and Associates, London, 1967-8), p. 14. Also D. Walton, *The Planning of*
Isfahan No 2; a Report to UNESCO (Shankland Cox and Associates, London,
1968); A. Meats, *The Planning and Conservation of Isfahan; a Draft Report to*
UNESCO (Shankland Cox Partnership, London, 1974).

35. G. Shankland, *The Planning of Isfahan*, p. 10.

36. This ill-conceived 'monument — object' approach has been adopted in
other Iranian towns, e.g. Mashhad, Hamadan and Shīrāz, where the policy has
been to 'free' major monuments and large public buildings from their surroundings by demolishing a 100 m zone around, thus removing them from their context
and historic setting. In some cases the monuments themselves have been rebuilt.

37. A. Meats, *Planning and Conservation of Isfahan*, p. 9.

38. N. Faghih, 'Rehabilitation in Dardasht' in *Isfahan* by S. Cantacuzino and
K. Browne, a special issue of *The Architectural Review* (1976) 315-19.

39. A. Meats, *Planning and Conservation of Isfahan*, p. 6.

40. G.H. Blake and R.I. Lawless, 'Continuity and change — the example of
Tlemcen, a pre-colonial town in western Algeria', *Architectural Association*
Quarterly, vol. 6, no. 1 (1974) 38-46.

41. On this subject see N. Ardalan, 'A new town in Iran: a case study of the
integration of traditional principles with contemporary needs and opportunities',
a paper presented to a Colloquium in the Islamic City, held in Cambridge,
England, 19-23 July 1976 (a description of the design process of Bandar
Sharpour, a new town under construction on the Gulf); and H. Fathy, 'Constancy, transposition and change', 332-3 (includes a description of a planning
experiment for New Baghdad in which old concepts of city and house design were
applied to high-rise buildings).

10 THE SMALL TOWN

G.H. Blake

Introduction

Small towns have been neglected to an astonishing degree in both academic studies and official planning documents concerned with Middle Eastern urbanisation. Many publications make no more than a passing reference to towns with fewer than 20,000 inhabitants, while those below 10,000 are likely to be ignored altogether. Yet small towns are neither unimportant nor uninteresting. In the last 25 years the number of settlements in the 5,000 to 20,000 population range has more than doubled, and in some countries they accommodate a higher proportion of the total national population than in the past, although their growth rates tend to be more modest than those of the large cities. A whole range of questions require investigation concerning both individual towns and the functions of small towns within urban networks and hierarchies. The regional functions of the traditional small town of the Middle East are still incompletely understood, with regard to the role of town-dwellers in agriculture and land ownership, and in marketing. The few studies attempted on both topics have proved extremely fruitful, but much remains to be done, particularly outside the Maghreb where urban studies are more plentiful than elsewhere.[1] Much uncertainty also surrounds the causes of population change in small towns, with some growing rapidly and others stagnating or in decline. Knowledge of the role of migration is very vague because of the inadequacy of census data, but even where figures are available they have not been put to effective use, except in a few isolated examples.[2] A number of small towns have lost substantial numbers of inhabitants as refugees. The Jews who left the Maghreb after 1948 had often represented a substantial proportion of the population of certain small towns, and the impact of their departure must have been profound.[3] Political upheavals have similarly disrupted the life of small towns in Libya, Turkey, Palestine and Lebanon, while the Kurdish rebellion is thought to have caused the rapid growth of certain northern Iraqi towns, such as Dhok and Zakho, between 1957 and 1965.[4]

It is not only geographers who neglect small towns. Studies of particular small towns are rare in all the social sciences, and for several Middle Eastern countries are virtually non-existent. In an extensive survey of urban studies in the Middle East covering 335 references, Bonine found scarcely a dozen directly concerned with small towns, and four of these were in Turkey.[5] The counter-attraction of village studies may explain why anthropologists and sociologists have had little time for small-town studies. Unlike the village, small towns cannot be studied as communities 'in the round'; to be properly understood their long and sometimes complex settlement history has to be un- ravelled, together with the spatial relationship of the town with neigh- bouring centres, and the intricate patterns of interactions between communities within the town.[6] Large towns are more amenable to research, with the possibility of access to documentation and basic statistics which are often unobtainable for small towns. In many ways, the smaller the town, the more difficult becomes the problem of data collection and interpretation. Small towns tend to be suffused with local cultural influences, and may reflect regional diversity associated with powerful rural links. In contrast the problems of the large cities are superficially similar to those of Europe and North America for which theoretical models and research techniques are available. Central governments have also reinforced the preoccupation with large towns by giving priority to them in planning strategies and capital investment.

How Many Small Towns Are There in the Middle East?

Incredibly, it is virtually impossible to estimate the number of small towns in the Middle East. In the first place, there is no universal defini- tion of 'urban', which is only to be expected in a region with such diversity in the origins and scale of national urban systems. Definitions use such different criteria that national statistics concerning numbers of towns and urban populations are not strictly comparable. Nine countries regard administrative status as a prime indicator of a town, regardless of population size. Iran for example counts all Shahrestan centres of any size, and all places with over 5,000 inhabitants as towns. Israel counts all settlements with over 2,000 inhabitants, except those in which at least one third of the heads of household earn their living from agriculture. The Jordanian definition is more elaborate, counting all district centres, localities of over 10,000 inhabitants (excluding Palestinian refugee camps in rural areas) and those localities of 5,000 to 9,000 inhabitants and the suburbs of Amman in which two thirds or more of the economically active males are not engaged in agriculture. Turkey includes all the localities which function as provincial or district capitals.[7] Such administrative criteria lead to the inclusion of some very small settlements in 'urban' statistics. The 1975 census of Turkey records 162 district capitals with fewer than 5,000 inhabitants, and 18 with fewer than 2,000 inhabitants.[8] The inadequacy of census data for certain countries is an additional obstacle to the accurate enumeration of small towns in the Middle East. No reliable data could be found concerning settlements in the 5,000 to 9,999 population range for Iraq, Jordan, Lebanon, Oman, Qatar, Saudi Arabia, and PDR Yemen, or for Lebanon, Oman, Qatar and PDR Yemen in the 10,000 to 19,999 population range.

For the purpose of attempting to give some idea of the number of small towns in the Middle East, all settlements in the 5,000 to 20,000 population range were counted. Table 10.1 shows that in those territories for which reasonable figures are available there are 738 settlements in the 5,000 to 9,999 range with 5.4 million inhabitants, an average size of about 7,300. In recent years there has been a considerable increase in the number of settlements in this category, particularly in the more populous countries. In Turkey the number rose from 113 in 1950 to 267 in 1975, and in Iran from 80 in 1956 to 163 in 1976.[9] Exactly how many of the total are genuine urban centres is an open question. Some are undoubtedly large villages with a high proportion of agricultural inhabitants and poorly developed regional functions. Many however are small mining towns, ports and the like, or rural centres which have managed to acquire urban functions. The processes whereby this transition occurs deserve investigation on a massive scale. What are the implications of the acquisition of local administrative functions for a small settlement? Who finances the new urban functions? What part is played by changes in local agriculture, or communications? Do rural migrants create fresh demands for goods and services? And what is the role of government planning, particularly regarding industrial location? The answers might throw light on the great variation in rates of growth of towns in this category. The majority appear to grow at about the rate of natural increase, but in some countries their growth rates have exceeded those of medium-sized towns.

Settlements in the 5,000 to 9,999 range tend to represent a rather smaller share of total national populations than previously, though the decline has been modest. In Egypt their share fell from 3.9 per cent in 1947 to 0.6 per cent in 1970; in Iran from 10.6 per cent in 1956 to 3.4 per cent in 1976; in Morocco from 1.3 per cent in 1960 to 1.2 per cent in 1971, and from 6.8 per cent in 1966 to 6.2 per cent in 1975 in Tunisia. Only Turkey shows an increase, from 3.6 per cent in 1950 to 4.4 per cent in 1975.[10]

It can be safely assumed that a high proportion of settlements with

Table 10.1: Settlements with 5,000 to 9,999 Inhabitants

Country	Year	Settlements	Population	Source
Algeria	1966	79[b]	950,900[b]	(A)
Bahrain	1971	3	19,400	(A)
Egypt[a]	1970	15	79,600	(B)
Gaza	1967	1	7,600	(C)
Iran	1976	163	1,123,100	(B)
Israel	1975	25	168,200	(E)
Jordan West Bank	1967	6	43,700	(C)
Kuwait	1970	18	134,600	(A)
Libya	1973	15	52,800	(B)
Morocco	1971	28	193,700	(B)
Syria	1970	58	400,400	(D)
Tunisia	1975	48	349,500	(B)
Turkey	1975	267	1,786,200	(B)
United Arab Emirates	1968	1	8,800	(A)
Yemen AR	1975	11	69,900	(B)

Notes
  a. Official towns only.
  b. Figures suspect, since the average size is over 12,000.

Sources
(A)   United Nations, *Demographic Yearbook 1971* (New York, 1972).
(B)   National censuses at date shown.
(C)   Central Bureau of Statistics, *Census of Population 1967* (West Bank, Gaza, Sinai, Golan Heights) (Jerusalem, 1967).
(D)   United Nations, *Demographic Yearbook 1973* (New York, 1974).
(E)   *Statistical Abstract of Israel*, no. 27 (1976) Jerusalem, 1977.

10,000 to 19,999 inhabitants are genuine towns. Only in Egypt are there likely to be rural settlements of this size whose urban status is dubious, and these are in any case excluded from Table 10.2. According to Table 10.2, there are more than 560 towns with 10,000 to 19,999 inhabitants. The total population of the countries listed at the dates for which figures are given was 182.5 million, 4.5 per cent of which lived in towns of this size. These figures are of limited value because of the absence of proper statistics for Lebanon, Oman, Qatar and PDR Yemen, and the variety of dates for which information was obtainable. The figure of one town in this category for the whole of Saudi Arabia also seems suspect, but was derived from authoritative sources by

Table 10.2: Towns with 10,000 to 19,999 Inhabitants

Country	Year	Towns	Population	Percentage of national population	Source
Algeria	1966	46	970,841	8.2	(A)
Bahrain	1971	2	21,883	10.1	(A)
Egypt	1970	57	579,500	4.1	(B)
Gaza[a]	1967	3	32,174	9.0	(C)
Iran	1976	93	1,277,296	3.8	(J)
Iraq	1965	19	266,487	3.2	(D)
Israel	1975	23	309,217	9.2	(E)
Jordan	1975	12	141,527	5.2	(F)
Jordan West Bank[a]	1967	3	36,828	6.1	(C)
Kuwait	1970	8	104,498	14.0	(A)
Lebanon	1977	5	75,000	2.7	(G)
Libya	1973	4	54,573	2.4	(J)
Morocco	1971	25	362,704	2.3	(J)
Oman	1977	2	40,000	5.0	(G)
PDR Yemen	1977	2	30,000	1.7	(G)
Qatar	1977	Nil	—	—	(G)
Saudi Arabia	1972	1	19,000	1.2	(K)
Syria	1970	28	372,931	6.0	(I)
Tunisia	1975	35	517,825	9.3	(J)
Turkey[b]	1975	194	2,886,806	7.2	(J)
United Arab Emirates	1968	Nil	—	—	(A)
Yemen AR	1975	3	52,393	1.0	(A)
Middle East		565	8,151,483	4.5	

Notes
a. Excluding refugee camps.
b. Towns with 10,000 to 25,000 inhabitants.

Sources:
(A) United Nations, *Demographic Yearbook 1971* (New York, 1972), pp. 382-7.
(B) W.A.E. Abd el-Aal, 'Spatial patterns of population dynamics in Egypt 1947-70', unpublished PhD thesis (University of Durham, 1977), Table 8.21.
(C) Central Bureau of Statistics, *Census of Population, 1967* (West Bank, Gaza, Sinai, Golan Heights) (Jerusalem, 1967), Tables 2 and 6.
(D) R.I. Lawless, in *The Populations of the Middle East and North Africa*, ed. J.I. Clarke and W.B. Fisher (ULP, London, 1972), p. 123.
(E) *Statistical Abstract of Israel*, no. 27 (1976) Jerusalem, 1977, p. 27.
(F) *Estimate of Population, Demographic Section, Department of Statistics*, Amman, 1976, 1 sheet (Arabic).
(G) Author's estimates.
(H) R. McGregor, in *The Populations of the Middle East and North Africa*, eds. J.I. Clarke and W.B. Fisher (ULP, London, 1972), pp. 31 and 224-8.
(I) United Nations, *Demographic Yearbook 1973* (New York, 1974), p. 390.
(J) National Censuses at date shown.
(K) N.C. Grill, 'Urbanisation in the Arabian Peninsula', unpublished MA thesis (University of Durham, 1977), p. 133.

Grill.[11] In spite of several defects, the aggregate figures for the Middle East are probably of the right order. It is worth noting that the number of people who live in towns of 10,000 to 19,999 inhabitants now greatly outnumber the nomads of the Middle East who continue to receive much attention from social scientists. A few years ago it seems likely that a higher proportion of the population of the Middle East inhabited towns of this size. Several countries have recorded a marked decline; in 1947 9.6 per cent of Egypt's population lived in towns of this class size, but by 1970 the proportion was 4.1 per cent. In Iran 14.7 per cent lived in towns of 10,000 to 24,999 in 1956, but by 1976 only 3.8 per cent lived in towns of 10,000 to 19,999, a difference not accounted for by the different bases for calculation. Other countries however show an increase: Turkey from 5.3 per cent in 1950 to 7.2 per cent in 1975, and Tunisia from 6.7 per cent in 1966 to 9.3 per cent in 1975.[12]

Taken together, Tables 10.1 and 10.2 speak volumes for the potential of small-town studies. If anything, they understate the position in 1978 since the number of centres in the 10,000 to 19,999 range has continued to rise through the 1970s. There are also many small towns which fall just outside this arbitrary size range. Some writers clearly regard towns of up to 30,000 as small towns.[13] Others, such as Bujra's anthropological study of Hureidah are concerned with populations well below 5,000.[14] Indeed the concept of 'small towns' is largely subjective. In the past, urban populations of over 10,000 were by no means regarded as small. They are perceived as small towns in the modern Middle East by virtue of being ranked towards the base of a hierarchy dominated by one or two cities with several hundred thousand inhabitants. It is astonishing that some of the leading cities of the past possessed quite small populations, yet their trade links and political influence may have extended for hundreds of kilometres.[15] Even today some small towns are the focal point for a hinterland of hundreds of square kilometres. Such towns loom large in the lives of the rural populations they serve, and in some instances, dominate.

Types of Small Town

The thousand or so small towns of the Middle East represent an immense variety of urban types fulfilling a great range of functions. In very broad terms, three categories may be recognised; modern foundations of the nineteenth and twentieth centuries; rural settlements which, for a number of reasons, have grown to acquire urban characteristics, and the old regional centres many of which have fulfilled urban functions, with fluctuating fortunes, for several centuries. In the absence of any serious study of the matter, one can only speculate as to the number of towns in each category. Probably a quarter are modern foundations, half are traditional regional centres, and the rest are urbanising rural settlements. The proportion in each category obviously varies greatly from country to country.

Many towns founded in the nineteenth and twentieth centuries have already grown far beyond the 20,000 mark, and others are destined to do so. During the French colonial period in the Maghreb a number of new towns were founded in regions of modern agriculture and European colonisation, particularly in Algeria. These were primarily market towns, and regional service centres some of which assumed the function of garrison towns. Most grew up from indigenous settlements, but others were entirely new foundations. In time all acquired the stamp of French colonial urban planning; Souk El Ghozlane (formerly Aumale) in Algeria, and Souk El Arba in Morocco are examples. Towns primarily associated with tourism were also a legacy of the French; Ifrane and Martil in Morocco, for example.[16]

A surprising number of new ports have appeared throughout the Middle East in modern times. These include ports specialising in mineral exports (e.g. Beni Saf in Algeria), and numerous oil-exporting terminals whose populations often remain small. Fao for example was originally a dredger port, but has become Iraq's chief oil-exporting port and a town of growing importance. Even in the last decade new ports have been built, notably in the Arabian peninsula, to cope with the spiralling volume of imports. Some, such as Jubayl (Saudi Arabia) and Jebel Ali (United Arab Emirates) are planned to become the focal point for new urban communities. Historically, changing patterns of trade have no doubt been the cause for the rise and fall of a great number of small coastal towns,[17] and the process is not over yet. Modern mining activities have also created small towns in the Middle East, most of which are likely to remain small and little known, for example Redeyef (Tunisia, phosphates), Divriği (Turkey, iron ore) and Maden (Turkey, copper). Small inland towns associated with the oil industry are of similar character, such as Abqaiq and Dhahran in Saudi Arabia (Figure 10.1).

The total number of small towns is also swollen by two other types of modern foundation. First, Israel has about 50 new towns in the 5,000 to 19,999 category. Israel's small towns were originally conceived as a way of achieving national population dispersion, and as local service centres for the rural population.[18] The results are not an unqualified

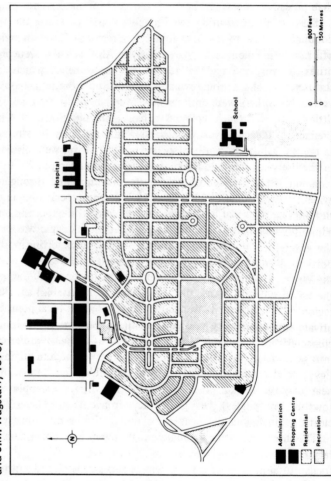

Figure 10.1: Dhahran in Saudi Arabia, Founded in 1935 as Headquarters of Aramco (P. Beaumont, G.H. Blake and J.M. Wagstaff, 1976)

success. Israel is such a small country that the smallest towns are easily by-passed in favour of larger centres. In the Negev, however, far from the big cities, half a dozen small desert towns are flourishing. Secondly, satellite settlements in the vicinity of certain major cities probably feature in small-town statistics, notably around Cairo and Baghdād. Unquestionably urban developments, usually constructed in the last two decades, they are parts of large metropolitan complexes rather than proper small towns.

Settlements in the 5,000 to 19,999 population range have probably doubled in number during the last 25 years or so, and there is plenty of evidence to suggest that a significant proportion of the total comprises established towns, or rural settlements in transition to urban status. Inquiry into the scale of this transition and the processes involved is probably the most pressing need in small-town studies, but little has been attempted. One notable exception is the recent work of Prenant in Algeria, who estimated that no fewer than 73 small centres in the 3,000 to 27,000 population range acquired urban characteristics in the 10 years 1966-76.[19] Prenant shows that different causes were paramount in different regions, although two influences were generally evident; the diffusion of industries largely through government activities and the creation of new *chefs-lieux* in the reorganisation of local administration (Figure 10.2). The improvement of social services by the government helped retain the populations of small centres, a proportion of whom had been uprooted from their village homes during the War of Independence. Similar factors may be underlying causes for the urbanising of rural settlements in other countries. In the Sahel region of Tunisia for example, manufacturing industries established by private entrepreneurs and overseas investors appear to be creating urban characteristics in several large villages.[20] The dispersion of industries into small urban centres or rural settlements has not been a feature of Egypt, but some villages are functioning as dormitories for workers near certain large industrial complexes. In one village near the steel town of Helwan, the urbanising influence of industrial employment is clearly evident.[21]

The third major category of small towns is the well-established regional centre. This includes oasis towns which may have been the focus for long-distance trade routes for centuries, and towns functioning as central places for a rural population, typically within a radius of 20 to 30 km. Most feature prominently as markets for local produce, and in some regions of the Middle East they are an integral part of a complex system of periodic markets, spatially and temporally

Figure 10.2: 'Urbanising' Villages in the Kabylia Region, Northern Algeria; Draa Ben Khedda and Kherrata (after A. Prenant, 1977)

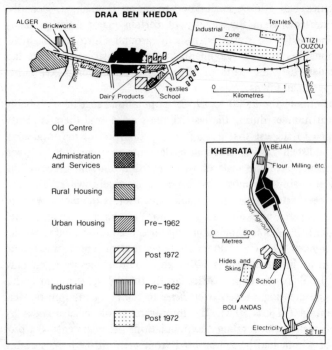

interlocking. These markets have received less attention in the Middle East than almost any other part of the developing world.[22] Many market towns are also the headquarters of the smallest unit of local government organisation. There are altogether several hundred such regional centres displaying an extraordinary variety of townscapes and activities. It is among these old centres that the biggest contrasts in economic and social status are encountered, and as a group they are most in need of effective planning strategies. As with the urbanising rural settlements discussed above, a few have benefited from industrial developments in recent years, or from some other revitalising economic impetus made possible by favourable location, or government intervention. Others have experienced a marked deterioration of economic fortune. The widespread decline of craft industries has profoundly affected many small towns. Nedroma in Algeria for example had 450 craftsmen in 1954 (population 7,600) compared with 332 in 1966 (population 12,600), but two-thirds of these were engaged in a new type of weaving largely controlled by interests outside the town.[23] Thus the real decline in Nedroma's traditional crafts was greater than these figures suggest.

The case of Tütüneli (a pseudonym), a small town in south-west Turkey admirably described by Benedict,[24] exemplifies the nature of decline resulting from the obsolescence of vital functions. With 4,600 inhabitants in 1965, the town was made the administrative centre (*Kaza merkazi*) for 13 villages in 1954. Benedict argues that Tütüneli's regional influence is weaker today than it was before the 1920s when urban-based landowners or *ağas* controlled most of the land and acted as community leaders in administrative and judicial affairs. Instead of being the seat of final authority for the villagers, Tütüneli has become 'but the first of many impersonal steps in initiating contact with a centralised bureaucracy'.[25] Visits to the town may be necessary for payment of taxes, land registration, obtaining credit, registration of births and deaths, and use of educational institutions. As with many small towns, Tütüneli's administrative role is being gradually eroded by the transfer of many of its duties to central government, including public health, education, welfare, public works, agriculture, security and transport. Even those functions it is obliged to fulfil cannot always be properly discharged because of shortage of funds. At the same time Tütüneli has declined as a centre for religious education. From the seventeenth century Muslim seminaries for training theological students had flourished in the town, but these were abolished in 1924. Another factor responsible for the economic decline of the town was the abolition of the once-powerful cobbler's guild in 1910. Cobbling survived as a craft specialisation in Tütüneli after the Second World War when Turkish factories began to turn out cheaper and more durable footwear. Tütüneli's other craftsmen suffered in a similar way – coppersmiths, blacksmiths, tanners, dyers and saddle-makers. At one time the town enjoyed an effective regional monopoly in the production of craft goods, but today it has to compete with other retailing centres, including retailers now established in the villages themselves. With improvements in road transport many villagers prefer to visit larger towns like Mugla, Aydin and Izmir, thus decreasing Tütüneli's commercial functions still further. The plight of Tütüneli is typical of a number of small market towns in Turkey and elsewhere whose function was to provide goods and services to an agricultural population. Few townsmen have been able to resort to farming in hard times, and a high level of emigration has resulted. From 1935 to 1965 Tütüneli's population increased by only 14.7 per cent, when it might have been expected to double.[26]

Unlike Tütüneli, the continuing prosperity of certain small Middle Eastern regional centres is a product of powerful urban links with their rural hinterlands. The oasis town of Tabas in Iran, for example, had a population of 13,000 in 1974,[27] serving a rural population of 28,000 in more than 300 tributary oasis villages and hamlets. E. Ehlers[28] found that Tabas benefits greatly from its rural hinterland through 'rent-capitalistic' mechanisms, in much the same way that has been found in larger Iranian cities.[29] Urban landlords take a substantial proportion of the value of the agricultural production, though less than before land reform when it was about 70 to 80 per cent. Farmers are often in debt to bazaar merchants for goods and services paid for in advance (*pish-foroush*), and Tabas merchants and craftsmen still sell most of their goods in the rural hinterland. Moreover, carpet-making, which began as a cottage industry only 25 years ago, is largely controlled from Tabas, which 'siphons off in typical rent-capitalist tradition up to 50 per cent of the values created by tedious labour at the loom'.[30] It seems probable that certain other small Iranian towns similarly dominate their hinterlands, while functioning as traditional central places. The phenomenon calls for more investigation.

Planning for Small Towns

The small towns of the Middle East have been generally neglected from a planning point of view. With few exceptions, largely confined to the oil-rich states, no master plans have been prepared for individual small towns, and their role in national urban strategy is either vague or unspecified. It is commonly agreed that small towns are to be 'developed', 'activated',[31] or 'encouraged',[32] but little indication is given as to how these objectives can be achieved. Indeed, until the current sketchy knowledge of the nature and functions of small towns is vastly improved, planning will continue to beg the question of what to do with them.

There are several reasons why small towns need to be more fully integrated into national urban planning. First, because the population of some is declining. While the number of small towns shows a net increase, there are probably a number which have declined in size since the turn of the century. Bharier's work in Iran revealed that out of 80 towns in the 5,000 to 20,000 bracket in 1900, 30 had declined in population by 1956.[33] More widespread than population decrease however is the gradual loss of regional influence being experienced by many provincial market towns, resulting in a marked decline in wealth and status. For over 2,000 years the Middle East has witnessed the rise and fall of urban centres in response to changing political and economic circumstances, and it is clearly not the task of modern planning to resist blindly the natural processes of urban decay. Investment resources are limited, and priority must be given to small towns showing evidence that they continue to function as effective regional centres. For those which have clearly seen better days, some investment in housing and services may be necessary to alleviate the social problems associated with decline. The possibility that some such towns may have inherited public and domestic buildings worthy of preservation should be borne in mind. The organic growth of some Middle Eastern towns has created visually stimulating spatial relationships which no amount of planning could produce. Sa'dah in Yemen AR (4,400 inhabitants in 1975) is a fine illustration of this (Figure 10.3).

Secondly, small towns deserve attention because many of them still function as vigorous regional centres, and they represent considerable potential for the implementation of the development policies of central governments. It is clear from the example of Tabas that the agricultural sector may be inextricably tied up with the influence of the regional town. Alternatively, as in Tütüneli, changes in agriculture may radically affect the fortunes of the regional town. Integrated regional planning would seem axiomatic in both cases. Geographical influences will ensure that Tabas has a future as a regional focus, which somehow needs to be shifted from one of dominance to interdependence. Here, agrarian reform may be the answer. In Tütüneli, and many towns like it, the greatest need is for the creation of more jobs to generate local wealth and stimulate retailing. The location of small-scale manufacturing industries in small towns has proved moderately successful in Algeria, Tunisia, Libya, Turkey and Israel. The best prospects are for those towns located reasonably close to major metropolitan regions, or along the major axes of growth between large cities. In more remote rural areas, however, the possibilities of agriculturally-based manufacturing and craft industries have yet to be adequately explored.

Abu-Lughod[34] has rightly drawn attention to the fallacy of expecting a 'balanced' hierarchy of settlement in the Middle East, with a broad base of small settlements supporting fewer small and medium-sized towns, culminating in one or two metropolitan cities with major regional functions. The countries of the Third World 'appear to be moving directly into the new larger scale of urban hierarchy, by-passing that intermediate stage which . . . we have mistakenly called "normal" or "balanced" urban hierarchies'.[35] Thus the existence of so many small towns in the Middle East is not the product of a malfunctioning

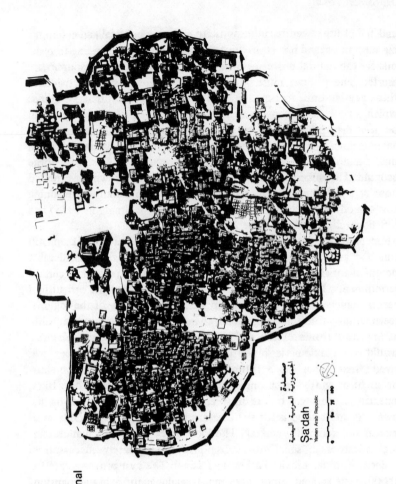

الجمهورية العربية اليمنية

Şa'dah
Yemen Arab Republic

Figure 10.3:
Sa'dah (Yemen AR);
a Fine Example of Spatial
Relationships in a Traditional
Small Arab Town
(Werner Dubach, Zurich,
1975)

system which has somehow prevented them from growing into medium-size centres. The more rapid growth of large towns at the expense of smaller towns is to be expected, and may well be in the national interest. These ideas are important since they give proper perspective to the role of small towns. Although possessing small populations, and growing slowly if at all, they may be exactly the right scale to perform the vital intermediate role between the large cities and the villages. Planning should be devised to stimulate the social and economic life of small towns, without striving to turn them into small cities. It must be recognised that their growth rates will nearly always be inferior to those of the large cities, but this is not indicative that their usefulness is at an end.

Studies of Misurata in Libya provide rather striking evidence of the extent to which a small town can change and grow in a short period of time if it is favourably located, and receives heavy government investment.[36] In 1966 Misurata had a population of about 9,000 and its periodic market functioned much as it had for very many years. The market commanded an extensive hinterland and operated three days a week within a regionally integrated system (Figure 10.4). On one market day in July 1966 nearly 7,000 people were counted entering the town to attend the market. There were 65 craftsmen at work, 250 pavement traders, and 136 'general' stores. Market day was the occasion for intense social and economic interaction, the success of which depended heavily on the concentration of activity at the centre of town. A proportion of the traders were part-time farmers; a few decades before all but a few would have been part-timers, exchanging local agricultural produce and craft goods.

Between 1966 and 1974 Misurata's population increased to about 40,000. Government funds were made available for urban expansion and reconstruction on an impressive scale. Vehicles registered in the town rose from less than 1,000 in 1966 to over 12,000. A new livestock market and slaughterhouse and a purpose-built complex for marketing fruit, vegetables, grain and wool were constructed in accordance with a physical master plan for Misurata drawn up in 1967. All these were located away from the town centre, and remained open six days a week. The three traditional market days had virtually disappeared. The number of craftsmen had fallen by half, only 70 general stores remained, and only 34 rather pathetic pavement traders appeared on market days. Part-time trading has been overtaken by the needs of a large population, best met by modern retailers. Thus in less than a decade traditional marketing patterns had been almost eliminated in

Figure 10.4:
The Hinterland of Misurata
Market in Libya in 1966;
a Small Town with
Important Regional
Functions
(G.H. Blake, 1968)

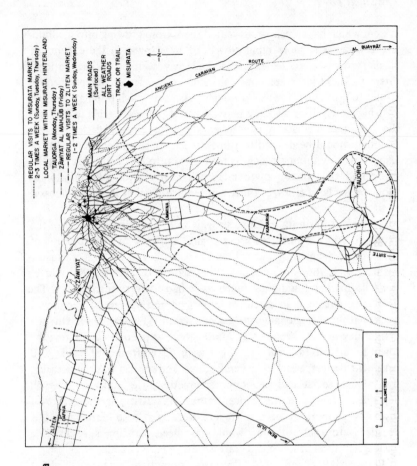

Figure 10.5: Proposals for a New Town Centre for Sur (Oman) Attempt to Blend Local Life-styles with Contemporary Planning Concepts (Gazzard Chipchase Consultancy Services BV)

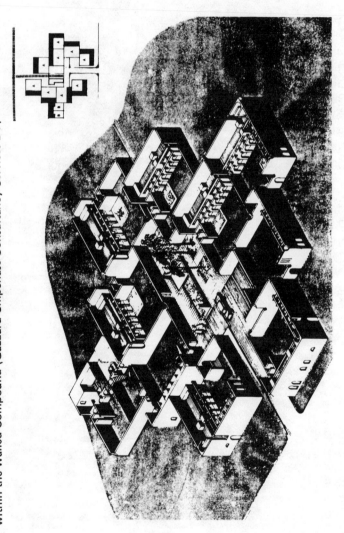

Figure 10.6: Low-income Housing Proposed for Sur (Oman). The Planner Allows for Progressive Addition of Rooms within the Walled Compound (Gazzard Chipchase Consultancy Services BV)

Misurata. The periodic market would have eventually died a natural death as the supply and demand for goods increased in the town itself, and the rural population became more mobile. In the event, planned physical changes, admirable as they were, greatly accelerated the process while powerful political and economic influences transformed the scale and character of the town.

Many Middle Easterners are becoming increasingly critical of the wholesale adoption of Western planning concepts and architectural styles in the big cities. It is equally important that planning for small towns should be in harmony with local life-styles and traditional forms of architecture. The right kind of physical planning can encourage community life within the town, and reinforce its external functions as a regional centre. Ill-conceived plans may undermine both. It is essential that adequate knowledge of the town is acquired before planning proposals are implemented. This may be a slow and expensive process, but it is a fundamental ingredient of successful small-town planning. Local cultural traditions are often powerfully reflected in the architecture of public buildings, house styles, street patterns, and the way in which public space is utilised for social and economic interaction. The incorporation of these in development planning is doubtless sometimes difficult. Too often, however, one suspects that their significance in maintaining the strength and character of neighbourhood and community interaction is simply not recognised.

Proposals for the development of Sur in Oman are an example of contemporary planning which successfully blends local urban life-styles with modern concepts (Figure 10.5).[37] Building designs owe much to traditional forms. The townscape of the new town centre is unmistakably Islamic and Omani. The scale is appropriate for a small town; all the amenities and institutions are located so as to encourage intense interaction at the town centre. Some limited income houses, with traditional courtyards and high walls, are proposed, grouped in traditional style with minimum road lengths, and space between buildings reduced to a minimum (Figure 10.6). Such painstaking planning could do much to preserve the ethos of the small Middle Eastern town.

References

1. See for example R. Duchac *et al., Villes et Sociétés au Maghreb, Etudes sur L'Urbanisation* (Centre National de la Recherche Scientifique, Paris, 1974).

2. A. Fadloulah and M. Belfquith, 'Profil d'une petite ville Marocaine à travers le recensement de 1971: le cas de Bouznika', *Table Ronde sur L'Urbanisation au Maghreb*, Tours (Novembre 1977) 87-98; H. Karoui, 'Mateur . . . lieu

228　The Small Town

d'immigration', *Revue Tunisienne de Sciences Sociales*, no. 23 (Dec. 1970) 119-42.

3. L.C. Briggs and N.L. Guède, *No More for Ever: A Saharan Jewish Town*, Peabody Museum Papers, vol. LV, no. 1 (Cambridge, Mass., 1964).

4. R.I. Lawless, 'Iraq: changing population patterns', in *Populations of the Middle East and North Africa*, ed. J.I. Clarke and W.B. Fisher (ULP, London, 1972), p. 119.

5. M. Bonine, 'Urban studies in the Middle East', *Middle East Studies Association Bulletin*, vol. 10, no. 3 (1976) 1-37.

6. P. Benedict, 'The changing role of provincial towns: a case study from southwestern Turkey', in *Turkey: Geographic and Social Perspectives*, ed. P. Benedict, E. Tumertekin, F. Mansur (E.J. Brill, Leiden, 1974), p. 246.

7. Definitions from United Nations, *Demographic Yearbook 1973* (New York, 1974), pp. 161-3.

8. Ministry of Statistics, *Census of Population October 1975* (Ankara, 1977), pp. 42-3.

9. For sources, see Table 10.2.

10. For sources, see Table 10.2.

11. N.C. Grill, 'Urbanisation in the Arabian peninsula', unpublished MA (University of Durham, 1977) 133.

12. For sources, see Table 10.2.

13. H. Benhalima, 'Sefrou, ville "predatrice" ou "animatrice" de sa region', *Table Ronde sur L'Urbanisation au Maghreb*, Tours (Novembre 1977) 99-119. (Sefrou has 29,000 inhabitants.)

14. A.S. Bujra, *The Politics of Stratification: a Study of Political Change in a South Arabian Town* (Oxford University Press, 1971). (Hureidah had 2,046 inhabitants.)

15. For examples, see T. Chandler and G. Fox, *3,000 Years of Urban Growth* (Academic Press, New York, 1974).

16. For a good summary of urban types in the Maghreb, see J. Despois and R. Raynal, *Géographie de l'Afrique du Nordouest* (Payot, Paris, 1967), pp. 43-67.

17. See M. Lombard, 'Une carte du bois dans la Mediterranée musulmane (VIIe-XIe siècles)', *Annales, Economies, Sociétés, Civilisations*, vol. 14, no. 2 (1959) 234-54.

18. J. Ash, 'The progress of new towns in Israel', *Town Planning Review*, vol. 45, 4 (1974) 387-400.

19. A. Prenant, 'Aspects de la croissance relative des petits centres urbains en Algérie', *Table Ronde sur L'Urbanisation au Maghreb*, Tours (Novembre 1977) 123-46.

20. H. Attia, 'Croissance et migrations des populations sahéliennes', *Revue Tunisienne de Sciences Sociales*, no. 23 (Dec. 1970) 91-117.

21. H. Fakhouri, *Kafr El-Elow: An Egyptian Village in Transition* (Holt, Rinehart, and Winston, New York, 1972).

22. See R.J. Bromley, B.W. Hodder, R.H.T. Smith, *Market Place Studies: A World Bibliography up to 1972* (School of Oriental and African Studies, London, 1972).

23. M.A. Prenant-Thumelin, 'Nedroma 1954', pp. 21-63 and D. Sari, 'Nedroma 1966', pp. 64-71, *Annales Algériennes de Géographie*, vol. 2, no. 4 (1967). See also D. Dari, *Les villes precoloniales de L'Algérie occidental; Nédroma, Mazouna, Kalâa* (SNED, Algiers, 1970).

24. P. Benedict, 'The changing role of provincial towns', pp. 241-80.

25. P. Benedict, ibid., p. 260.

26. P. Benedict, ibid., p. 273.

27. On 16 September 1978 Tabas was severely damaged by an earthquake, and a high proportion of its inhabitants were killed.

28. E. Ehlers, 'City and hinterland in Iran: the example of Tabas/Khorassan', *Tijdschrift voor Economische en Sociale Geografie*, vol. 68, no. 5 (1977) 284-96.

29. E. Ehlers, 'Dezful and its hinterland; observations on the relationships of lesser Iranian cities to their hinterland', *Journal of the Association of Iranian Geographers*, vol. 1, no. 1 (1976) 20-30.

30. E. Ehlers, 'City and hinterland in Iran', p. 292.

31. P. Zaremba, *The Outlines of the Strategies of Spatial Development in Iraq* (Ministry of Planning, Baghdad, September 1974), pp. 1-43.

32. S. El-Shakho, 'Urbanisation and spatial development in Libya', *Pan-African Journal*, vol. VIII, no. 4 (1975) 371-86.

33. J. Bharier, 'The growth of towns and villages in Iran, 1900-1966', *Middle Eastern Studies*, vol. 8, no. 1 (1972) 51-61.

34. J.L. Abu-Lughod, 'Problems and policy implications of Middle Eastern urbanisation', in *Studies on Development Problems in Selected Countries of the Middle East 1972* (United Nations, New York, 1973), pp. 42-62.

35. Ibid., pp. 51-2.

36. G.H. Blake, *Misurata; a Market Town in Tripolitania*, Research Paper No. 9, Department of Geography (University of Durham, 1968); G.H. Blake, 'Misurata's periodic market: tradition and change', *Proceedings, First Geographical Conference in Libya 1975* (University of Benghazi, forthcoming).

37. Gazzard Chipchase Consultancy Services, *Sur: Development Plan Report* (Gravenhage, 1976).

11 URBAN WATER PROBLEMS

Peter Beaumont

The Environment

In any study 'of water and environmental management problems in the Middle East it is essential to realise from the outset that one is dealing with a wide range of environments rather than with a single and uniform one.[1] While it is obvious that urban areas tend to avoid the most extreme environmental conditions the contrasts which are to be found in the region are considerable.

In terms of altitude one finds towns such as Jericho situated 300 m below sea level, while at the other extreme Erzurum in eastern Turkey is situated at over 1,500 m above sea level. It should not be forgotten either that Tehrān and Ankara, the capital cities of Iran and Turkey respectively, are both located at a height of over 1,000 m above sea level, and are many kilometres away from the sea. Others like İstanbul, Beirūt, Tel Aviv and Kuwait City have coastal sites.

Associated with these marked topographical differences are great climatological variations. In the southern part of the region along the Indian Ocean a town like Aden experiences July mean temperatures of 32°C and January mean temperatures of 25°C. In contrast, Erzurum situated high on the Anatolian Plateau, although it records July mean temperatures of 18°C, experiences very severe January conditions when the mean temperature falls to as low as − 9°C.

Another interesting feature of the region is the way in which the mean annual temperature range increases away from coastal locations. Minimum annual temperature ranges of less than 5°C are experienced by the coastal towns of southern Oman, while over the highland areas of eastern Turkey and central Iran the annual temperature range exceeds 25°C.

Precipitation, the source of all fresh water within the region, also reveals great spatial differences. Highest annual totals are recorded along the coastal strip of the Black Sea coast of eastern Turkey. Here Rize has a mean annual total of 2,440 mm, with significant amounts falling in each month. At the other extreme at Aswan in upper Egypt the mean annual rainfall is only 1 mm.[2]

Throughout most of the Middle East the summer season is a period in which little or no rainfall occurs. The only exceptions to this are the

230

coastal regions of the Black and Caspian Seas where precipitation falls all the year round and the southernmost parts of the Arabian peninsula which receive only summer monsoonal rainfall.

The lack of precipitation during summer means that water supplies, in terms of groundwater recharge and river flow, are totally dependent on precipitation inputs falling in a three- to five-month period during the cooler part of the year.

Fortunately this does provide an advantage in so far as a high proportion of the precipitation occurring in the highlands of Turkey and Iran falls as snow. This means that large volumes of water are stored in the mountains as snowpacks to be released as flood flows when temperatures rise in late spring and early summer. The result is that maximum water availability in terms of river flow occurs in April and May, whereas maximum precipitation usually takes place in December and January.[3]

The maldistribution of precipitation throughout the year does mean that man has always relied heavily on water storage systems to safeguard his water needs for the long dry summers. Undoubtedly the most important storages have been the natural aquifer systems of the Middle East which are recharged each year by the infiltrating winter precipitation.

These storages are used in two ways. Indirectly, they are used in the sense that it is the slow groundwater discharge from these aquifers which makes many of the rivers of the region perennial. This is particularly true in the Zagros Mountains of Iran and the Taurus Mountains of southern Turkey. A variety of aquifer systems are found, but in general it is the carbonate ones which tend to be the more important in the highland areas.

The storage and water release characteristics of these aquifers can be seen from a study of the hydrographs of certain rivers. For example in the Zagros Mountains the Zāyandah River, on which the city of Eşfahān is built, clearly exhibits a long period of continuously declining discharge during summer when the river is supplied with water entirely from groundwater sources.[4] The flow of this river also clearly illustrates the snowmelt effect on rivers draining from highland areas (Figure 11.1).

In the more arid interior parts of the Middle East, such as the Arabian peninsula, urban development has only been possible as the result of the tapping of groundwater supplies. Over the years oasis settlements have evolved where groundwater flowed out at the surface. Al-Hufuf in the eastern part of Saudi Arabia provides a good example

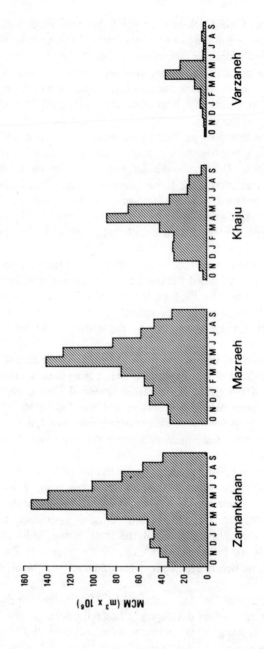

Figure 11.1: Downstream Variation in Water Discharge along the Zāyandah River, Iran

of this type of development. More recently the growth of Riyadh, the capital of Saudi Arabia, has only been possible through the extraction of water by deep wells from the Biyadh and Al-Minjūr aquifer systems.

Water Supply

Throughout the Middle East water provides a key to explain the distribution of towns and cities, for in the more arid parts permanent settlement was only possible where adequate and reliable water resources were to be found.

The nature of the water sources varies considerably. Jericho, one of the oldest towns in the world, dating back at least 10,000 years owes its existence to a spring, known as Ain es Sultan, which issues forth from the foot of the escarpment bounding the Dead Sea lowlands.[5] Eṣfahān, one of the world's greatest oases, in contrast depends on the waters of the Zāyandah River on which it stands for the cultivation of its gardens and fields.

Modern urban water management can be divided into two complementary and essential parts. The first consists of the discovery, conservation and distribution of water supplies to the consumer, while the second involves the collection, treatment and eventual disposal of waste water. In itself this demands a tremendously expensive infrastructure of water mains and trunk sewer systems, as well as related water treatment plants and sewage works.

In the developed countries of Western Europe and North America this infrastructure has been built up gradually since the mid-nineteenth century. By way of contrast many of the countries of the Middle East are striving to install water distribution and sewage collection networks in the larger urban areas in a matter of a few years.

The supply of water has always been of crucial importance to the urban centres of the Middle East, whereas sewage disposal has tended to be taken for granted. Even for drinking water supply purposes little treatment of water to improve quality was attempted until recently. In many cases drinking water was obtained from groundwater sources by a well or qanat and so water quality was often high.[6]

When water was transported long distances through aqueducts, as was the case with the supply to Kairouan, Tunisia, during the rule of the Aghlabites in the ninth century AD, it was led into large storage tanks. These tanks acted as sedimentation basins, allowing the finer grained material in suspension to settle out. The fact that they were open to the sky allowed the penetration of ultra-violet light into the water which tended to kill off bacteria and other organisms. Given the windy nature of the steppe climate around Kairouan it seems likely that dust and other small pathogenic organisms might also have been blown into the water supply.

Currently the urban areas of the Middle East are drawing their water supplies from both surface and groundwater sources which are often polluted by the entry of domestic sewage effluents. This has necessitated the widespread utilisation of water treatment systems similar to those used in the West.

The first major stage of water treatment usually consists of the addition of a range of different chemicals. The most commonly used are iron and aluminium salts which cause particles to form, flocculate and then settle out. To improve taste and reduce odours carbon can also be added at this stage. The treated water is then led into primary settling tanks where the sludge produced by the addition of chemicals can accumulate and be drawn off for disposal. Rapid sand filters are then generally employed to remove any suspended material which may still be present in the water. Finally, prior to distribution through the mains, chlorine or a related chemical is added to provide a terminal disinfection of the water. Ozone is now being used more for disinfection purposes and this has the advantage that it instantly kills those viruses which may be resistant to the addition of chlorine.

Until very recently the domestic per capita consumption of water in the Middle East, even in urban environments, remained low. Few reliable figures for use are available, but it seems reasonable to assume that it was nearly everywhere less than 50 litres/day.

Over the last 50 years or so, and especially since the Second World War, water resource managers in the Middle East have been faced with the twin problems of rapidly rising urban population numbers and as the result of increasing standards of living, a marked growth in the per capita domestic consumption of water. The result has been a desperate struggle to obtain new sources of water to meet these ever growing demands. Inevitably it has meant that water has had to be transported ever greater distances towards the growing urban centres.[7]

Little accurate and detailed information has been published on water use within the countries of the Middle East. One of the few comprehensive studies was that undertaken by the World Health Organisation for 1970.[8] Its accuracy varies from country to country, but it does at least give an indication of the very wide range of conditions which are experienced throughout the region. In an urban context it was noted that there are large differences in per capita consumption of water between users having house connections and those who have to obtain

Table 11.1: Freshwater Consumption in Middle Eastern Countries (litres/capita/day)

Country	Present consumption Urban With house connections Min.	Max.	With public standposts Min.	Max.	Rural Min.	Max.	Future consumption Urban With house connections Min.	Max.	With public standposts Min.	Max.	Rural Min.	Max.
Afghanistan	60	70	20	30	15	20	60	100	30	50	30	50
Algeria	20	200	10	30	10	60	80	200	50	60	50	60
Bahrain	220	420	23	140	110	340	230	360	–	–	140	280
Cyprus	145	275	–	–	90	145	185	320	150	250	145	185
Egypt	100	260	30	40	30	40	250	350	–	–	40	60
Iran	75	150	–	25	40	75	150	190	–	–	110	150
Iraq	90	200	–	–	65	130	160	360	–	–	90	145
Jordan	60	120	–	–	30	60	80	150	–	–	40	80
Kuwait	150	220	70	220	–	–	180	410	150	220	–	–
Lebanon	150	200	–	–	80	125	200	250	–	–	100	150
Morocco	60	260	10	20	–	70	100	300	20	30	20	80
PDR Yemen	50	180	10	23	10	18	140	230	18	36	50	70
Qatar	150	300	80	110	40	80	230	300	80	150	80	150
Saudi Arabia	50	400	25	50	25	50	150	250	25	50	100	200
Sudan	45	900	23	32	14	42	110	1140[a]	–	–	18	45
Syria	150	200	–	–	50	–	–	250	–	–	–	75
Tunisia	100	150	5	10	–	–	150	–	5	10	–	–
Turkey	120	170	60	70	50	60	–	–	–	–	–	–
Yemen AR	50	80	30	50	20	40	–	–	–	–	30	60

a. Includes garden watering.

Source: World Health Organisation (1973).

their water supplies from public standposts (Table 11.1). In general consumers with house connections use approximately twice as much water as those who have to collect it from public sources.

Wide differences in urban water consumption were seen from one country to another. Some of these differences are undoubtedly the result of statistical inaccuracies and ambiguities in the data collected. However, it is interesting to note that some countries such as Bahrain, Saudi Arabia and Sudan do have maximum urban use values in excess of 400 litres/capita/day. These values are, of course, comparable with water use figures for many of the developed countries of the West.

Perhaps more important though is the predicted rise in water consumption in the future. In many countries it would seem that the average urban use of water (with house connection) is likely to be between 150 and 250 litres/capita/day. Given the fact that urban populations are growing rapidly this increasing water demand will place an ever more severe burden on available water supplies.

Recent studies from Israel have shown that family size and income per capita are the dominant controls of urban water use.[9] Other factors of importance were the actual urban area involved, the country of origin of the person concerned, the type of metering and educational level of the inhabitants. Of all the factors family size seemed to have the dominant effect. In all income groupings per capita water consumption declined with increasing family size (Table 11.2). With small families in the highest income grouping average water consumption per capita was about 240 litres/day. In contrast large, poor households had water use rates of only 94 litres/capita/day. Although income levels seemed to influence water use in small families, it did not appear to exercise as much effect with larger household sizes.

The level of access to satisfactory water supplies by many urban residents is still unsatisfactory in many parts of the region. The poorest towns from this respect tend to be the smaller regional centres which have not benefited to the same extent from the infrastructure investment that has often gone into the capital cities and other larger cities.

The World Health Organisation has made estimates of the water supply facilities which will be needed in the urban areas of the region by the 1980s (Table 11.3). In general costs, at early 1970 prices, suggest that house connections for water supply average between 20 and 50 US dollars per capita, while for public standposts the figure is from 6 to 15 US dollars/person.

The objective of the World Health Organisation is to ensure that 60 per cent of the urban populations are supplied with house connections

Table 11.2: Freshwater Consumption in Israel per capita/litres/day

	Income per capita		
Persons/dwelling	£0–249	£250–399	£400 +
1–2	179.5	199.5	239.5
3–4	137.5	135.3	160.5
5+	94.0	132.9	123.6

Source: P. Dorr, S.L. Feldman and C.S. Kamen, 'Socioeconomic factors affecting domestic water demand in Israel', *Water Resources Research*, vol. 11, no. 6 (1975) 805-9.

by 1980 and that the remainder have access to public standposts. The vital importance of adequate safe water supplies is that it is one of the best ways to improve and maintain public health standards in the urban environment. Many illnesses are water related with often the greatest problems being caused by water-borne and water-washed diseases.[10] Given the fact that sewage systems still, and are likely to remain, rather rudimentary in many areas, it is imperative that adequate piped water supplies are made available to urban populations. It is also important to ensure that water costs are not too great as this will mean that some families will tend to look elsewhere for water to wash plates and cooking utensils. Such water might well be contaminated and so give rise to health problems.[11]

One of the best examples of the difficulties involved in urban water supply is provided by Tehrān, the capital of Iran. As late as 1920 the population of Tehrān was only about 200,000. Since then the growth rate has been extremely rapid to a figure in excess of 3.5 million people at the present day. Initially water was supplied to the city through 34 qanats which tapped the shallow aquifer systems.[12] These supplies soon proved inadequate and so it became necessary during the 1920s to abstract water from the River Karaj, some 30 km to the west of the city. After the Second World War water in Tehrān was once again in short supply and so a well-drilling programme was initiated. At the same time a new piped water distribution system was installed in parts of the city.

In the early 1960s the construction of the Karaj Dam and a pipeline system to the city provided Tehrān with an extra 144 million m^3 of water each year. Later in the same decade this was further supplemented by the building of the Latian dam on the River Jaji which supplied

Table 11.3: Availability of Water Supply Facilities in the Middle East

Country	House connections				Public standposts			
	Population to be served 1980 (000)	Increase over 1970 (000)	Cost US dollars per consumer	Total million US dollars	Population to be served 1980 (000)	Increase over 1970 (000)	Cost US dollars per consumer	Total million US dollars
Afghanistan	1,150	1,025	10	10.3	767	567	6	3.4
Algeria	6,589	2,089	120	250.7	4,392	2,392	25	84.8
Bahrain	125	—	6	—	83	70	11	0.8
Cyprus	221	—	50	—	148	148	11	1.6
Egypt	13,524	2,354	20	47.1	9,016	6,186	11	68.0
Iran	11,424	4,933	32	157.9	7,616	4,378	7	30.6
Iraq	4,651	1,051	35	36.8	3,101	2,135	11	23.5
Jordan	1,034	62	30	1.9	690	582	11	6.4
Kuwait	612	492	32	15.7	408	128	11	1.4
Libya	1,032	382	32	12.2	688	488	11	5.4
Morocco	5,743	3,543	120	425.2	3,829	829	25	20.7
PDR Yemen	393	159	20	3.2	262	162	12	1.9
Qatar	52	2	55	0.1	34	30	60	1.8
Saudi Arabia	2,090	590	32	18.9	262	1,064	11	11.7
Sudan	1,549	409	45	18.4	338	1,022	15	15.3
Syria	2,748	293	32	9.4	1,032	1,588	11	17.5
Tunisia	2,138	938	32	30.0	1,832	575	11	6.3
Turkey	12,808	7,102	120	852.2	8,538	7,112	25	177.8
Yemen AR	415	335	32	10.7	276	201	11	2.2

Source: World Health Organisation (1973).

Tehrān with another 80 million m^3 of water/annum.

Even this, however, has not been sufficient to satisfy the growing water needs of the capital's population and so another major dam scheme has been embarked upon. This is being built on the River Lar near Puloor. From the reservoir a tunnel under the Elburz Mountains will transport water to a river which eventually flows into the lake behind the Latian dam on the River Jaji. Water is, of course, already extracted from this reservoir for Tehrān's water supply, and so no new distribution network will be required. Once the Lar dam is in operation in the 1980s it is expected that 180 million m^3/year will be sent on average through the tunnel to the Latian reservoir.[13]

There seems little doubt though that even more water will be needed for Tehrān by the late 1980s and so new water sources will have to be found. As there are no more untapped sources in the vicinity of Tehrān it will mean that whichever site is chosen will necessitate the construction of a major pipeline system to bring the water to the capital. This will need tremendous investment of capital.

Kuwait is an urban society of about one million people which has chosen an unusual solution to its water supply difficulties. Climatically Kuwait is very arid with average precipitation totals averaging only 100 mm/annum. Almost all of this water is lost by evapotranspiration, and as a result surface run-off is virtually non-existent. Some groundwater recharge probably does occur during the heaviest rainfalls.

Until the twentieth century the only source of fresh water in the country was obtainable from sand aquifers in the coastal region. In these the water table was reached at depths of about 7 metres in hand-dug wells. As the population of the town grew during the early part of the twentieth century the yield of water from the shallow aquifers was insufficient to supply the demands. To alleviate this problem barrels of fresh water from the Shatt al'Arab were shipped in on dhows. This proved a successful operation and by 1948 364 m^3/day of water were being imported from this source.

It was, however, after the Second World War, when the first export of oil took place that the economy began to expand rapidly and that the water supply problem became crucial. In 1946 the Kuwait Oil Company had installed a private desalination plant to supply its own needs. This distillation plant proved so successful in operation that the Kuwait government decided to embark on a major desalination programme to supply the water needs of the country as a whole.[14]

As electricity demand for air conditioners was increasing markedly at this period it was decided to construct the desalination plant in association with an electricity generating station. This would permit the low pressure steam exhausted from the power generating process to be used to heat the incoming water supplies for the desalination plant. In this way energy costs could be minimised.

The first desalination plant at Shuwaykh, with a capacity of 4,546 m^3/day, began operation in 1957. Since then another plant has been constructed at Shu'aiba and the capacities of both of them increased on a number of occasions. The current position is that the installed desalination capacity is now in excess of 280,000 m^3/day. Kuwait is now totally dependent upon desalted water for drinking purposes.

Although the desalination programme has progressed smoothly since its inception, the costs of the water produced are high. Besides high energy and running costs, the capital investment required for such plants is large. The Kuwait government has heavily subsidised desalinated water production by a policy of writing off the initial capital investment of the plant over a 15-year period and by only charging a 5 per cent interest rate against the outstanding capital balance. This together with other subsidies has meant that the consumer has not been charged a realistic economic rate for water. Partly as a result of this and partly as a result of higher standards of living, potable water consumption in Kuwait has shown an almost fourfold per capita increase between 1957 and 1975 from 41.5 to 151.7 litres/ day.[15]

Kuwait is unusual also in that it employs a dual quality water distribution system. Potable water is distributed through one pipe network, while brackish water, used for toilet flushing and other cleaning purposes, is distributed through a separate one. This obviously increases infrastructure costs, but permits potable water to be used only for certain essential purposes.

Kuwait's present rate of population growth is one of the highest of all countries in the world. As a result it has been estimated that the population is likely to at least double by the end of the century to a figure between 2.1 and 3.5 million. Using a figure of about two million people, consultants have suggested that mean daily demand of potable water could rise to as high as about 800,000 m^3/day. This figure, it will be noted, is about 2.8 times the 1975 value for installed desalination capacity. While it is true that some extra water may be obtained from deep aquifer sources, the only major alternative to desalinated water supplies available to Kuwait is a pipeline system transporting water from the Shatt al'Arab. Although this is technically feasible the prevailing political relationship between Iraq and Kuwait make this solution seem unlikely.

Unless Kuwait is able to control either its population growth or the rise in per capita water consumption it appears inevitable that the country will have to continue with its policy of constructing new desalination plants to meet growing demands. Whether even Kuwait can afford such a costly policy of water provision once oil revenues begin to decline before the end of the present century is uncertain. At the moment the only option available to the government would appear to be a policy of strict water management using high-price water tariffs and perhaps even rationing of supplies.

Nearby Saudi Arabia has also chosen the high-technology alternative of desalination as a solution to the water supply problems of its coastal urban regions. Unlike Kuwait, Saudi Arabia did not enter the desalination field until the late 1960s. The first plant at Jiddah on the Red Sea coast, with a capacity of 19,000 m^3/day, was only commissioned in 1970. Four years later a larger plant of 28,500 m^3/day was opened at Al Khubar on the Gulf. Both of these plants are being enlarged as part of the desalination programme.

The proposed rate of growth of desalinated water production in Saudi Arabia is quite remarkable. If construction schedules are met it is expected that by 1980 the country could be producing about 516,000 m^3/day of desalted water, while during the 1980s this production is planned to rise to a capacity of 1,224,000 m^3/day.[16] The scale of the investment involved in this desalination programme is huge. For example during the current Second Development Plan, 1975-80, 34,000 million Saudi Riyals have been allocated to be spent on water and desalination projects.

The new desalination plants are to be built on both the Red Sea and Gulf coasts. However, when the current desalination programme is complete almost two-thirds of the water production capacity will be located on the Gulf coast. Wherever possible the plants are to be connected by pipeline so that water can be transferred more easily to the demand areas. One of the largest water users on the Gulf coast will be the new urban/industrial complex at Jubayl.

Waste Water Disposal and Water Pollution

Perhaps the greatest problem facing the towns and cities of the Middle East at the present time is to provide adequate sewage transport and treatment systems. Although water supply has always played a big role in urban development, the disposal of human wastes has been almost totally neglected. The result is that only the most rudimentary sewer systems have existed until recently in many of the region's urban areas.

The World Health Organisation made estimates in the early 1970s of the likely costs of improving sewage facilities in certain Middle Eastern countries to levels such that 40 per cent of the urban population are connected to the public sewerage system; 60 per cent of the urban population are provided with household systems and 25 per cent of the rural population provided with adequate sewerage facilities (Table 11.4).

For the urban areas the costs to provide new connections to public sewerage systems vary between US $29 and US $100 per user. To provide only household systems the costs are much lower ranging from US $5 to US $28 per person. In absolute terms the costs of providing 30.1 million people in the seven countries of Table 11.4 with sewage facilities of one form or another by 1980 is likely to cost US $1,124.6 million. This averages out at about US $37 per person.

Table 11.4: Costs to Meet Sewage Disposal Targets Suggested by the World Health Organisation for 1980 in the Middle East

Country	Population to be served 1980 (000)	Increase over 1970 (000)	Cost (million US dollars)
Algeria	13,296	12,336	161.0
Iran	24,128	7,184	534.5
Iraq	9,357	3,270	240.9
Libya	1,952	700	40.4
Morocco	12,828	8,174	51.1
Saudi Arabia	4,138	2,488	58.2
Tunisia	4,870	1,714	63.6

Source: World Health Organisation (1972).

The objectives of modern sewage works are surprisingly limited given the technological possibilities available. In essence all they attempt to do is to reduce the settleable solids within the waste waters and at the same time to reduce the oxygen demand caused by the presence of human waste products.

The operation of sewage works is divided into primary, secondary and tertiary treatment. Primary treatment is basically physical in nature. It consists usually of the screening of incoming waste waters to remove coarse solids, such as dead animals, large pieces of wood and other material. The waste waters are then led through a grit chamber so designed that sand, grit and related inorganic material are deposited. Following this the waters are put into large sedimentation basins, which are the most important part of primary treatment. In the sedimentation tanks coarse organic material sinks to the bottom and is then pumped to storage chambers for further treatment.

This simple sedimentation process can lower the BOD (Biochemical Oxygen Demand) of an effluent by as much as 33 per cent, and will remove between 60 and 80 per cent of the settleable solids present. In the more rudimentary sewage works primary treatment is all that occurs prior to the effluent being returned to a water course. In most sewage works, however, the clarified waters from the sedimentation tanks are taken for secondary treatment, which is biological in nature. The most common method used today for large sewage works is the activated sludge process. With this the effluent is aerated with paddles to produce an optimum environment for aerobic bacteria and other organisms to grow. These organisms then consume the organic matter which is held in suspension in the waste waters and so help to reduce further the BOD (Biochemical Oxygen Demand).

For smaller installations, percolating or trickling filters are utilised in place of the activated sludge process. These consist of large circular tanks filled with an inert material, which has a large surface area relative to the area it occupies. The effluent from the sedimentation tanks is sprayed on to the filters through revolving arms. This liquid soaks through the medium, coming into contact with films of bacteria and fungi which have developed on the surface of the particles. These bacteria and other organisms cover the breakdown of unstable organic matter by oxidation in the same way as occurs in the activated sludge process. These filters have the great advantage that they do not require any energy input for their operation and are, therefore, especially suitable for small community systems. For large urban areas, however, the activated sludge process is invariably used today. In most sewage works in the developed countries of the world the effluent is passed through a final sedimentation tank after it has been through the activated sludge process, or through a trickling filter. It is then discharged directly to the nearest water course. In England and Wales the effluent has to meet a standard which requires a BOD of less than 20 mg/litre and a suspended solids level of less than 30 mg/litre.

It is, however, possible to improve the quality of effluent still further by tertiary and other advanced treatments to produce a BOD

Table 11.5: Sewage Treatment — Beneficial Effects and Costs

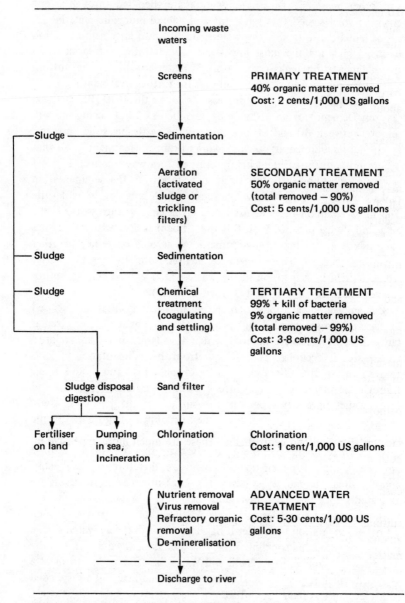

Source: B.A. Whitton (ed.), *River Ecology* (Blackwell Scientific Publications, 1975), Figure 2.31, p. 592.

of less than 10 mg/litre and a suspended solids content of less than 10 mg/litre. Such methods are normally very expensive in both energy and money terms, but will probably become of growing importance in the Middle East where water shortage is a problem (Table 11.5).

The treatment and disposal of sewage sludge, which accumulates as a result of the primary and secondary sedimentation processes, poses particular problems. Usually this sludge is confined in tanks heated to about 35°C in which anaerobic digestion occurs. In this process the sludge is converted into an inoffensive organic material and carbon dioxide and methane are given off. The methane can be used for heating the digestion tanks or for other uses. Although many pathogenic organisms are destroyed in the digestion process, the fact that some may remain means that subsequent disposal may be a problem in the Middle Eastern context where so many virulent endemic diseases occur.

At this stage of the digestion process the sludge has a solids content of only about 4.5 per cent. It is, therefore, essential to dewater it further prior to disposal. The commonest method in the West until recently has been the use of drying beds into which the sludge is run and the water is then lost by evaporation.

In a Middle East context this would work well during the summer months, but during winter in many parts of the region evaporation rates would be low and a build-up of sludge would result. The drying bed method also suffers from the disadvantage that considerable quantities of water are lost through evaporation and also that birds and small animals coming into contact with the sludge may act as carriers for any pathogenic organisms still remaining.

More advanced methods of sludge dewatering include pressure and vacuum filtration and centrifuging. These are much more expensive in both energy and monetary terms but do allow the recovery of water. The dewatered sludge is now much less bulky and so transportation costs to the ultimate disposal point are reduced.

A common way to dispose of the sludge is to spray it onto agricultural land. This can have beneficial effects in terms of the small amounts of fertilising chemicals which are present and the organic matter helps to improve the soil structure. This is particularly useful in Middle Eastern soils which are often deficient in organic matter as the result of high oxidation rates.

Provided that the sewage has been collected largely from domestic sources the only likely problems to be generated are those associated with potential disease transmission. On the other hand, if industrial effluents are being discharged into urban sewage systems it is possible for a wide range of toxic chemicals to be present in the sludge and this could have very serious deleterious effects on crop production. It is, therefore, essential that a monitoring of sewage sludges is carried out in the larger urban centres if they are to be used for agricultural purposes.

An example of the types of sewage problems experienced by the large cities of the Middle East can be provided by a study of the coastal city of İzmir in western Turkey. The sewerage system in operation in İzmir in the early 1970s was of the combined type. In most cases waste waters and storm run-off were collected in the same sewer and then discharged into the nearest natural water course or body, without any form of treatment. Only about half of the total population was served with sewage collection and disposal facilities. Many of the sewers were too small to conduct storm flows adequately, and maintenance of the systems was often poor. The lack of regulations governing the disposal of effluents meant that there were many discharge points and that as a result of lack of any form of treatment pollution could be very severe. A 1970 survey suggested that on a BOD content the industrial wastes being discharged were the equivalent to a population of about 600,000. By the end of the century it was thought that this loading might increase by up to two and one half times.

At this time all the rivers and creeks passing through the industrial and urban areas were often severely polluted by effluents. In the Bay of Izmir pollution was often a problem where outfalls occurred and fears were already being expressed about nutrient build-up in the near shore waters. To cope with these increasing problems it was felt necessary to construct a major new sewage treatment facility to handle the urban/industrial effluents. With this it was proposed that following treatment the effluent should be discharged into the middle section of İzmir Bay. It was felt that this could not lead to serious nutrient build-up, but if it did a longer submarine outfall would be designed to carry the effluent into the deeper and more exposed waters of the outer bay.

The scarcity of water in the region as well has led many people to consider the various ways in which the treated sewage effluents could be used for beneficial purposes. Suggested uses include irrigation of crops, fish-farming, and even complete reclamation and recyling for drinking-water purposes.

The use of sewage effluent for irrigation purposes has been widely employed in places such as Melbourne, Australia and in Mexico City. Outside Israel, though, it has not been widely used as yet in the Middle

East. However, the irrigation potential using those waters around cities such as Tehrān and Ankara appears great.

The reclamation and re-use of sewage effluent for drinking water purposes has been carried out for a number of years, apparently quite successfully in Windhoek, South-West Africa. Here the population of 84,000 recycles about 4 million litres/day of its sewage back into the potable supply system to provide about one-third of the total daily needs. Many experts however, have expressed worry about the re-use of waste waters for drinking-water supply as the result of our lack of knowledge of the long-term effects of their usage. Three main areas of concern seem to arise. There are fears about the possible presence, even after treatment, of pathogens, inorganic chemicals such as the heavy metals lead, mercury and cadmium and organic chemicals as represented by pesticides and herbicides. It is interesting to note that over 1,000 chemicals can be present in waste waters, yet the drinking-water standards of most countries specify limits of concentration for only 50 or less.[17] To date it has been the Israelis who have expressed the greatest interest in the re-use of sewage effluents. Even they, however, have not yet embarked upon any major projects to re-use these waters for drinking supply purposes as they feel that enough information is not yet known about the long-term health effects.

Over the last 50 years or so Western sewage technology has been introduced into the arid areas of the Middle East almost without any thought being given as to whether this represents the optimum solution for the region. We tend to overlook the fact that most of these effluent disposal systems were designed initially in the abundant rainfall regions of Western Europe and eastern North America. Almost all of them depend on the dilution of the final effluent by disposal into a perennial stream or river. Such conditions are, of course, only found in a relatively small proportion of the Middle East and this has given rise to speculation as to whether the water-borne sewage system might not after all be the best solution to the problem of human waste disposal.

The composting toilet has been proposed as an alternative for use in less crowded urban as well as rural situations. This eliminates the need for expensive sewage systems and sewage works and at the same time reduces the pollution hazard. Other positive benefits are the production of about 30 kg of fertiliser per person per year, as well as a reduction in water use by as much as 40 m^3/household/year.[18]

In coastal locations a partial solution to the difficulties of operating the water carriage sewage system can be achieved by having a dual quality water supply system with sea water being used for toilet flushing purposes. Such a system alone is likely to cut the potable water demand by about 40 per cent.

Conclusion

It is sometimes forgotten that in areas of water deficiency severe competition exists for the suppliers of water for different uses. Until recently agricultural demand for water has dwarfed domestic and industrial needs in nearly all parts of the region. However, with the rapid growth of urban centres and the increasing importance of industrial activity new demands have been created. Nowhere is this better illustrated than in Israel which is now facing a very serious water problem.[19] Although it is difficult to estimate the actual easily developable freshwater resources of the country, it seems to be generally accepted that the likely figure is somewhere between about 1,400 and 1,700 million m^3/annum. What is interesting though is that estimates of likely future demand made at the same period suggest that by 1985 water demand in Israel could be about 1,960 million m^3/ annum. If these figures are approximately correct it suggests that further urban, industrial and agricultural development in the country will only be possible by the extensive re-use of available water resources. However, estimates suggest that by 1990 Israel is likely to be able to reclaim about 360 million m^3/year of water to give an annual supply of 1,900 million m^3/year.

At the present, agriculture is by far the largest user of water in the country, accounting for about 72 per cent of the total water abstracted. Unfortunately, this water, which is used for irrigation purposes, is almost all applied by the efficient sprinkler method. This means that further water savings will not be easy to make, though some benefits could be achieved by the extension of drip irrigation methods. However all these modern irrigation methods do suffer from the very marked disadvantages of high energy and capital costs.[20] A possible alternative is, of course, to enter upon a large desalination programme similar to that pioneered by Kuwait. This is capable of making new supplies of water available but costs are high, so limiting the uses to which the water can be put.

It seems more likely though that in Israel water will be diverted from those uses which produce a relatively low monetary return to those which produce a much higher one for each unit of water utilised. This could result in a reduction in the area of irrigated agriculture so that greater amounts of water can be supplied to industries in the main urban centres. Such a change in use also has the advantage that most industrial waste waters can be re-used whilst almost all irrigation water is lost through evapotranspiration.

In the future there does seem to be little doubt that the urban centres of Israel will have to be supplied with a greater proportion of the total water used within the country. By 1985 this figure is likely to be about 33 per cent of total compared with only 20 per cent in the early 1970s.

As water does become more difficult to supply it is inevitable that costs will rise, whether as a result of extra treatment facilities necessary to reclaim waste waters or the high capital and energy costs associated with the installation and operation of desalination plants. In time this will mean that the industrial products for which the water is utilised will have their profit margin reduced, so making competition on the international market more difficult.

The problems which Israel is now facing in terms of water use are likely to become important in many other countries of the Middle East within the next decade.[21]

References

1. P. Beaumont, 'The Middle East – environmental management problems', *Built Environment Quarterly*, vol. 2, no. 2 (1976) 104-12.

2. P. Beaumont, G.H. Blake and J.M. Wagstaff, *The Middle East: A Geographical Study*, see section on climate, pp. 49-90 (John Wiley, London, 1976).

3. P. Beaumont, *The River Regimes of Iran* (Department of Geography, University of Durham, Occasional Publications), New Series, no. 1, 1973, 29 pages; W.H. Al-Khashab, *The Water-Budget of the Tigris-Euphrates Basin* (University of Chicago, Department of Geography, Research Paper no. 54, 1958), 105 pages.

4. P. Beaumont, 'Hydrology and water resources of the Iranian plateau', *Encyclopaedia Persica* (Iran Centre, Columbia University, New York, 1978, in press).

5. K. Kenyon, 'The origins of the Neolithic', *Advancement of Science* (London), vol. 26 (1969) 144-60.

6. P. Beaumont, 'The qanat systems of Iran', *Bulletin of the International Association of Scientific Hydrology*, vol. 16 (1971) 39-50.

7. P. Beaumont, 'Water resource development in Iran', *Geographical Journal*, vol. 140 (1974) 418-31.

8. World Health Organisation, *World Health Statistics Report*, vol. 6, no. 11 (1973).

9. P. Dorr, S.L. Feldman and C.S. Kamen, 'Socio-economic factors affecting domestic water demand in Israel', *Water Resources Research*, vol. 11, no. 6 (1975).

10. R.G. Feachem, 'Infectious disease related to water supply and excreta disposal facilities', *Ambio*, vol. 6, no. 1 (1977) 55-8.

11. P.L. Rosenfield, *Development and Verification of a Schistosomiosis Transmission Model* (Agency for International Development, Washington, 1975).

12. P. Beaumont, 'A traditional method of groundwater extraction in the Middle East', *Ground Water*, vol. 11 (1973) 23-30.

13. R. Marwick and J.P. Germond, 'The River Lar multipurpose project in Iran', *Water Power and Dam Construction*, vol. 27, no. 4 (1975) 133-41.

14. T.G. Temperley, 'Kuwait's water supply', *Journal of the American Water Works Association*, vol. 57 (1965).

15. P. Beaumont, 'Water in Kuwait', *Geography*, vol. 62, part 3 (1977) 187-97.

16. P. Beaumont, 'Water and development in Saudi Arabia', *Geographical Journal*, vol. 143, part 1 (1977) 42-60.

17. H.I. Shuval, 'Direct and indirect wastewater re-use for municipal purposes', *Ambio*, vol. 6, no. 1 (1977) 63-5.

18. Anonymous, 'U.N. assesses water saving toilet', *Middle East Water and Sewage*, April/May, vol. 2, no. 2 (1978) 72.

19. A. Wiener, 'Comprehensive water-resources development – case history: Israel', in A. Wiener, *The Role of Water in Development* (McGraw-Hill, New York, 1972), pp. 401-11.

20. A. Wiener, 'Coping with water deficiency in arid and semi-arid countries through high-efficiency water management', *Ambio*, vol. 6, no. 1 (1977) 77-82.

21. See for example C. Gischler, *Water Resources in the Arab Middle East and North Africa*, MENAS Resource Study (MENAS Press, Wisbech, 1979).

12 THE URBAN FUTURE
G.H. Blake and R.I. Lawless

A recurrent theme of the preceding chapters has been the sketchiness of present knowledge and understanding of the Middle Eastern city, at least as represented in the writings of Western geographers and other social scientists. Urban studies conducted by Middle Easterners and published in local languages are an increasingly rich source of information and ideas, but they are similarly unable to provide any answers to many of the outstanding questions. Workers both within and from outside the Middle East are faced with the same difficulties. Data analysis and interpretation is hampered by the paucity of official statistics, lack of adequate cartographic material, and often by bureaucratic controls. Concepts derived from research into Western cities are found to be inappropriate when applied to the Middle East. A typical example is the problem of defining unemployment, with the result that misleading figures are often cited showing low levels of unemployment, when the reality is otherwise. Bartsch's pilot survey of employment in a poor district of Iran showed that over 70 per cent of all the economically active population were either unemployed, in disguised employment, or intermittently employed, far in excess of official estimates.[1]

The scale of what needs to be done in urban research in the Middle East is massive, but the total number of investigators in all disciplines is minute. Useful progress has been achieved by the near-heroic efforts of individuals working in isolation with minimal official encouragement, but their findings have generally been of little practical value. Much research is probably never seen by the decision-makers, while some is doubtless too academic or limited in scope to be of use in planning strategies. Urban research in the Middle East not only needs to be stepped up dramatically, but also made more applicable to local decision-making processes. Master plans for urban research should be drawn up at national level to guide and co-ordinate the work of individuals and teams of workers. Priority areas of research should be established at various scales, from regional and national network analysis to neighbourhood studies in small towns. Many of the tasks thus defined would be best carried out by interdisciplinary teams including no doubt both local and expatriate specialists. On the other hand, the efforts of individuals and small groups need not be wasted if their objectives are carefully chosen and their findings integrated into an overall pattern of inquiry. The aim of all such inquiry would be to supply the data upon which coherent national urban policies might be based. With the exception of Israel, no Middle East state has evolved a detailed national urban strategy, and even in Israel it has not been very effective. Urban life in the region is fast approaching crisis point, and if the quality of urbanism is to improve and not deteriorate, the processes at work must be understood. Those able to interpret what is happening should be encouraged to work alongside planners and administrators so that the full implications of their actions can be carefully monitored.

This chapter does not attempt to forecast the future shape and style of Middle Eastern urban life. For one thing, generalisations about states with such diverse economic, social and political personalities would be meaningless. Indeed, as time goes by the urban structures of each Middle Eastern state acquire more distinctive national characteristics. The absence of rigorous planning strategies, and the very pace of change make forecasting doubly difficult. Above all, history shows that environmental disasters, political events (including war), and fluctuating economic fortunes can bring about abrupt changes in patterns of settlements and living standards in the urban Middle East. The aim of the following paragraphs is to underscore the need for vigorous inquiry, integrated planning and massive investment, without which the region could shortly enter a grim period of environmental degradation and social upheaval in its towns and cities.

Urban Growth and Concentration

One fact about the future urban scene in the Middle East which seems beyond dispute is that the level of urbanisation will continue to increase. At present about 44 per cent of the inhabitants of the region live in towns. Only 30 years ago the figure was below 30 per cent; within a decade or so the figure could exceed 50 per cent. It is interesting to speculate where this expansion will end. The Middle East could well become as heavily urbanised as Western Europe or North America with some 75 per cent urban dwellers, unless there is a radical transformation of attitudes to agricultural and rural development. No Middle Eastern country has sought to emulate the essentially ideological commitment to 'deurbanisation' as practised with dramatic effects in Cambodia and Vietnam.

Some states are already highly urbanised (Table 2.3). Although the percentage of town-dwellers is unlikely to go on rising rapidly in these states, the *scale* of urban populations will continue to increase. With average annual rates of natural increase around 2.8 per cent in the Middle East, the population of the region will double in 25 years. The populations of many of the larger towns will accordingly double in this period, and in many cases in a much shorter period because of the continuation of high rates of rural to urban migration. Efforts to create alternative poles of attraction in rural areas have proved disappointing, while efforts to reduce high rates of increase among the urban population through family planning have so far had only limited impact.

The desirability of continued urban growth is a matter of some debate. There is general agreement that very high rates of urbanisation set up stresses which are undesirable from social and economic points of view. On the other hand it is not always accepted that prevention of rural to urban migration is the best solution to the problem. This viewpoint has been strongly argued by Abu-Lughod who stresses that problems arising from rapid urban growth are not sufficiently clearly distinguished from problems resulting from rural to urban migration.[2] In her view, urban growth rates should be reduced by tackling high rates of natural increase which currently contribute more than half the annual urban growth in the Middle East. One of the most important ways of achieving this should be through female education. Rural to urban migration however, is both inevitable and necessary for national economic growth, since agriculture cannot support a large population. Most rural migrants are better off in the city, and make a greater marginal contribution to the economy than is possible in overcrowded rural areas. Moreover, the rural migrant, unlike the established urbanite, is able to help solve housing shortages through his own efforts, and much more could be done to utilise these skills and energy. Abu-Lughod does not see any solution to the growth of primate cities, though it might be possible to channel the natural forces at work to create new directions of growth. In most countries it is clear that the forces of growth are concentrated along certain axes, as between Cairo and Alexandria, Baghdād and Basra, Casablanca and Rabat. These axes could become the location for a series of semi-self-sufficient satellite communities, 'strung out like beads' along the major lines of communication which could relieve the pressure on the major cities at either end. Towns located along these axes have experienced impressive growth, whereas towns located equally close to the major cities but off the dominant axes have tended to show relative decline. Elongated metropolitan regions are likely to emerge as the cities of the future in the Middle East, and according to Abu-Lughod, they should be planned for now.

Ibrahim[3] however, has argued the opposite, at least as far as the Arab world is concerned. He believes that most Arab countries reached an 'optimum' level of urbanisation of 10 to 20 per cent in the 1940s and 1950s in relation to the current stage of their economic development. That level was sufficient to stimulate a healthy economic, 'take-off', but the rapid urbanisation of the 1960s intervened, and economic development was seriously retarded. Migration from villages contributes to *urbanisation* but not necessarily to *urbanism*, and it is urbanism which is the key to modernising societies, especially through industrialisation.[4] Urbanism implies literacy, orderliness, rationality, tolerance of change and universalism; probably only 30 to 40 per cent of the urban populations of the Middle East can be described as having these characteristics. The rest are in effect urban-dwelling villagers for whom there is rarely productive employment. Ibrahim advocates some planning to control and slow down current rapid urbanisation to avoid the 'social dynamite' which lies ahead if nothing is done. He also emphasises the cost of maintaining overpopulated cities. These views are hardly new, but they deserve restatement because of the growing tendency to regard rural to urban migration with too much complacency.

Evaluation of the role of urbanisation in development must also include the consequences of rapid growth for the quality of life in particular towns and cities. In the majority of areas, rapid growth has had detrimental consequences, particularly in cities outside the oil-rich states where the public sector is only able to provide a fraction of housing needs, especially for low-income groups. As in the past, many urbanites, both newcomers and established urban dwellers, will be forced to seek shelter in areas of expanding spontaneous settlement often on the fringes of the city. Increased numbers will aggravate already serious pressures on urban infrastructures such as water supply, sewage disposal, electricity and public transport. The plight of Cairo is well known in this respect. Built to house no more than two million inhabitants, the city is now home for nearly nine million. In parts population densities exceed 150,000 per km^2. Hundreds of thousands live on rooftops, and squat in the tomb-houses of the City of the Dead. There is overcrowding everywhere, in the buses, on the pavements and in homes. Some three and a half million commuters battle their way into the city daily on roads and using transport which is totally inadequate. The infrastructure of the city is in an appalling state of decay, and electricity, water, sewerage and telephones are all subject to periodic failures which are both dangerous and frustrating.

At one time it was true to say that at least refuse collection was efficiently performed by armies of *zabbaleen*, squatters who earn a living by sorting refuse and selling all re-usable matter. Nowadays however, they tend to concentrate on refuse collection from the wealthy areas because it is more profitable, and the poorer neighbourhoods are neglected.[5]

Cairo's appalling problems are the result of hopelessly inadequate investment over a period of years, and its continued rapid growth of population, currently put at 4.6 per cent per annum. If present trends continue the city could have 20 million inhabitants before the end of the century. The implications of this are profound and manifold. Here however, it is merely intended to draw attention to the colossal investment which will be required to maintain the present services, apart from providing for twice the present population. Even low-cost housing schemes now being adopted for Cairo and Alexandria will absorb huge sums of money. Unfortunately there is no low-cost alternative when it comes to transport systems, telephones, water supply, sewerage and electricity; the bill for these over the next decade or so will add to Egypt's economic troubles on a considerable scale. The price of urbanisation in Egypt must also be measured in terms of the loss of precious agricultural land; between 1952 and 1977, 243,000 ha were lost to agriculture through building.[6] This is almost half the total amount of land reclaimed for cultivation – at great expense – during the same period. It has been suggested that the total built-up area of the Middle East will double in 10 or 15 years, much of it at the expense of agricultural land.[7]

The continued concentration of urban growth in the major cities, in many cases the capital, is also predictable. A few countries have developed national spatial strategies, e.g. Iran and Iraq, aimed at creating alternative growth poles either by building satellite settlements around the major metropolitan centres or encouraging decentralisation (especially of manufacturing industry) to strengthen the economies of some secondary urban centres. Where efforts have been made to implement such policies the impact has been minimal. The continued dominance of capital cities, which has deprived provincial towns of much needed financial resources, is likely to continue. If set within the concept of core-periphery relationships, this situation can also be seen as part of a chain of exploitative relationships that link metropolitan countries (the industrialised nations) to the major cities and dominant classes of the dependent country, and significantly restricts the freedom of choice of the less-developed nations in determining their economic policies.

The ever-increasing polarisation of national and urban population into one or two dominant metropolitan regions is perhaps the most publicised aspect of the changing spatial pattern of urban population in the Middle East today. It is not however the only significant change taking place, nor is the concept of changing urban status anything new. Indeed the long history of urban development in the region is the story of changing fortunes, and dynamic interurban relationships. The interplay of political, economic and environmental influences has brought about the decline of once powerful centres, and the region abounds with the ruins of abandoned cities. In the modern Middle East, a significant number of small urban centres are losing their regional functions, and are in the process of stagnation and decline. On the other hand a surprising number of new towns have been founded during the twentieth century, some of which seem destined to grow into medium-size cities. The spatial implications of these towns for existing urban networks have yet to be properly examined. The most notable example in recent years has been the construction of new ports, particularly around the Arabian peninsula; Saudi Arabia's colossal new port and industrial complex at Jubayl on the Gulf could support an urban community of about 300,000 by the end of the century. Several other existing urban centres have been chosen for government projects which will bring about a sharp increase in population. Yanbu, on the Red Sea, is being developed as an industrial town and port for some 200,000 inhabitants in 25 years time. Similarly, the Libyan government is to develop Misurata as an industrial town with a steel works of seven million tonne capacity by 2005. A population of 180,000 is forecast, which makes an interesting comparison with its 10,000 inhabitants during the 1960s.

In the longer-term future, it is possible that almost unimaginable new urban developments will be added to the map of the Middle East. The most spectacular might be the construction of new towns around the Qattāra depression in Egypt after it has been flooded to form a large inland sea to create both HEP (hydro-electric) potential and a favourable micro-climate for north-west Egypt. Feasibility studies for the Qattāra project had already begun in 1978. Some Egyptians have also proposed the construction of a new capital city in the Western Desert, to supersede an overgrown and decaying Cairo.[8] In the more distant future, a revolution in transportation could bring about spectacular changes in the contemporary geography of the region. A new generation of ocean-going skimmers capable of moving at high speed over land and sea could deprive many conventional ports of their major *raison d'être*, and inland towns could become the most important centres for the collection and distribution of goods as in the days of the caravan trade. Eventually one must also assume an end to the supply of oil from the Middle East, which could leave a number of small centres as ghost towns, and the towns of the Suez Canal in serious decline. At the same time increasing dependence upon solar energy, and desalinated seawater could lend significance to urban locations at present regarded as of limited value. These ideas are of course all in the realms of fantasy, but they serve as reminders that nothing is final or static concerning urban patterns and urban populations in the Middle East.

Architecture and Planning

Middle Eastern architecture and urban planning are already showing encouraging signs that the wholesale adoption of Western styles and forms may give way in future to greater emphasis on indigenous traditions. Since the beginning of the century modernisation has been largely equated with Westernisation, and much ancient fabric has been swept away in the name of 'beneficial demolition'. Many Middle Eastern cities have forfeited their characteristic skylines and compact ground plans for a skyline of high-rise buildings and sprawling outward expansion. A few architects and planners are now expressing grave concern over the destruction of the region's unique urban heritage, and disillusionment with the alien urban environments so widely imposed in the Middle East. There are those who believe that it is only possible to live the life of a good Muslim in the traditional type of urban environment, and that the progressive secularisation of Middle Eastern society may be partially the product of the Westernisation of urban environments. There have as yet been few signs of popular opposition to modern urban development and redevelopment, though after the 1979 Islamic Revolution in Iran, this should not be ruled out for the future. Those interests favourable to Western-style modernisation however remain powerful, and it would be foolish to underestimate the influence of property developers, urban landlords, planners, consultants, architects and their political allies. Where financial interests are not directly involved, as in the case of important national monuments, conservation has proved easier to implement. Nevertheless, the preservation and restoration of historic buildings has hitherto been generally slow, with some notable exceptions. The twin incentives of the revival of national and Islamic cultural values, and the prospects of tourist revenues could bring about more vigorous action with regard to urban conservation. Conservation and restoration are of course very costly, and it must be remembered that in many large cities municipal budgets already fall far short of what is necessary, and demands for finance increase all the time.

Tangible evidence of this new concern for indigenous values was the initiation in 1978 of a programme of discussions designed to lead to the presentation in 1980 of the first Aga Khan award for architecture. The aim of the award is to encourage the creation of architecture suitable for the modern world, but in the spirit of Islam. Participants at the first seminar recognised that the unprecedented rate of urban building is presenting the Islamic world with an urgent opportunity to determine its own future environment. The problem is easily stated: 'The major modern urban environments of the Islamic world are suffering from a crisis which is directly reflected in their ugliness and are in stark contrast with the serenity and beauty of the traditional Islamic city. Islamic architecture has been eclipsed by a conglomeration of often hideous styles or at best bland ones, in both cases imitated from foreign models . . .'[9] The difficulty is knowing how to set about reintroducing 'the spirit of Islam' in contemporary terms. While the Islamic past undoubtedly has much to teach the urban planner and architect, the idea of simply recreating old forms was rejected. Certain successful features of Islamic architecture need to be scientifically evaluated, such as natural cooling devices and local building materials. It is not easy to decide what constants in the built environment can be identified as 'Islamic'. While Islam clearly imposed certain unifying attributes, the variety of distinctive regional interpretations related to the local physical environment were probably even more important. Predictably perhaps, this significant seminar ended with a call for further inquiry, including a study of Islamic texts to identify attitudes and principles governing the built environment, and a thorough survey of indigenous building materials and skills to determine their potential for meeting contemporary needs. If such inquiry leads to a fresh infusion of some of the finest qualities of Islamic architecture, the urban life of the region could be immeasurably enriched. What is needed goes far beyond the mere accretion of spurious Islamic facades to what are essentially Western constructions, in the manner currently the vogue among certain architects. The Islamic city was an organic whole which functioned efficiently, and succeeded in preserving close interaction between its inhabitants. The privacy of the courtyard house was complemented by the life of the neighbourhood, and the central mosque and bazaars. The form of individual buildings and the pattern of streets was aesthetically subtle, using space and light and shadow to create variety and interest, while building styles were often rich with religious symbolism.

Significantly, a conference on housing problems in developing countries at Dhahran in 1978 also called for a return to traditional architectural forms in the Islamic world. The delegates at this conference encountered a different problem; that the low-cost housing made possible by modern technology is difficult to reconcile with beautiful designs which conform with local social and religious beliefs. More research and experiment will be required.[10] A partial solution to the dilemma might be in a reappraisal of what constitutes low-cost housing. Roberts has pointed out that the adoption of traditional courtyard-house styles can obviate the need for energy-hungry air conditioning and air filtration systems. More expensive to build, such houses may be cheaper to run. He also advocates a revaluation of the merits of the dry toilet which works successfully in certain places such as San'a in the Yemen AR, and represents enormous savings on installation costs, water consumption and inevitable repairs.[11]

There are great dangers inherent in concentrating upon architectural and physical aspects of urban redevelopment without coming to terms with the social and economic well-being of the people themselves. This is particularly the case in the ancient *medinas* of many Middle Eastern cities which have become overcrowded with many of the urban poor. The aim of urban renewal is not to build 'a Disneyland reconstruction of folk museums in which anachronistic activities are staged for the edification of jaded tourists', but a living city, with economic and social activities thriving together at the local level, constantly renewing themselves.[12] The old residential-commercial-industrial complexes of Cairo known as *rab'*, or the small neighbourhood units centred upon the local mosque in so many towns and cities, deserve serious reappraisal. The existence of small subsystems in the traditional Islamic city may have gone far to avert the social problems associated with the contemporary city — anonymity, impersonal social relations, absence of family ties, loneliness and anomie. It is not necessarily large numbers or density that generate anomie, but the increased randomness of human contacts that comes from participating in large-scale social systems. Small subsystems could play an indispensable role in mediating between the individual and large-scale society, and future physical planning should encourage their survival rather than hasten their destruction as so often happens.

Urbanisation and Welfare

A major defect of the collected views expressed in this volume is the absence of discussion on urbanisation and economic development, and urbanisation and politics. In future both will play a far greater part in the evaluation of urban planning. It must be acknowledged how little we know about the relationship between economic development and urbanisation and about the performance of Middle Eastern economies and urban occupational trends. Much of the research on these important themes has been carried out in Latin American cities,[13] but it provides some useful indicators of possible trends and processes in the Middle East. Even in those countries which have experienced impressive rates of economic growth, a significant part of the urban population has been excluded from the material benefits — jobs, housing, welfare. Growth it seems has succeeded in 'marginalising' sections of the urban population so that they cease to be important factors in influencing events. Contemporary economic growth based essentially on industrialisation concentrates upon the large-scale sector of the urban economy which offers the best profits, salaries and wages. Yet a small-scale sector of the urban economy continues to thrive, though on low wages and low profits through the interdependency of the two sectors. The large-scale or 'formal' sector makes use of the small-scale or 'informal' sector as a reserve of unskilled and casual labour, as a means of putting out work and as a means of providing cheaply services such as transport, commerce and repairs, all of which facilitate the expansion of the large-scale sector. The small-scale sector absorbs labour, using income opportunities provided by the large-scale sector, but within it there is much concealed underemployment and involvement in essentially non-productive occupations.

Economic and social marginality in the city, defined as the exclusion of part of the urban population from better paying jobs, a say in politics, and adequate housing, is seen by some observers as a permanent irreversible result of capitalist development — thus distinguishing contemporary marginality from previous patterns of urban poverty such as in nineteenth-century British cities where marginality was ultimately reversed by the expansion of employment opportunities in the urban economy. One view claims that contemporary industrialisation which is capital-intensive in nature, cannot absorb the increase in the population of underdeveloped countries who are seeking work.[14] According to this view, the possibility of industrial expansion in the Third World is limited by external control from the industrial West. Thus the urban population marginalised by the current economic policies must continue to find work in the tertiary sector of the urban economy, and this marginal employment is likely to continue in the large cities where there is a higher concentration of high-income earners and where improved access to education and welfare make possible a wider range of strategies for survival. Eventually, as modern capitalism expands to provide capital-intensive services for higher-income urban groups, the smaller enterprises will be relegated to servicing the needs of the poorest segment of the urban population, restricting upward mobility out of the marginalised classes. As most capital-intensive and much government employment is concentrated in the largest cities, factory production is not attracted to provincial centres whose survival will depend on the proliferation of small-scale labour-intensive activities. In this way the whole economy of secondary urban centres could in time become marginal.

Others have criticised this view however, arguing that it under-estimates the extent to which even capital-intensive industrialisation generates employment opportunities and contributes to the capitalist transformation of an underdeveloped country.[15] Their evidence on employment creation and on the productivity of the large-scale and small-scale sectors of the economy does not suggest an increasing marginalisation of the urban population with capital-intensive indus-trialisation. For them industrialisation develops on the basis of labour-intensive services which are not well-remunerated and which add to capitalist accumulation – in effect the existence of marginal occupa-tions subsidises capitalist production. According to this approach, the large-scale sector does not invade the small-scale sector but uses it to reduce directly and indirectly its own costs of production.

The existence of urban economic dualism in the Middle East is well attested. The contrast of skyscrapers, luxury shops and sumptuous offices surrounded by unpaved streets, squatter settlements and open drains is typical of cities in both the capital-poor and in the capital-rich countries. Tehrān provides probably the most striking example of this phenomenon. A significant proportion of the urban population have become marginalised, although as yet we know little about the processes involved. Whether or not increasing marginalisation will take place in the future is open to debate. Are Middle Eastern cities in a stage through which urban society must pass to achieve balanced urban-industrial development or will large sections of their population remain excluded from the material benefits of economic growth? Is the future a city of workers integrated into the modern urban economy or a city of peasants who exist on the fringes of the modern economy yet excluded from participation in it? We still know very little about these marginalised classes – the characteristics of squatter settlement and their likely responses to problems such as food shortages. Yet these are constant preoccupations of certain governments and elites in the Middle East, e.g. Sadat's Egypt, where the apparatus of the state is oriented to information-gathering about the underprivileged and any potential disturbances. Though it is unlikely that the low-income urban population will spontaneously organise against authoritarian rule, they represent a force which is potentially mobilisable – a situation to which Middle Eastern governments may become increasingly sensitive. Social and economic inequalities and tensions within the Middle Eastern city are manifest; whether or not they will find political expression in the future remains to be seen. If they do, it is conceivable that urban planning in the Middle East will begin to be influenced by considerations of security and controls in ways hitherto unfamiliar to the region. Meanwhile, some observers have noted a growing 'ruralisation' of towns as new immigrants from the countryside have difficulty in assimilating into the urban economy and society. Even where the majority are integrated into the modern urban economy, it should not be assumed that the attitudes and values which they acquire will be those of traditional urban dwellers, and certainly not those of Western urban society.

The immediate future will no doubt see the continuation of an urban bias in Middle East development with the towns receiving priority in development strategies, thus tending to reinforce rural-urban disparities. Since most of the decision-makers are urban dwellers, it is not surprising that, in the past, urban areas have received the major share of investment from both private and public sources. This is particularly evident where there is emphasis on rapid industrialisation. Even in those countries which have recorded high rates of economic growth, the standard of living of the majority of the rural population has scarcely improved, in spite of land reform and the implementation of major irrigation projects. Not only has agriculture been neglected, but there has been little thought given to the improvement of rural housing and rural services. In some parts of the Middle East, the small agro-town may provide some of the answers to the problem, particularly if their functions as service centres can be reinforced by the creation of light agro-industries. Several countries pay lip-service to this concept, but there has been little progress, presumably because of the diversion of scarce resources into large urban centres.

In the medium term however, this urban bias might change, if it is recognised that the need for a shift of resources from the urban to the rural sector is the overriding development task, as Lipton has convincingly argued:

> The most important class conflict in the poor countries of the world is not between labour and capital. Nor is it between foreign and national interests. It is between the rural classes and the urban classes. The rural sector contains most of the poverty, and most of the low-cost sources of potential advance; but the urban sector contains most of the *articulateness, organisation* and *power*. So the urban classes have been able to 'win' most of the rounds of the struggle with the countryside . . . Resource allocations within the city and the village as well as between them, reflect urban priorities rather than equity or efficiency.[16]

Thus development in most Third World countries is deemed to imply a move out of agriculture and away from villages, since this has been the Western experience. For national elites, the creation of an urbanised, industrialised society after Western or Socialist models is the accepted goal. A major appraisal of development goals along lines advocated by Lipton and others would clearly bring about unexpected convulsions in the patterns of the urban growth expected for most Middle Eastern countries. Small and medium-sized regional centres located in agricultural areas might experience a new lease of life, and the growth of metropolitan regions could at last be restrained. The chances of such an urban revolution occurring are very remote. What we must realistically expect is a continuation of contemporary trends to breaking-point.

References

1. W.H. Bartsch, 'Unemployment in less developed countries: a case study of a poor district of Tehran', in D.J. Dwyer (ed.), *The City in the Third World* (Macmillan, London, 1974), pp. 159-68.

2. J. Abu-Lughod, 'Problems and policy implications of Middle Eastern urbanisation', in *Studies on Development Problems in Selected Countries of the Middle East* (United Nations, New York, 1972), pp. 42-62.

3. See for example S.E.M. Ibrahim, 'Over-urbanisation and under-urbanism: the case of the Arab world', *International Journal of Middle Eastern Studies*, vol. 6 (1975) 29-45.

4. A. Schnaiberg, 'Rural-urban residence and modernism: a study of Ankara Province', *Demography*, vol. 7, no. 1 (1970) 71-85.

5. J. Antoniou, 'The urban problems facing Egypt', *Middle East Construction*, vol. 4, no. 3 (March 1979) 18-19.

6. J. Smit, 'Which future for Alexandria', *Geoforum*, vol. 8, no. 3 (1977) 135-40.

7. H. Roberts, 'Townplanning: looking beyond the year 2000', *Middle East*, no. 30 (April 1977) 64-8.

8. 'Egypt: in search of a new capital', *Middle East*, no. 22 (August 1976) 27-9.

9. S.H. Nasr, 'The contemporary Muslim and the architectural transformation of the urban environment of the Islamic World', in R. Holod (ed.), *The Aga Khan Award for Architecture*, Proceedings of Seminar One (Aiglemont, France, April 1978, Philadelphia, 1978), pp. 1-4.

10. F. Dakhil, O. Ural and M.F. Tewfik (eds.), *Housing Problems in Developing Countries: Proceedings of IAHS International Conference 1978* (John Wiley & Sons Ltd, New York, 1979).

11. H. Roberts, 'Townplanning', 64-8.

12. J. Abu-Lughod, 'Preserving the living heritage of Islamic cities', in R. Holod (ed.), *The Aga Khan Award for Architecture*, Proceedings of Seminar One (Aiglemont, France, April 1978, Philadelphia, 1978) 27-35.

13. Admirably summarised in B. Roberts, *Cities of Peasants: The Political Economy of Urbanisation in the Third World* (Edward Arnold, London, 1978).

14. For example, A. Quijano, 'The marginal pole of the economy and the marginalised labour force', *Economy and Society*, vol. 3, no. 4 (1974), 393-428.

15. For example, V.E. Faria, 'Occupational marginality, employment and poverty in urban Brazil', unpublished PhD thesis (Harvard University, 1976) and L. Kowarick, *The Logic of Disorder: Capitalist Expansion in the Metropolitan Area of Greater Sao Paulo*, Discussion Paper (Institute of Development Studies, University of Sussex, 1977).

16. M. Lipton, *Why Poor People Stay Poor: A Study in Urban Bias in World Development* (Temple Smith, London, 1977), p. 13.

NOTES ON CONTRIBUTORS

Peter Beaumont, Professor of Geography, Saint Davids University College, University of Wales, Lampeter

J.S. Birks, Honorary Research Fellow, Department of Economics, University of Durham

G.H. Blake, Senior Lecturer in Geography, University of Durham

B.D. Clark, Senior Lecturer in Geography, University of Aberdeen

J.I. Clarke, Professor of Geography, University of Durham

V.F. Costello, Lecturer in Geography, Bristol Polytechnic

D.W. Drakakis-Smith, Research Fellow, Department of Human Geography, Australian National University

A.M. Findlay, Lecturer in Geography, University of Glasgow

T.H. Greenshields, Mapping and Charting Establishment (re) Tolworth

R.I. Lawless, Assistant Director, Middle East Centre, University of Durham

C.A. Sinclair, Research Fellow in the Economics of the Middle East, University of Durham

J.M. Wagstaff, Lecturer in Geography, University of Southampton

265

INDEX

266